FOOD LOVERS' SERIES

Food Lovers' Guide Connecticut

*Best Local Specialties,
Markets, Recipes, Restaurants,
Events, and More*

Patricia Brooks and Lester Brooks

The
Globe
Pequot
Press

GUILFORD, CONNECTICUT

The prices and rates listed in this guidebook were confirmed at press time. We recommend, however, that you call establishments to obtain current information before traveling.

Text design: Nancy Freeborn
Page layout: M. A. Dubé
Maps created by Rusty Nelson © The Globe Pequot Press
Illustrations © Jill Butler; with additional illustrations by Carleen Moira Powell. Illustrations by Carleen Moira Powell on pages 4, 113, 123, and 238 have been rendered from photographs taken by Lynda Morgenroth.

ISSN 1546-6728
ISBN 0-7627-2861-2

Manufactured in the United States of America
First Edition/First Printing

For Jim, Jonathan, and Christopher for
their supportiveness, enthusiasm, and
willingness, from childhood, to be
"tasters" and participants in our various
gastronomic adventures

HELP US KEEP THIS GUIDE UP TO DATE

Every effort has been made by the authors and editors to make this guide as accurate and useful as possible. However, many things can change after a guide is published—establishments close, phone numbers change, facilities come under new management, etc.

We would love to hear from you concerning your experiences with this guide and how you feel it could be improved and kept up to date. While we may not be able to respond to all comments and suggestions, we'll take them to heart and we'll also make certain to share them with the authors. Please send your comments and suggestions to the following address:

The Globe Pequot Press
Reader Response/Editorial Department
P.O. Box 480
Guilford, CT 06437

Or you may e-mail us at:

editorial@GlobePequot.com

Thanks for your input, and happy travels!

Contents

Preface

Watching the fast-evolving food revolution here in Connecticut is like having ringside seats at a major three-ring sporting event. It couldn't be more electric, exciting, and head-on.

When we moved from New York City to Connecticut to root our young family in a suburban terrain, one thing we missed was the glorious ethnic-food variety of a big city. Even finding good bread locally was a challenge. Ingredients for a Chinese dinner involved a trip to New York's Chinatown. Favorite herbs like basil and cilantro, ubiquitous today, were unavailable locally. A book like this one wouldn't even have been pamphlet-size in the Connecticut of 1956.

That was then. Now one of the joys of our lives has been the slow (at first), then rapidly accelerating growth of food sources in our town and county and throughout our state. We have seen supermarkets expand their produce departments and have watched specialty food markets open and routinely stock not just basil and cilantro but lemongrass and galanga. We have reveled in the arrival of scores of new restaurants of wide-ranging specialties. When we first moved to New Canaan, there were perhaps four restaurants in town, only one of high caliber. Now there are more than thirty eateries, some very good, including one Indian, one Japanese, three pan-Asian, a French bistro, several Italian, and one for seafood. Our little town is by no means unique; similar changes have taken place in many towns in the state.

Our observations in this book are based on both personal and professional experience. Since 1977, Pat has been the restaurant reviewer for the *New York Times*, covering the entire state of Connecticut. This has involved sampling, analyzing, and reporting about food at more than 1,400 restaurants statewide—always anonymously. This experience has led us to delightful discoveries as the restaurant scene has grown in sophistication and diversity. We have observed the arrival of notable French chefs and the expanding number of expert home-grown ones. Les, as a wine writer and oenophile, has noted with pleasure the development of a fast-growing wine industry and wine events in our state and increasingly better wine selections in our restaurants statewide.

Together we have enjoyed the growth and range of farmers' markets and the increasing variety of crops that Connecticut family farms now produce. From our early roots in Minneapolis (Pat) and Des Moines (Les), we especially cherish the wondrous flavors of fresh, natural foods such as those we recall from childhood. Years of roaming the globe on food and travel article assignments for *Bon Appétit, Travel & Leisure,* and other national publications have made us appreciate the emergence in Connecticut of many seafood, gourmet, cheese, specialty food stores, and bakeries, catering to an ever more knowledgeable clientele. We marvel also at the many food events that all of us can enjoy, from wine tastings to pizza, apple, strawberry, and even garlic festivals.

It has been our pleasure to discover, explore, sample, and take note of many of these food-related phenomena and gather them together here. We hope this book will help you, the reader, find, use, and enjoy many of these diverse food resources yourself, as most of them are available within a short drive. That is an added advantage of living in this small state—so much is so easily accessible. Go for it.

Acknowledgments

The first thing we found in researching this book was that people in the food business are among the most generous on Earth—or at least the Earth in Connecticut. Virtually everyone we talked to was willing and often eager to share sources and ideas and offer helpful suggestions.

Leading the list of food colleagues whose general helpfulness extended far "beyond the call" were the following:

Lee White, cookbook author, food consultant, and warm-hearted friend, whose passion for good food is matched only by her ingenuity in finding it;

Linda Giuca, food editor of the *Hartford Courant*, whose willingness to share her vast repertoire of sources and suggestions made our work easier and more fun;

James O'Shea, proprietor of West Street Grill in Litchfield, who volunteered with gusto some of his favorite secret sources;

Christopher Prosperi, chef-owner of Metro Bis restaurant in Simsbury, whose wide knowledge and dedication to the best local food sources was unstintingly shared;

Stuart London, chef and cheesemaker at Sankow's Beaver Brook Farm in Lyme, whose excitement about his cheeses, lamb dishes, and other creations was infectious.

Our heartfelt thanks and appreciation go especially to Laura Strom, our unflappable editor at The Globe Pequot Press, for her encouraging words, helpful ideas, and enthusiastic suggestions. Thanks also to project editor Cary Hull, who "rode herd" on our manuscript through the entire production process with patience, graciousness, and wisdom. We are grateful as well to the following Globe Pequot staffers for their quick responses to our queries about food preferences: Michelle Brown, Shana Capozza, Brett DeMello, Larry Dorfman, Mimi Egan, Melissa Evarts, Joy Hall, Kathryn Mennone, Katy O'Brien, Casey Shain, and Stefanie Ward.

We are appreciative also of various folks at Connecticut tourism departments for their advice and information. Deserving special mention are: Renny Loisel, director of public relations at the Greater New Haven Convention & Visitors Bureau, whose expertise on her city and critical astuteness were our lodestars in navigating New Haven's culinary landscape; Heidi Bieter, communications specialist at the Connecticut River Valley & Shoreline Visitors Council, whose lengthy list of food resources was invaluable; Anne Lee, group marketing manager at the Greater Hartford Tourism District, for her rapid response and helpful information; and Janet Serra, executive director of the Litchfield Hills Visitors Bureau, whose in-depth Litchfield County experience led us down many rewarding culinary paths. Thanks also to Karen Staples, Deborah J. Donovan, and Ellen Jacobs Sweeney for their suggestions.

Our admiration is endless for the many farmers we visited and spoke with, who took time away from their demanding chores to share their experiences and farm histories. Their dedication and hard work have helped make living in Connecticut a pleasure and joy for so many of us who benefit from the fruits of their labor. Special thanks as well belongs to Rick Macsuga, marketing representative, Connecticut Department of Agriculture, whose information on farmers' markets and farm stands was an essential guidepost in our research, and to Elizabeth Wheeler, director of agricultural programs at the Hartford Food System, whose dedication to Connecticut farmers, their farms and farm products led us to valuable sources.

Thanks as well to the following individuals and establishments for graciously sharing their recipes, many of which were adapted for home cooks. These individuals and companies are not responsible for any inadvertent errors or omissions.

Adelma Simmons's Spicy Pumpkin Bread: Adelma Grenier Simmons, adapted from *A Witch's Brew* Caprilands cookbook

Adrienne's Roasted Apple and Pumpkin Soup: Adrienne Sussman, Adrienne

Belgique's Tarte Tatin: Pierre Gilissen, Belgique Chocolatiers

Boneless Veal Breast: Ann Howard and Jeff Gantkin, Ann Howard Apricots

Brendan Walsh's Fabulous Indian Pudding: Brendan Walsh, The Elms

Buells Orchard's Apple Walnut Cake: Patty Sandress, Buells Orchard

The Cannery's Eggplant Ravioli: William O'Meara, The Cannery

Chaiwalla's Famous Tomato Pie: Mary O'Reilly, Chaiwalla

Good Food Good Things's Cranberry Walnut Tart: Good Food Good Things, Darien

Hopkins Inn Rösti Potatoes and Tiroler Gröstl: Franz Schober, Hopkins Inn

Jacques Pépin's Honeyed Sweet Potatoes: *Jacques Pépin's Simple and Healthy Cooking* cookbook

Jim Dougherty's Easy One-Dish Pork and Peppers: Jim Dougherty, The Egg & I Pork Farm

Jimmie Booth's Broccoli Salad: Jimmie Booth, Golden Lamb Buttery

Lee White's Super Simple Salad Dressing: Lee White

Metro Bis Pear Panna Cotta: Christopher Prosperi, Metro Bis

Oatmeal Zucchini Bread: University of Connecticut, adapted from Cooperative Extension System's *From the Farm to the Table*

Pasta with Cauliflower, Oil, Garlic, and Hot Pepper: Sally Maraventano, adapted from her *Festa del Giardino* cookbook.

Ronnie Fein's Fresh Apple Brown Betty: Ronnie Fein

Sandi Rose's Microwave Raspberry Cobbler: Sandi Rose, Rose's Berry Farm

Silvermine Tavern's New England Clam Chowder: Frank Whitman, Silvermine Tavern

Stonington Red Shrimp Cocktail: Christopher Prosperi, Metro Bis

Sundial Gardens Ginger Brandy Tea Cake: Tom Goddard, Sundial Gardens

Susan Goodman's Talk-of-the-Party Hors d'Oeuvres: Susan Goodman

Tipsy Pudding: Diana Jackson, Mrs. Bridge's Pantry

West Street Grill's Brandade of Salt Cod: James O'Shea, West Street Grill

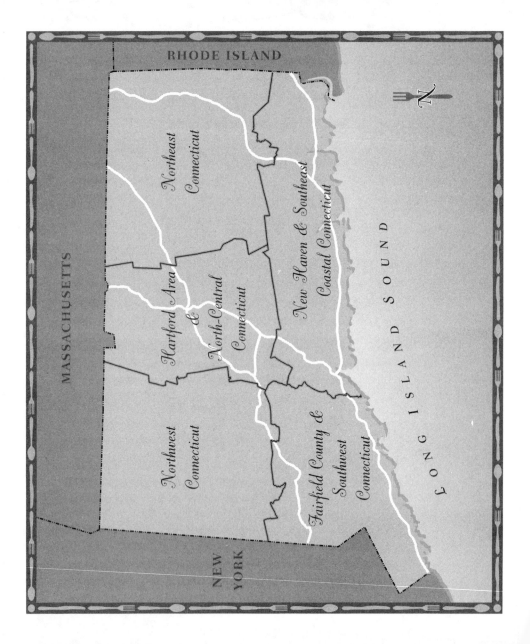

Introduction

Situated as it is between New York and Massachusetts, our state of Connecticut may sometimes be overlooked. Yet small as it is, it fairly bursts with gastronomic treasures, agricultural resources, ethnic diversity, and entrepreneurial spirit. Historically, Connecticut Yankees were great entrepreneurs and suppliers and purveyors of food— selling nutmeg from the West Indies gave us a lasting nickname as "Nutmeggers"—and still are. The state sometimes seems to be a beehive of small towns where exciting food things are happening in producing, selling, or celebrating tasty edibles. The food revolution that has been sweeping across America for the past twenty years has taken hold with tenacity and exuberance in our state. Scores of new restaurants have opened and now thrive here. Gourmet food stores, bakeries, cheese shops and special ethnic-food markets are now part of our state's topography. Recent years have brought new wineries, once a rarity in our state, now a welcome stop on the food-and-beverage landscape.

Some of the resources in this book may be familiar to you; many others may not. It is our pleasure to introduce new ones to you. Even though we have been crisscrossing the state in a quest for new food sources for more than thirty years, we continue to marvel at the new food enterprises, specialty food stores, and restaurants that continue to pop up, in the optimistic spirit of true Yankee ingenuity.

While we hope we are bringing new information to you, we have another purpose as well: to acquaint you with good fresh foods within easy reach. We exult in the many natural resources of our state, the native clams and other fresh seafood, the produce grown here, and its many outlets, like farm stands selling fresh fruits and vegetables and local festivals featuring homemade food specialties. Especially noteworthy is the relatively recent return of old-fashioned farmers' markets, encouraged by the state's department of agriculture. These markets convene throughout the growing season, with their farm-to-consumer fresh produce and farm products like honey, cheese, fresh eggs, maple syrup, and fruit jams and preserves. Our nation is proud of being a major industrial society, but at the local "people" level, we in Connecticut are able each summer and autumn to reach back to reclaim our country's roots, to relish the direct contact between the growers and consumers of wonderful, farm-fresh natural foods.

How to Use This Book

This guide has been organized into five chapters, beginning with the Fairfield County area at one end of the state, radiating upward to the northwest, then to Hartford and the north-central area around it, south to New Haven and the southeast coast, and finally concluding with the northeast area of the state. Each chapter includes a map of the region, enabling you to plan day trips for visiting and exploring. Within each chapter you will find the following categories:

Made or Grown Here

You may be surprised to find the large number of food producers in Connecticut. Some are huge enterprises, like Munson's Chocolates; others are mere "cottage industries" of food products—individuals who have come up with a superior salsa, cheesecake, or a recipe for pesto. Some of these producers sell their specialties to wholesalers and/or retailers—in which case we have cited several sources in the area where you may buy them—whereas many others sell directly to the consumer, via e-mail, their Web site, or their catalog. We have included prize-winning dessert makers, bakers, and cheesemakers, among many other entrepreneurs.

Specialty Stores & Markets

This section of each chapter features a wide variety of specialty food stores, which range from bakeries, candy shops, and ice-cream parlors to ethnic-food markets, gourmet delicatessens, and fish markets. Included are stores selling cheese and chocolates, bangers and bouillabaisse, olive oils and oregano, teas and tamales—virtually every imaginable good thing to eat that can be packaged, marketed, and sold. Many of these shops are like undiscovered treasures, known only to locals—until now. Generally, we have not included chain stores, even unusual ones, but you will find a list of several very good ones in Appendix D in the back of the book.

Farmers' Markets

In Connecticut there are some sixty-five farmers' markets operating throughout the state, most of them in the smaller towns. These offer shoppers a chance—one or two days a week—to buy seasonal, field-fresh fruits and vegetables directly from the grower. The wares are limited to state-grown or home-produced products, whether fresh produce, eggs, preserves, baked goods, meats or cheeses, fresh and dried flowers, ornamental gourds, Indian corn, and cockscomb. No middlemen are involved, which is why you will not find bananas, mangos, avocados, or other such tropical non-natives. Most of the markets operate from late spring to the end of October, but check beforehand, in the various chapters, for specific dates and times.

Part of the fun of shopping at a farmers' market is the camaraderie between sellers and buyers. Many of the same farmer-growers travel to several market days in various Connecticut towns. Information about farmers' markets is available through the state Department of Agriculture.

Be aware that it is cash only at most farmers' markets and farm stands, but occasionally someone will accept a check with proper ID.

Farm Stands

There are hundreds of small farms in Connecticut, and many have roadside stands where, in season, they sell their crops, freshly picked from the field. Some stands are literally that; others are ensconced in barns or outbuildings. Many sell, in addition to their produce, fresh eggs, honey, maple syrup, home-baked pies, breads and pastries, homemade preserves, and pickles. Although most of the farm stands we have listed keep regular, seasonal hours, it is always prudent to call ahead.

If you choose to take advantage of the pick-your-own opportunities offered at many of the farms, be sure to bring along sunscreen and water bottle and wear old clothes, a hat, and comfortable shoes.

Food Happenings

Each year's Connecticut calendar brings a surprising number of annual food events: festivals, fairs, and fund-raisers in which food dominates. This section in each chapter tells you about happenings throughout the year and where, whether it is Adam's Garlic Fest in Pawcatuck or the Dionysos Greek Festival in New Britain.

Learn to Cook

Cooking courses in Connecticut range from a professional school in New Haven with a full-fledged academic curriculum to recreational classes, demonstrations, and hands-on workshops. You will find everything from the basics of cooking to instruction in esoteric ethnic cuisines.

Learn about Wine

Under this heading in various chapters, you will find information about wine tastings and sources helpful to novice and serious oenophiles alike. In addition, the following Web sites may help you track wine tastings, seminars, and other wine-related events that occur from time to time throughout the state:

LocalWineEvents.com offers what it calls the "largest wine and spirits calendar in the world," which does list a few Connecticut wine tastings and events.

Oxfordwineroom.com focuses on New England, with notes about a few upcoming Connecticut wine events such as tastings and dinners, reviews of wines, listings of wine specialty shops, area vineyards, and comments by three wine columnists.

Connecticut Wine Club, www.ctwineclub.com, is a Web site–only organization that provides information about wine shops, tastings, wine reviews, wine dinners, auctions, vineyard tours, "informal tastings" at dozens of wine stores in various parts of the state, wine "dos and don'ts."

Landmark Eateries

Connecticut now has an abundance of restaurants of every imaginable type, approximately 12,000 of them, according to the Connecticut Restaurant Association. But because this book is not a restaurant guide, we have limited ourselves in each chapter to recommending those restaurants renowned for certain cuisines, specialties (like the sticky buns at Silvermine Tavern and the Spanish tapas of Ibiza), or a particular ambience. Considering the number and variety of restaurants in the state, our selection represents a relatively small forkful of gastronomic gems. What our restaurant choices have in common, in addition to terrific food, is character, personality, uniqueness—call it what you will—that adds to the sheer pleasure of being there.

RESTAURANT PRICE KEY

$ = inexpensive; most entrees under $15

$$ = moderate; most entrees in the $16 to $22 price range

$$$ = expensive; most entrees over $22

Brewpubs & Microbreweries

Fond as we are of fresh-tasting craft beers and ales with real flavor and complexity, we wish there were more microbreweries and brewpubs in Connecticut. Those that we have are listed in this section of the appropriate chapters.

Wine Trail

Connecticut's wine industry has been a growth stock (no pun intended) in recent years, especially in the northwest, southeast, and northeast regions of the state. Established wineries are included in these sections, along with information about their tasting facilities and special events. We have also, in Appendix B, noted additional events held at various wineries around the state throughout the year.

Recipes, Etc.

Folded into the book are recipes harvested from various Connecticut sources. Some came from chefs and restaurateurs, others were provided by farm growers, still others by specialty-shop owners. We have also included a few of our own gustatory heirlooms, which we passed along to our children and now to you.

Connecticut's Best

Here also you will find a few choices we deem to be "Connecticut's Best," restaurants or foods we prefer to all others in a given category. Declaring "Bests" reflects personal taste and is bound to be controversial, so don't hesitate to send us your comments and suggestions for the next edition of *Food Lovers' Guide to Connecticut*.

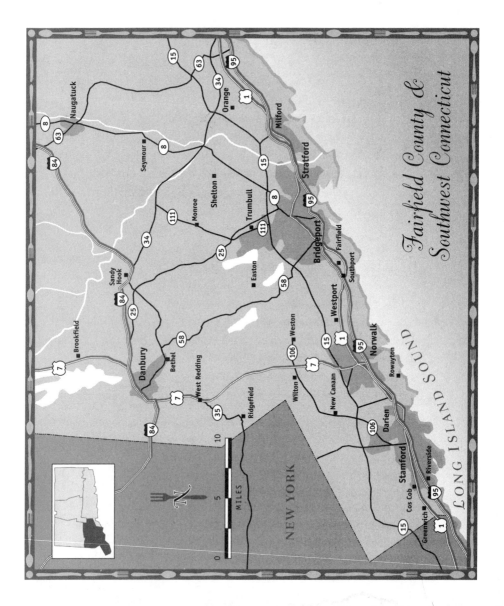

Fairfield County & Southwest Connecticut

Fairfield County and Southwest Connecticut

The home of Bridgeport, Connecticut's largest city, this southwestern region encompasses Fairfield County, one of the nation's richest suburbs. Despite its dense population, the area is still, surprisingly, a terrain of woods, rivers, ponds, and wildlife preserves. Its Long Island Sound coastline has been dubbed the "Gold Coast" because of the CEOs, moguls, and celebrities who live in expensive homes and mansions on and near its shores, from Greenwich all along the coast to Westport, Southport, and as far east as Stratford. Once known as the "bedroom" of New York, the area now has a vibrant life of its own, as many national corporations and businesses have settled here, allowing many officers and employees to work closer to home. New ethnic groups have also migrated here.

This affluence and diversity have changed the dining landscape, attracting notable New York City restaurateurs and chefs. Some have opened their own restaurants, whereas others have grasped the reins (or range, ahem) at historic village inns and have brought new levels of culinary expertise and sparkle to what had often declined into staid, predictable fare. As a result, the number of authentic French restaurants, bistros, and cafes in this southwestern region exceeds that in any other part of the state. Gastronomic tastes have evolved from so-called "vanilla" or "white bread" into discerning gourmet, with almost every imaginable type of ethnic restaurant now available; Indian, Japanese, Thai, Spanish, Chinese, Portuguese, Mexican, Greek, Middle Eastern, Italian are all here now. Here too is Martha Stewart, who began her catering business in Westport, where she still lives. Towns formerly with a single decent restaurant—our own New Canaan (population 18,000) comes to mind—now have literally dozens, which range from good to excellent. Deluxe restaurants are on a par with those in major cities all over the United States.

In tandem with this welcome restaurant expansion have come new food-supply and specialty shops, food enterprises, ethnic markets, elegant take-out services, catering businesses, and other gustatory innovations. Southwest Connecticut is no longer a pale imitation of Manhattan, but a bona fide, reliable, and exciting source of fine food in and of itself. This "Gold Coast" now boasts a new, freshly burnished patina.

Made or Grown Here

Bear Naked Granola, 25–13 Old Kings Highway North, P.O. Box 110, Darien, CT 06820; (203) 655-9212; www.bearnakedgranola.com. New in 2002, this all-natural granola (with 35 percent fruits and whole nuts, but no preservatives or refined sugars) was developed by two twentysomethings, Brendan Synnott and Kelly Flatley. Brendan says, "We wanted to prove granola could be sexy, not something only hippies eat." The orange label proclaims, "Go bear naked wild . . . it's natural," and the sturdy, clear plastic package bares everything: oats, hazelnuts, pecans, walnuts and almonds, dried cranberries, apricots, raisins, flax and sesame seeds, honey, maple syrup, and canola oil. The granola is now in full frontal view at more than seventy-five retail outlets in Connecticut and New York State, including Food for Thought in Westport and the Firehouse Deli in Fairfield.

Boulder Brownie Company, 59 Halloween Boulevard, Stamford, CT 06902; (203) 323–1945; www.boulderbrownie.com. These all-natural brownies, made from high-grade Belgian chocolate, are sinfully rich and fudgy. Besides the fine chocolate, the other all-natural ingredients are eggs, wheat flour, butter, pure vanilla extract, and unbleached, unrefined sugar. The brownies come in seven types: the basic brownie, pecan, espresso, blondie, peanut butter, rocky road, and raspberry. All are kosher, have no additives or preservatives, and are packaged individually. They are sold at Wild Oats Market in Westport and Whole Foods Market in Greenwich and can also be ordered on the company's Web site.

Briar Patch Enterprises, 322 New Haven Avenue, Milford, CT 06460; (203) 876–8923. Nancy Follini and Joseph Gilbert have dug clams for years. Since 1982, their business of harvesting the juiciest, tastiest littleneck clams, bluepoint oysters, and scallops grown in Long Island Sound has flourished. Local and area restaurants—Corvino's and

Armellino's in Milford, La Riviera in West Haven, and Mezzanotte in Monroe come to mind—gobble up almost their entire "crop."

Bridgewater Chocolate, 559 Federal Road, Brookfield, CT 06804; (800) 888–8742; www.bridgewaterchocolate.com. Chocolatier Erik Landegren's small company expanded from Bridgewater to Brookfield, where it produces American style handmade chocolates from pure premium ingredients. The chocolates won the Connecticut Specialty Foods Association award in 2002 for "most outstanding overall food product" and "best confection" award in 1999, 2000, and 2001. In 2002, the chocolates were featured by the Food Network on its "Food Finds" television show. The line includes chocolates, toffees, truffles, mints, chocolate-dipped dried apricots and orange peel, chocolate bark, and chocolate bars, all handsomely boxed and packaged, as well as tins of Gourmet Peanuts and Crunchy Butter Toasted Gourmet Peanuts. All are for sale in the factory, at gourmet shops in this part of Connecticut (including Carol Peck's Good News Café in Woodbury), and via the company's Web site and catalog.

Chocolate Lace, 14 Clark Circle, Bethel, CT 06801; (203) 792–1234. If you like Florentines (those dark chocolate cookies formed over crisp caramelized sugar), you will love Chocolate Lace. Its original recipe was created in, no, not Italy, but Imperial Russia, and these sheets of handcrafted Chocolate Lace—like delicate brown snowflakes—are made in Bethel in limited quantities and shipped to candy shops and gourmet food stores all over the United States, including The Pantry in Washington Depot. The lace comes in best-selling dark

In Connecticut Candy Has Always Been Dandy

In our peregrinations around the state, it continues to surprise us how many chocolate makers there are in Connecticut. But Nutmeggers have always had a sweet tooth, dating back to the taffy pulls of colonial times. It wasn't until the early twentieth century that candy making became a big deal here. Like many of present-day Connecticut candymakers, Peter Paul Halajian started out small. An Armenian immigrant living in the Naugatuck Valley, he began making chocolates at home. In 1919 this led him to launch a wholesale candy business, the Peter Paul Manufacturing Company in New Haven. His most memorable products were the best-selling Mounds and Almond Joy chocolate bars. Although the company was eventually sold, both these bars are still made today in Naugatuck, along with Classic Caramels.

chocolate, dark-chocolate mint, and toasted-almond milk chocolate, each packed in a gold box. Also produced here are Florentine lace cookies and white chocolates.

Hardwoods Gourmet Specialties, 35 Brentwood Avenue, Fairfield, CT 06432; (888) 468–9303; e-mail: oaksalmon@aol.com. Bill Marinelli was working as a chef-caterer when he developed his oak-grilled salmon. He sent a sample to Williams-Sonoma, who ordered it immediately for their mail-order catalog. Bingo! He was in business. That was five years ago, and he has been marinating salmon (in soy, ginger, rice vinegar, and garlic), oak-wood grilling it, and popping it into vacuum packs for quick, safe, sealed shipping ever since. His four-ounce and two-pound whole fillet packages are sold at Trader Joe's stores, at Whole Foods Market in Greenwich, and directly (via e-mail or phone orders), with overnight shipping all over the United States. The smoky, wood-grilled flavor is memorable, whether you eat the fish plain or with pasta.

Hauser Chocolatier, 137 Greenwood Avenue, Bethel, CT 06801; (203) 794–1861; www.hauserchocolatier.com. Ruedi Hauser Sr. was making chocolates as a teenager in his native Switzerland, long before he emigrated to the United States. In 1983 Ruedi and his wife, Lucille, started producing their handmade chocolate truffles in Bethel. The line now includes twenty-four to thirty different types of assorted choco-lates, chocolate dessert sauces, chocolate-covered nuts and coffee beans, almond toffee, truffle shells and cups, sugar-free chocolate and cocoa, baking powders, and supplies. The Hausers also create beautifully boxed assortments for corporate gifts, weddings, and special occasions like Valentine's Day. The chocolates in the shape of miniature Swiss gold ingots make an especially attractive gift box. Hauser chocolates are sold at retail outlets around the state and United States, and through their Web site and catalog. Although the main factory has moved to Rhode Island, the fudge and solid chocolates are still made in Bethel, right behind the Greenwood Avenue shop, with its old pressed-tin ceiling.

Knipschildt Chocolatier, 4 New Canaan Avenue, Norwalk, CT 06851; (203) 849–3141; www.Knipschildt.com. When we first encountered Knipschildt chocolate truffles, we could hardly believe how ambrosial they were, the memory of each bite lingering lusciously on the tongue. The chocolates come in some twenty flavors. They are made with Valrhona and Michel Cluizel French raw chocolate and a high amount of cocoa butter, and they are 100-percent natural, free of additives and preservatives. Founded in 1999 by Danish-born Fritz Knipschildt, the company now sells its truffles and other chocolates to upmarket stores like Aux Délices in Riverside and Darien Cheese & Fine Foods in Darien. There is also a line of dessert sauces with intense flavors (chocolate, raspberry pepper, passionfruit ginger, Amaretto mocha, butterscotch, and *dulce de leche*) and chocolate sticks to stir into coffee.

Middlesex Farm, P.O. Box 2470, Darien, CT 06820; (800) 779–FARM; www.middlesexfarm.com. Bobbi Stuart found that adding glazes can transform the most mundane cut of pork, beef, or chicken on the barbecue grill. She developed perky Ginger Jazz (a spicy pineapple glaze), Pepper Pizazz (red-pepper jelly) and Apricot Ginger Jive glazes, all of which also make tasty spreads on toast. Middlesex Farm glazes can be purchased from the Web site.

Newman's Own, 246 Post Road East, Westport, CT 06880; (203) 222–0136; www.newmansown.com. Actor Paul Newman and author A. E. Hotchner started this business in 1982 as something of a lark (the Web site says, "Fine foods since February" in Newman's wry style). It took off immediately with an initial high-quality salad dressing that featured Paul's smiling face. Since then, the company has grown phenomenally, and the natural-foods line now includes Tomato and Roasted Garlic Pasta Sauce, three flavors of Old Style Picture Show Microwave

On the Half Shell—Raw Bar Heaven along the Southwestern Shore

Less than a century ago, Norwalk was known as "the oyster capital of the nation," and hillocks of shucked shells lined the Norwalk River on Water Street. Though no longer the industry it once was, the bivalves are still found at six or more Norwalk oyster farms, and the bluepoints can be savored along the entire Connecticut coast. In these two intriguing seafood places, you will find varieties of tasty oysters fresh from local and other chilly waters east and west.

Elm Street Oyster House, 11 West Elm Street, Greenwich, CT 06830; (203) 629–5795; $$. Former luncheonette space has been converted into an attractive, modern, all-white cafe with sea-blue trim and a separate barroom with a long, long bar. The mostly seafood menu is especially strong on oysters, and the raw bar features a dozen types a day, among them Chesapeake, Malpeque, briny Kumomoto, Chincoteague, Louisiana, and bluepoint. Dips include horseradish, standard cocktail sauce, and a tangy mignonette of shallots, red wine vinegar, and cracked black peppercorns. Pan-fried oysters are also wonderful here, as are the littleneck clams, steamed mussels, poached salmon, grilled shrimp, and pan-fried catfish.

Ocean Drive, 128 Washington Street, South Norwalk, CT 06854; (203) 855–1665; $$. As you step inside this lively bar and restaurant, whose entire facade opens to the street in warm weather, you might think you are in Miami's South Beach, with the tropical white and ocean-blue interior and simulated porthole windows. A huge, orange-and-teal, handblown glass sculpture by Dale Chihuly hanging from the ceiling adds even more pizzazz. While all the seafood is ocean-fresh, oyster mavens belly up to the raw bar for the evening's five daily oyster specials from both East and West Coasts, as well as iced littlenecks, lobster cocktail, and spicy scallop-and-shrimp ceviche. It is easy to make a meal of the daily oyster harvest (we have), but Ocean Drive has other nautical delights, such as fresh tuna tartare, pan-fried rock shrimp, seared diver scallops, and steamed or broiled Maine lobster.

Popcorn, steak sauce, fruit salsas, lemonades, and Red Wine and Vinegar Salad Dressing. New products include Vodka Pasta Sauce, three new light dressings, and three fruit juices. Taking the company motto to heart—"Shameless Exploitation in Pursuit of the Common Good"—all Paul Newman's profits after taxes, some $125 million since 1982, go to a variety of charities. Newman's Own products, available nationally as well as via the company Web site, are recognizable by their clever labels, showing Paul in a variety of hats and outfits that are different with each product.

Pearl's Salad Dressing, P.O. Box 2098, Westport, CT 06880; (203) 226–6003; www.pearls.com. Paula Scholler began producing this special mustard vinaigrette during her thirteen years as a local Westport restaurateur. Her Pearl's Restaurant was a favorite on Westport's celebrity dining-out circuit, attracting Paul Newman, Robert Redford, and others. Redford, Don Imus, and other notables are fans of sugar-free Pearl's Original House Dressing and Pearl's Light Salad Dressing, which are available via mail order, at Gold's Delicatessen in Westport, the Village Market in Wilton, and through her Web site. Both dressings make tasty marinades for chicken, shrimp, and pork and even work with potato salad. Why the name Pearl? Because Paula, modestly, did not want her name to become high profile.

Rick Trading Company, 199 Ethan Allen Highway, Ridgefield, CT 06877; (203) 431–0505; www.rockingrogers.com. What do you get when you blend the honey-and-mustard tradition of the Carolinas with the spiciness of the Southwest and the tomato and molasses of the

Deep South? Rockin' Roger's Barbecue Sauce of course! It is the creation of Roger Kaufman, a rock musician and barbecue fanatic who lives in Weston. He took the tangy, sweet, and hot styles of three different barbecue-famous regions and combined them in a single "soulful" sauce, which, since 1989, has been selling all over the United States and on his Web site.

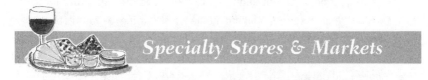

Specialty Stores & Markets

Abbondanza, 30 Charles Street, Westport, CT 06880; (203) 454–0840. The large showroom of Abbondanza, whose name means "abundance" in Italian, is part espresso bar, part catering, part takeout foods (salads, pasta dishes, desserts), and part store. The store section displays an eclectic mix of products, such as imported dried pastas, Provençal jams from Les Confituriers de Haut, Esprit du Sel gray sea salt, L'Estorvell caperberries and Arbequina olives, tomato paste in tubes, dried corn and lentils, chocolates, and other sundries.

Asia Bazaar, 131 Cove Street, Stamford, CT 06902; (203) 961–1514. Packed into a cluttered, distinctly utilitarian corner store is a huge variety of Indian products. If you are serious about preparing authentic Indian food, Asia Bazaar is a valuable resource for all kinds of rice in bulk (basmati, long, brown, jasmine, among others), Indian teas, a variety of beans and lentils, cardamom seeds, coriander, cloves, garam masala and other Indian spices, hot peppers, different kinds of flours, fresh produce,

Indian soft drinks, spicy snack foods, and much, much more. An Indian nostalgic for home can even find Bollywood videos here.

Aux Délices, 1075 East Putnam Avenue, Riverside, CT 06878; (203) 698–1066; www.auxdelicesfoods.com. When Debra Ponzak, former executive chef at Montrachet, a top New York City restaurant, opened this stylish gourmet take-out shop in late 1995, she raised the bar for local take-out and catering, making home entertaining a gourmet experience. Her Provençal-influenced menu changes daily and can be faxed to you for ordering ahead. There are usually six entree choices, more than a dozen side dishes, and at least six desserts to choose among. Sample entrees might be peach-and-shallot-stuffed pork loin, pesto mushroom lasagna, crab cakes with roasted yellow-pepper sauce. A few burnished copper-topped tables in the tiny shop are handy for noshing on soups, sandwiches, salads, and coffee while waiting for your order. The shop also sells directly, on-line, and via mail order a number of blue-chip delicacies like aged balsamic vinegars, capers, roasted red peppers, dried fruits, chocolate truffles, fondues, dessert sauces, Aux Délices spiced nuts, and famous labels in biscotti, biscuits, almond macaroons, crispy crepes, and butter cookies. Gift baskets and homemade cakes and tarts are available for overnight delivery. A second Aux Délices is now at West Elm Street in Greenwich (203–622–6644).

Darien Cheese & Fine Foods, Goodwives Shopping Center, Old Kings Highway North, Darien, CT 06820; (203) 655–4344. Compact, narrow, and full of alluring edibles, this immaculate shop is so tempting we want to scoop up everything in sight, like the dozen types of olives

fastidiously lined up in their crocks, capers and caperberries, a hanging array of sausages (that includes the Spanish jamón Serrano), and, as a centerpiece, dozens and dozens (at least fifty at any given time) of imported cheeses (mostly from France and Italy) and even a few Connecticut ones. Shelves along the wall contain delights to dream about, many from England and France: dessert sauces, rarefied chocolate truffles, jams, preserves, biscuits, and teas. In the rear are bins of coffee and a few nonfood items like cheese knives, cheese trays, and assorted baskets.

Deborah Ann's Homemade Chocolates, 453 Main Street, Ridgefield, CT 06877; (203) 438–0065. Chocolates made by two New York lawyers? An unlikely scenario, right? Wrong! That's what Deborah Ann and Mike Grissmer's candy shop is all about. Both Grissmers wanted a change of scene and a job that would make people happy. Drop by their wonderful all-white, tin-ceilinged shop, which reminds us of the movie *Chocolat*, with its intoxicating aromas and big open kitchen, and you will understand "happy." Though the main candy production has just moved to Brookfield, you can see the hand-rolled truffles, turtles, best-selling butter crunch, caramels, and other chocolates being made in the shop and watch as the Enrober machine coats the soft centers, Besides offering seventy varieties of their own chocolates, the Grissmers tempt the kid in all of us with sixty five-gallon glass jars of hard candies (Gummi Bears, jelly bellies, and the like), as well as Leonides Belgian chocolates. The sweet smell of chocolate that fills the air here is contagious.

Dr. Mike's, 158 Greenwood Avenue, Bethel, CT 06801; (203) 792–4388. Don't let appearance fool you. Inside this modest-looking ice-cream parlor, tucked into the rear of an old frame house, lurks some of the richest, tastiest ice cream in Connecticut. Since 1975, Robert Allison has been churning out as many as fifty flavors of ice cream, with a butterfat content of 16 percent. At any time, there are eight flavors—four regulars (vanilla, rich chocolate, strawberry, and chocolate lace-and-cream) and four daily specials. In warm months, thirty different flavors rotate during a given week. Among them are Swiss almond fudge, vanilla raspberry swirl, Oreo, and fudge swirl. Most popular are rich chocolate and chocolate lace-and-cream, which use 22- to 24-percent cocoa butter and Belgian Bensdorf chocolate. There are several tables and a handful of places to sit on the porch. The parking lot holds sixty cars, which gives you an idea of Dr. Mike's popularity. A second Dr. Mike's (444 Main Street, Monroe; 203–452–0499) is equally small, also with ample parking. And who, you might ask, is Dr. Mike? The man who lent Robert the money to begin this flourishing business so many years ago.

Drotos Brothers Market, 849 Kings Highway, Fairfield, CT 06432; (203) 333–7530; e-mail: drotos@bigplanet.com. The display space in this small, plain, freestanding Hungarian butcher shop is limited, but in the meat case are roasts and chops cut Hungarian style, Hungarian salamis, and Hungarian sausages of various types made on the premises. Limited shelf space is crowded with Hungarian and Polish imports: jars of plum and apricot butter, mushrooms, roasted peppers, gooseberries, sauerkraut; dried soup noodles in a variety of shapes; tins of diverse Hungarian paprikas and spices. A huge container on the floor is filled with poppy seed in bulk. For thirty years or more, Drotos Brothers has been a culinary "lifeline" to the many Hungarian immigrants in this area. It is located directly across the street from St. Emery's Church.

Fuji Mart, 1212 East Putnam Avenue, Cos Cob, CT 06807; (203) 698–2105. Compact and neatly organized, this tidy market is a rarity in Connecticut: a grocery dedicated solely to Japanese food products. Salmon, horse mackerel, and other fresh fish; sushi-ready maguro, tako, hirame, and other raw favorites; daikon, tofu, and other fresh vegetables; a variety of seaweeds, teas, rice, canned and dried goods—all these and much more are here. Fuji Mart is in the ground-floor, left-hand corner of a glass low-rise office building, just off exit 5 of I–95.

Good Food Good Things LLC, 865 Post Road, Darien, CT 06820; (203) 655–7355; www.goodfoodgoodthings.com. Formerly the Good Food Store, this large space, with its white pressed-tin high ceiling, brick walls, and painted wood floor, is an olfactory treat, especially if you enter from the rear parking lot where the open kitchen is located. The rear of the store, partitioned from the home-accessories front section (with elegant china, fresh flowers, and other gifts), is devoted to the kitchen, dessert display case, and counter where you can buy freshly made muffins, scones, croissants, bagels, pastries, cookies, and yummy breads (olive, rosemary, multigrain, and French baguettes among others), and unusual sandwiches and salads. There are a few tables where you may munch your goodies and sip coffee, and a small nook with gourmet mustards, oils, dressings, and jams. The new owners

Good Food Good Things's Cranberry Walnut Tart

Diane Browne, food manager of Good Food Good Things in Darien, shared this recipe with us. Cranberries are so New England that we like to make this dessert in autumn and early winter, when the fresh berries are widely available in the markets.

Tart Dough

½ pound unsalted butter

1 cup confectioners' sugar

1 teaspoon salt

1 teaspoon vanilla extract

1 egg

2 cups all-purpose flour

Cream butter and sugar together with an electric mixer. Add salt, vanilla, and egg. Mix well; then add flour. Mix until combined. Chill, wrapped in plastic wrap, until firm enough to roll. Roll dough between sheets of plastic wrap. Press into a 7-inch tart pan, making

are Michael and Beth duPont; Diane Browne is in charge of the kitchen and catering.

Kaas & Co., 83 Washington Street, Norwalk, CT 06854; (203) 838–6161; www.kaasnco.com. Also known as "A Taste of Holland," Jan Schenkels's spic-and-span shop has specialized, since 1990, in foods

sure all the air bubbles are pressed out of the corners. Bake at 350°F until set. Remove from oven and fill with tart filling.

Tart Filling

⅛ cup all-purpose flour

⅓ cup brown sugar

½ teaspoon cinnamon

⅓ corn syrup

1 large egg

½ teaspoon vanilla extract

5 tablespoons unsalted butter, melted and cooled to room temperature

⅔ cup walnut pieces

⅔ cup whole cranberries

Blend flour, brown sugar, and cinnamon in a bowl. Add corn syrup, egg, vanilla, and butter. Blend well. Stir in nuts and cranberries. Pour into partially prebaked tart shell. Bake at 350°F until light brown and mixture is set, approximately 25 minutes.

Makes 1 7-inch tart.

Good Food Good Things

865 Post Road
Darien, CT 06820
(203) 655–7355

and decorative items from the Netherlands and Indonesia. Walls are lined with blue-and-white Dutch tiles, and there are tables full of blue-and-white china jars and plates, tea towels, and other gift items. Homesick Netherlanders come from as far away as Pennsylvania and New Jersey for the Dutch cookies, jams, Droste cocoa, Pickwick teas, de Ruijter chocolates, Indonesian spices, honeycakes, *speculaasbrokken*,

Here's the Scoop on Southwest Connecticut's Best Ice Cream

Scoop! In a minuscule shop in the rear of a large building facing Main Street, accessed through a rear parking lot, you will find a chilling fact: some of the most delicious ice cream ever. Though Connecticut is blessed with many wonderful ice-cream parlors, ice-cream producers, and a mouthwatering variety of flavors, our vote for the best ice cream in this region goes to Mr. Shane's, which is rich, creamy (16-to-18 percent butterfat), and made from the best ingredients. Especially ambrosial is the chocolate (and we don't usually swoon over chocolate ice cream). Vanilla, the most popular, is heavenly, too. Also high on our list is Mud, an assemblage of coffee ice cream, Oreo cookies, fudge swirl, and almonds—in short a Wow! Prune armagnac, toasted almond, chocolate malt, and toasted coconut are other cold comforts. Since 1988 John Shane has been scooping up sixteen different flavors on any given day, from a total repertoire of more than eighty, all made on the tiny premises. The child's dip is like a regular single scoop elsewhere, the single dip is really a pile-on of scoops, and the largest size is so huge that a cone really cannot contain it. The shop is open from April to the week before Thanksgiving, but the ice cream is sold wholesale to various shops and restaurants in Connecticut (River Cat Grill in Rowayton, for one) and New York all year long.

Mr. Shane's Homemade Parlour Ice Cream

409 Main Street
Ridgefield, CT 06877
(203) 431-8020

marzipan cakes, candies, eighty-five types of Dutch licorice, as well as mixes and crackers. In the deli cases are Dutch cheeses—low-fat, regular, and aged Gouda, Leyden, Old Amsterdam, baby Edammer, farmers cheese, raw milk cheese, Friese Nagel, and Rookvlees—as well as ham, herring, and mackerel. Kaas & Co. even sells mettwurst, a smoked sausage shipped from a Dutch butcher in Michigan. There are six small tables-for-two where you can lunch on simple sandwiches and Dutch hot chocolate.

La Sorpresa, 61 Cedar Street, Norwalk, CT 06854; (203) 838–9809. This modest little shop-bakery reveals the ethnic diversity of Connecticut's southwestern region, which has recently attracted many immigrants from Latin America. Owned and run by Colombians, the shop (whose exterior resembles a Spanish-style house with red tile roof) features freshly made sweet rolls, apple turnovers, crisp "pig's ears" pastries, breads, and rolls. Our favorite item is *arepesa chocolo*, a loose-textured corn cake, which, when warmed slightly, makes a tasty morning snack. A minuscule, no-frills restaurant is part of La Sorpresa, with a separate entrance and very simple Colombian food at Depression-era prices.

Oriental Food Market & Deli, 109 New Canaan Avenue, Norwalk, CT 06850; (203) 847–0070. This great source for Chinese, Japanese, and Philippine foods also has products from Korea, Thailand, and India. Revel in the fresh snowpeas, tofu, Chinese parsley (cilantro), Chinese cabbage, bok choy, bean sprouts, sweet pickles, Japanese pumpkins, and Chinese squash, as well as frozen Chinese dumplings, Filipino pampango lumpia, and Chinese sweet sausage. Shelves are crammed with soy sauces, oriental noodles, nori (seaweed), dried beans, roasted sesame seeds, nuts, dried mushrooms, sugar palm, pickled garlic, mung beans, rice vinegars, tamarind seasoning, kim chee mix, Madras curry powder, and twenty-pound sacks of rice. The canisters of China lychee black tea (a favorite of ours) save us a trip to New York's Chinatown. A small housewares section carries electric rice cookers and Chinese tableware. There is even a small take-out section with sushi and a few Chinese dishes.

Scandia Food & Gifts, 30 High Street, Norwalk, CT 06851; (203) 838–2087; www.scandiafood.com. We would expect an emporium of Scandinavian foods to be bright and cheerful, and Scandia is, with neat displays of cookies, crackers, crisps, breads, pudding mixes, and refrigerated cases with frozen fish (including lutefisk), tubes of salmon and herring paste, and cod-roe caviar. Scandinavian cheeses include Gräddost, Herrgårds, Greve/Emmentaler, Norvegia, Jarlsberg, Prästost, Västerbotten, and Gjetost, as well as mushroom, shrimp, and ham cheese spreads. A large adjoining room displays sweaters, clothes, dolls, calendars, books, copperware, party supplies, Christmas ornaments, candleholders, candles, and other gifts and accessories from Sweden, Norway, Denmark, and Finland.

Simpson & Vail, 3 Quarry Road, Brookfield, CT 06804; (203) 775–0240 or (800) 282–TEAS; www.svtea.com. All about tea, this restful haven tucked into a rock quarry is ideal for sampling a huge variety of teas, which include green, black,

TRADING UP

All five of Trader Joe's Connecticut stores are in this part of the state. Trader Joe's is not a typical food chain or we would not include it in this book. We know devotees who travel across the state for the many unusual items at these unique gourmet bazaars, whose prices are often well below those of supermarkets. Trader Joe's specializes in organic, vegetarian, kosher, fat-free, sugar-free, gluten-free, sodium-free, and sybaritic foods, some of which are not available elsewhere. Great buys are imported cheeses, crackers and breads, nuts and dried fruits, dried pastas, jams and preserves, salsas and sauces, chocolates, candies, and cookie assortments. Natural cereals, tofutti, fresh soy milk and other soy products, organic blueberries and other fruits and vegetables, pasta sauces, olive oils and specialty vinegars, smoked salmon, organic fresh chickens, wasabi peas, soy nuts, and other snack items are among scores of products sold here, many with the Trader Joe label. Vitamins, herbal soaps, and shampoos are also available. The frozen cakes and pies are exceptional; our all-time favorite is the chocolate ganache torte with a chocolate mousse center. What makes Trader Joe's such a habit is that every week new, irresistible products arrive to tempt us.

Trader Joe's

436 Post Road
Darien, CT 06820
(203) 656–1414

400 Post Road East
Westport, CT 06880
(203) 226–8966

2258 Black Rock Turnpike
Fairfield, CT 06430
(203) 330–8301

113 Mill Plain Road
Danbury, CT 06811
(203) 739–0098

560 Boston Post Road
Orange, CT 06477
(203) 795–5505

www.traderjoes.com

and white teas, aromatic, blended, organic, flavored, herbal, even decaffeinated. All kinds of tea accompaniments you might crave are here—shortbreads, cookies, scone mixes, jams, honey, and Devon creams—as well as tea accessories—teapots, tea cozies, and strainers, and other related products. These include Bunzlauer stoneware from Poland and English Victorian bone-china mugs. Flavored, organic, and decaffeinated coffees, salsas, and other specialty food products are sold here as well.

Versailles, 315 Greenwich Avenue, Greenwich, CT 06830; (203) 661–6634. Sometimes it seems as though the cake at every wedding or special event we attend in Fairfield County comes from Versailles. No, not the royal estate in France, but a small patisserie, where Maurice Versailles has for decades been specializing in superb cakes, tarts, and breads, which are clearly worthy of being served in *any* palace. The Versailles repertoire includes French classics like Opera, Casino, Madeleine, Clairefontaine, Strawberry Montmartre, and Pont Neuf, along with individual delights like Paris Brest, St. Honoré, and assorted fruit tarts. A small cafe in the rear is popular for breakfast, lunch, and dinner, with salads, quiches, fish dishes, and those yummy pastries. Catering is another Versailles talent.

Farmers' Markets

For the most up-to-date farmers' market locations, days and times, call Connecticut Department of Agriculture at (860) 713–2503, visit the Web site at www.state.ct.us/doag/, or e-mail at ctdeptag@po.state.ct.us.

Bethel Farmers' Market, 67 Stoney Hill Road, Bethel. Saturdays from 9:00 A.M. to 1:00 P.M., mid-July through October.

Bridgeport Farmers' Market, Wall Street, Bridgeport. Fridays from 9:00 A.M. to 2:00 P.M., last week of July through October.

Bridgeport Farmers' Market II, United Congregational Church, 877 Park Avenue, Bridgeport. Thursdays from 2:00 to 6:00 P.M., last week of July through October.

Danbury City Center Farmers' Market, Danbury Green, between Delay and Ives Streets, Danbury. Thursdays, from 3:00 to 6:30 P.M., mid-July through October.

Darien Farmers' Market, parking lot behind CVS, one-half block from Boston Post Road at Corbin Drive, Darien. Wednesdays from 11:00 A.M. to 4:00 P.M., mid-June through mid-November.

Fairfield Farmers' Market, Greenfield Hills, 1950 Bronson Road, Fairfield. Saturdays from 1:00 to 4:00 P.M., mid-July through October.

Greenwich Farmers' Market, Horse Neck parking lot, Greenwich. Saturdays from 9:30 A.M. to 1:30 P.M., mid-May through mid-November.

Naugatuck Farmers' Market, lot next to post office, corner of Maple and North Water Streets, Naugatuck. Fridays from 11:00 A.M. to 3:00 P.M., early July through October.

 **New Canaan Farmers' Market,** Center School parking lot, South Avenue and Maple Street, New Canaan. Saturdays from 10:00 A.M. to 2:00 P.M., mid-June through the Saturday after Thanksgiving.

Norwalk Farmers' Market, North Water Street parking lot at the Maritime Center, South Norwalk. Wednesdays from noon to 6:00 P.M., last week in July through October.

Sandy Hook Farmers' Market, 5 Glen Road, Sandy Hook. Sundays from 9:00 A.M. to 1:00 P.M., mid-July through October.

Seymour Farmers' Market, Old Seymour Middle School, Pine Street, Seymour. Tuesdays from noon to 6:00 P.M., late May through October.

Shelton Farmers' Market, corner of Cornell and Canal Streets, Shelton. Saturdays from 9:30 A.M. to 1:00 P.M., mid-July through October.

Stamford Farmers' Market, Columbus Park, Main Street and West Park Place, Stamford. Mondays and Thursdays from 10:00 A.M. to 3:00 P.M., mid-July through the first week of November.

Stratford Farmers' Market, Deluca Field, Main Street, Stratford. Mondays from 1:00 to 5:00 P.M., mid-July through October.

Trumbull Farmers' Market, Long Hill Green, Trumbull. Thursdays from 3:00 to 6:00 P.M., early June through October.

Weston Farmers' Market, School Administration parking lot, School Road, Weston. Saturdays from 8:00 to 11:00 A.M., first week in June through first week in October.

 Farm Stands

Beardsley's Cider Mill & Orchard, 278 Leavenworth Road (Route 21), Shelton, CT 06484; (203) 926–1098; e-mail: cbeardsley01@snet.net. Dan is the third-generation Beardsley managing this one-hundred-acre farm, and the apple of his eye is—apples, twenty acres and forty-two varieties of them. Some trees planted in 1918 are still producing old-fashioned apple types like Summer Rambeo, Baldwin, Blue Pearman, Wagner, and Sheep's Nose. From late September to Christmas Eve, you can watch the cider-making process in Dan's cider mill, then buy some of the fresh, cold cider, made from McIntosh apples. The farm store sells other fruits—peaches, pears, and quince—as well as fresh honey and nine kinds of apple pies made from Northern Spies. Call ahead for hours and fruit in season. In spring, stop by for the maple-syrup processing.

Blue Jay Orchards, 125 Plumtrees Road, Bethel, CT 06801; (203) 748–0119; www.bluejayorchards.com. You'll find blue jays (and other birds) on plum trees at this 120-acre farm, where the Pattersons invite

FOOD LOVERS' TIP

Ever hear of wineberries? They resemble raspberries but are sweeter, and they are believed to be grown only between the Hudson River and Connecticut River Valleys. Beardsley's may be the only farm producing them in quantity large enough for sale. They sell them only at the Trumbull Farmers' Market on Long Hill Green.

you to pick-your-own apples from thirty varieties. Most popular is the Macoun, followed by the Mutsu (the big yellow Japanese hybrid sometimes called Crispin); there are McIntosh, Gala, Cortland, Granny Smith, Empire, and Winesap, too. Then browse the farm's Store & Gift Shop for apple pies, cider doughnuts, and fresh cider (August through October), pastries from the farm's bakery, as well as maple syrup, honey, peaches, pears, and pumpkins. There are hayrides to the pumpkin patch in September and October. The Pattersons also have a luncheonette and a Sample Tasting Corner for sampling the various types of apples. The store and cider mill are open daily, August through December, from 9:00 A.M. to 5:30 P.M.

Jones Family Farms, 555 Israel Hill Road, Shelton, CT 06484; (203) 929-8425; www.jonesfamilyfarms.com. Philip Jones began farming here in the 1850s, and six generations of Joneses have worked the land ever since. Terry and Jean Jones and their son Jamie are the current "family in charge" of the 400 acres in these rolling hills. They have grown

Christmas trees since 1947 and now have strawberries, blueberries, pumpkins, squash and gourds, all awaiting pick-your-own-ers. Just hop aboard the "Berry Ferry" wagon and ride to one of two locations—Strawberry Valley or Pumpkinseed Hill—for picking from June through August, depending on crop conditions (call ahead for days and times).

Shortt's Farm & Garden Center, 52-A Riverside Road, Sandy Hook, CT 06482; (203) 426–9283. On a mere four acres, Jim and Sue Shortt produce an amazing variety of organic vegetables and fruits. For sale at their farm store during the growing season are beets, brussels sprouts, caulifower, broccoli, beans, hot and mild peppers, Heirloom and hybrid tomatoes, six types of eggplants, summer and winter squash, radishes, carrots, leeks, onions, celery, spinach, bok choy, cucumbers for eating and pickling, six types of lettuces, vitamin lettuce, cantaloupes, watermelons, basil and other herbs, as well as fresh eggs, honey, and jams. They also have 125 blueberry bushes where you may pick-your-own. The store is open year-round, but hours vary, depending on the season. Check ahead.

Silverman's Farm, Inc., 451 Sport Hill Road, Easton, CT 06612; (203) 261–3306; www.silvermansfarm.com. You want apples? Peaches? Nectarines? Plums? They're all here in many varieties (twenty-five types of apples alone), and you can pick-your-own from July to September. But there's more: Irv Silverman's "Animal Farm" has sheep, goats, deer, emus, pigs, buffalo, llamas, and exotic birds and is open year-round, as is the farm market for fresh pies and jams. There are picnic tables in the park area and tractor rides through the orchards from August to October. The "pumpkin patch" in fall sports twenty varieties of squashes and gourds, as well as pumpkins, cornstalks, scarecrows, and sunflowers. In November you can watch the pressing of the apples at the cider mill—one of the state's oldest—and enjoy the resulting *hot* cider. Open year-round; check for hours.

Treat Farm, 361 Old Tavern Road, Orange, CT 06477; (203) 799–2453; e-mail: treat.farm@snet.net. Owner Jeff Wilson grows and sells field-fresh sweet corn, tomatoes, pumpkins, squash, peppers, and eggplants, plus various other veggies. His stand is open from July through October and in December for Christmas trees, on Saturday and Sunday from 9:00 A.M. to 6:00 P.M. and Monday through Friday from noon to 7:00 P.M.

Warrup's Farm, 51 John Read Road, West Redding, CT 06896; (203) 938–9403. This organic farm's roadside stand sells organic lettuces, tomatoes, peppers, zucchini, garlic, potatoes, eggplant, broccoli, beans, and other vegetables and herbs, from the farm, as well as fresh flowers and maple syrup. You may also pick your own vegetables, herbs, and flowers as they come into season, from late July on. You will find Warrup's at the Weston Farmers' Market each Saturday in season. Open from July through October, but check ahead for hours. In March, during maple-syrup season, visitors to the sugarhouse can watch the syrup-making process from sap to "liquid gold."

February: Taste of Ridgefield, Ridgefield Community Center, 316 Main Street, Ridgefield, CT 06877; (203) 438–4585. Sponsored by the Rotary Club, this annual fund-raiser is usually held the first Sunday of February (check ahead to be sure). This event offers a chance to critique specialties of twenty-two of Ridgefield's most fabulous eateries (it is a great restaurant town) in a worthy cause. More than a "taste," the admission ticket permits unlimited samplings of appetizers, entrees, wine and beer on the main floor, leisurely sit-down bites of desserts with tea or coffee in a cafe-like setting upstairs. Live jazz and chamber music alternate through the day at two sessions: 11:30 A.M. to 2:00 P.M., 4:00 to 7:00 P.M. Each session is limited to 300 attendees because of fire-code restrictions; 100 percent of the proceeds, some $30,000, goes to thirty-two local philanthropies.

February: Annual Taste of Stamford, Stamford Marriott, 2 Stamford Forum, Stamford, CT 06901; (203) 359–4761. On your mark, go! In a three-hour period, from 5:30 to 8:30 P.M., on a single day in the last week of February, you can eat your way through Stamford's finest. For a set price, you might pick, choose, or wolf down the wares of some thirty area restaurants, bakeries, caterers, and others in the food establishment, as well as samplings from various vineyards, beer importers, and specialty-coffee distributors. It is munching for a worthy cause, as the proceeds go to the Stamford Chamber of Commerce for a host of educational and community services.

Pasta with Cauliflower, Oil, Garlic, and Hot Pepper

Sally Maraventano, Wilton cooking-school instructor, adapted this delicious easy-to-make vegetable dish from her attractive cookbook, Festa del Giardino, to share with us. Its centerpiece is cauliflower—cavolfiore in Italian—which Mark Twain jokingly called "cabbage with a college education." As the saying goes, you don't need to be Italian to enjoy Italian food.

1 head of cauliflower
1 slice white bread
2 large garlic cloves
Crushed red pepper flakes to taste
½ cup olive oil (preferably extra-virgin)
Salt to taste

1 pound conchiglie (fluted shells) or other short macaroni
2 tablespoons minced Italian flat-leaf parsley
½ cup freshly grated Romano cheese
4 ounces pitted Gaeta black olives, chopped (optional)

1. Remove all leaves from the caulifower and rinse in cold water.
2. Put the whole cauliflower in a pot with 4 quarts salted water. Place the white bread slice on top of the cauliflower to absorb the strong odor

April–May: Taste of The Nation, Italian Center of Stamford, 1620 Newfield Avenue, Stamford, CT 06905. An annual fund-raiser (since 1989) for SOS (Share Our Strength), an antihunger, antipoverty organization, this corporate-sponsored event is held in late April or early May. Contact is Linda Kavanagh at (203) 323–4185, e-mail at Linda@maxexposure.net. Some sixty area restaurants, wineries, brew-

during the cooking. Cover the pot, bring the water to a boil, lower the heat, and cook until fork-tender but not mushy (about 20 minutes). Remove the bread and drain the cauliflower. Remove the hard core of the cauliflower.

3. Sauté the garlic cloves and red pepper flakes in olive oil until golden; then remove the garlic. For a more intense flavor, mince the garlic cloves beforehand and do not remove them from the oil. Add the cauliflower to the oil, breaking it into small pieces with a fork. Turn it until it is thoroughly coated with the oil. Add salt to taste and cook over high heat for 3 to 4 minutes. Turn off the heat and set aside.

4. Meanwhile, cook the pasta in 6 quarts of boiling water to which 2 tablespoons of salt have been added, until al dente, about 8 to 10 minutes. Drain, reserving ½ cup of the cooking water.

5. Toss the cauliflower with the pasta in a warm serving bowl. Add the reserved hot water if mixture is too dry. Top with the minced parsley and serve at once, passing the grated Romano separately.

Note: To make the dish spicier, add the chopped black olives when you toss the cauliflower and pasta together.

Serves 4–5 as a first course.

eries, and specialty-food shops participate. A single entrance fee enables you to sample an extravaganza of delicious food and cooking demonstrations.

***June*: Secrets of Great PBS Chefs,** Norwalk, CT. This special late-June event, held annually since 2001, is sponsored by and benefits the

Public Broadcasting System. For specific date and locale, call the PBS Special Events Department at (800) 287-2788 or check the PBS Web site at www.specialevents@CPTV.org. This high-powered, three-hour evening lets you rub elbows and lift forks with famous chefs who have been on the PBS television series. The chefs (who in 2003 included Rick Bayless, Joanne Weir, and Michael Colameco) provide a live demonstration and dinner at a set price.

July: **Chef's Festival,** Columbus Park, Stamford, CT 06901; (203) 348-5285; www.stamford-downtown.com. Held on four consecutive Thursdays, beginning in mid-July, from noon to 2:00 P.M., this popular happening, sponsored by the Stamford Downtown Special Services District, gives browsers a chance to sample the fare of ten to fourteen local restaurants, with proceeds going to benefit community social services. There is no entrance fee, just a modest per-plate charge.

August: **Annual Milford Oyster Festival,** Fowler Field & Town Green, Milford, CT 06460; (203) 878-5363; www.milfordoysterfestival.org. If it is the third Saturday in August, you must be in Milford, on the Green or at Fowler Field. Billed as the largest one-day event in New England, this festival began in 1974; now between 50,000 and 60,000 people attend. Some seventy-five nonprofit organizations man (or woman) booths in the huge food court, where you can buy anything your palate desires from burgers and hot dogs to, yes, oysters, which come raw, fried, stewed. Headline entertainers, canoe races, art and crafts exhibits (with 225 vendors), a Classic Car Show are all part of the day's fun. Hours are from 9:00 A.M. to 5:00 P.M.

September: Annual Norwalk Oyster Festival, Veterans Park, Seaview Avenue, Norwalk, CT 06854; (203) 838–9444; www.seaport.org/oysterplaces. Circle the dates: the weekend after Labor Day. This "biggie" started small in 1978 and now draws as many as 80,000 visitors over a three-day period. Oysters are definitely in the swim, with oyster boats and tall ships in the harbor, an "oyster pavilion" with displays commemorating the decades of oystering in Norwalk, an oyster-shucking contest, and "Celebrity Oyster Slurp-Off," in which dignitaries demonstrate their oyster-downing prowess. Oysters star in the twenty food booths, too, along with clams, soft-shell crabs, lobster, shrimp, fish, calamari, jambalaya, pizza, Belgian waffles, and a host of international favorites, with proceeds to go to community groups, social services, and scholarship programs. Skydiving, marching bands, entertainers on three stages, and arts-and-crafts exhibits keep the crowds entertained. Call for hours or check the Web site.

Learn to Cook

Aux Délices, 23 Acosta Street, Stamford, CT 06905; (203) 326–4540. In new corporate headquarters, chef-owner Debra Ponzak has installed an all-new, all-modern 5,000-square-foot kitchen with stainless steel tables. Cooking classes for adults and also for children will feature courses on basics, ethnic recipes, and easy entertainment, among other subjects.

Cucina Casalinga, 171 Drum Hill Road, Wilton, CT 06897; (203) 762–0768; www.cucinacasalinga.com. Sally Maraventano has conducted

Ronnie Fein's
Fresh Apple Brown Betty

This delicious dessert is from food writer/cooking-school instructor Ronnie Fein. It makes a great treat any time of year but seems especially appropriate during the fall harvest season, when Connecticut's apple crop is at its crisp-and-crunchiest. This is an easy dessert you can make in less than 30 minutes.

5–6 pie apples, such as
  Granny Smith, Rhode
  Island Greenings, or
  Golden Delicious
Juice of ½ lemon
4 cups diced home-style
  white bread

¾ cup brown sugar
½ cup unsalted butter, melted
¾ teaspoon ground cinnamon
¼ teaspoon freshly ground
  nutmeg
Pinch of salt

1. Preheat the oven to 375°F. Peel the apples and remove the cores. Cut the apples into bite-size pieces and squeeze lemon juice over the pieces. Place apples in a baking dish.

2. Combine in a bowl the diced bread, brown sugar, melted butter, cinnamon, nutmeg, and salt. Toss ingredients to coat the bread completely. Put the coated bread mixture on top of the apples.

3. Bake for 50–60 minutes or until the top is golden brown and crusty. Cool slightly, then serve warm, preferably topped with vanilla ice cream.

Serves 6.

cooking classes in her home since 1981. Her kitchen has a Tuscan wood-burning pizza oven. Sally's emphasis is on Italian regional cooking, especially Sicily, the home of her grandfather. Each class, which is sometimes conducted by a guest chef, stands alone, with a theme covering a complete meal, which the class enjoys afterwards. Recent themes: Thirty Minute Italian Meals, Hearty Do-Ahead Italian Meals, and Fabulous Fish. Check her Web site or call for the upcoming schedule. Classes of fifteen are held year-round and there are classes for children eleven to sixteen years old. Sally also leads tours to the Italian markets of Arthur Avenue in the Bronx and conducts annual culinary tours to three regions of Italy, where classes are taught by notable Italian chefs. Sally's enthusiasm for the foods of Italy is infectious, whether in teaching or tour guiding.

Ronnie Fein School of Creative Cooking, 32 Heming Way, Stamford, CT 06903; (203) 322–7114. Since the 1970s, food writer Ronnie Fein has been teaching individually designed, one-on-one cooking workshops in her home, at sessions lasting three to three and a half hours. Usually six recipes are developed in the hands-on, single-day sessions.

Two Steps Downtown Grille, 5 Ives Street, Danbury, CT 06810; (203) 794–0032. Seasonal cooking classes, held in the kitchen of the restaurant, are conducted by owners Tom Devine and Keith O'Marra. Usually there are four sessions, in each of which four dishes are prepared. Participants may partake of any or all of the four, with a price reduction for the entire series. Each session includes tasting of all the prepared dishes, recipes, and wine. Though the classes are serious,

Susan Goodman's Talk-of-the-Party Hors d'Oeuvres

Susan Goodman has been in the catering business in Connecticut for years and has a repertoire of fifty or more creative hors d'oeuvres recipes. The following trio, which she was happy to share with us, are easy to make for a small gathering of six to eight people or a large party.

Connecticut Crab Cakes

½ cup mayonnaise

1 cup cracker meal

2 tablespoons fresh lemon
   juice plus the zest

2 tablespoons chopped fresh
   parsley

2 eggs, beaten

2 teaspoons Old Bay seasoning

1 pound fresh crabmeat,
   drained and picked over

2 finely chopped green onions

Mix half the mayonnaise and half the cracker meal with the remaining ingredients. Shape mixture into 15 large cakes or 30 tiny ones. Roll each in the remaining mayonnaise and then the remaining cracker meal. Bake in a 425°F oven about 15 minutes. Serve immediately with fresh lemon slices and tartar sauce.

Grilled Walnut-Stuffed Prunes

1 pound pitted prunes

1 cup Marsala wine

1 cup walnut halves, toasted

1 pound thick-cut bacon, cut into
   thirds (Susan prefers Nodine's)

Marinate prunes in the Marsala wine for about 1 hour. Drain prunes, pat dry, then stuff each one with a walnut half, wrap in bacon, and spear with a toothpick. Brush lightly with oil and grill about 5 minutes, or until bacon is cooked, turning once or twice. This can also be done on a cookie sheet in the broiler.

Roasted Plum Tomato with Confit of Ripe Olives, Fresh Basil, and Parmesan

5 ripe plum tomatoes, cut into
 ¼-inch slices
1 tablespoon olive oil (or
 enough to coat the tomato
 slices)
Bunch of fresh basil, coarsely
 chopped

¼ cup grated Parmesan cheese
½ cup sliced ripe olives
6 cloves garlic, finely chopped
¼ cup olive oil
1 baguette of bread cut into ¼-
 inch slices, brushed with
 olive oil, and toasted

Brush tomato slices with tablespoon of olive oil and roast in a 350°F oven about 1 hour. Mix chopped basil with Parmesan, olives, and garlic. Add ¼ cup olive oil and mix well. Top the toasted baguette slices with the roasted tomatoes and then sprinkle with the confit of olives, Parmesan, and basil. Serve immediately.

Serves 6–8.

Susan Goodman Catering

327 Old Norwalk Road
New Canaan
CT 06840
(203) 972-3793

there is a great deal of chatter, joshing, and wine imbibing, proof that you can have fun while learning.

Learn about Wine

Grapes, 10 Cross Street, Norwalk, CT 06851; (800) 434–9463; www.grapeswine.com. This bunch of grapes is a trio of wine experts: John Caplan, Jim Winston, and Holt Gollatz. They began operations in 1986 as "wine selection specialists" and proudly claim to have tasted more than 5,000 wines in the process of selecting the ones they favor and sell. You can visit their Norwalk store, select from their wine displays, or check them out on the Web site. Grapes specializes in wine-tasting dinners at hotels, restaurants, and special events—all listed on the Web site, along with menus, wines selected, and other details. Their typical wine dinners traverse the state, with recent ones at Pierpont's in Hartford and Versailles in Greenwich. Information about upcoming tastings, discussions, and dinner reservations is available by phone or Web site.

Silvermine Tavern, 284 Silvermine Avenue, Norwalk, CT 06850; (203) 847–4558; www.silverminetavern.com; $$. Each monthly wine dinner in this historic old tavern-restaurant-inn spotlights a wine theme and includes nine wines and a five-course dinner for a fixed price. Themes are organized around wine regions—such as Tuscany, the Rhone Valley, Australia, or Napa Valley—or single wineries like Beringer, Mondavi, or Kendall Jackson, or wine types, like the Annual Fall

Harvest Zinfandel dinner. Many participants are regular habitués, but newcomers are warmly welcomed, and there is always an animated discussion of the wines, usually led by an expert. If you want to be on the mailing list, call or sign up via the Web.

Landmark Eateries

Baang Café and Bar, 1191 East Putnam Avenue, Riverside, CT 06878; (203) 637–2114; $$$. The first to introduce Asian fusion cooking to Connecticut, this unusual restaurant opened in 1995 with a (yes) bang! Its eclectic decor (designed by avant-garde architect-designer David Rockwell) vibrates with colors and unusual shapes. Even so, it plays second banana to the food, which is so fresh it crackles, from wok or grill in the open kitchen directly to table. East really does meet West here, as western cooking techniques combine with Asian ingredients. The result is a series of palate-awakening taste combinations. Our steady favorites are the pan-fried pepper oysters, grilled Szechuan beef, and gossamerlike crispy spinach deep-fried in soy oil. Much copied by other restaurants is the crackling calamari salad with ever-so-lightly breaded squid, a hint of hot chile oil, and frisée and baby lettuces in a lime-miso vinaigrette. In peak hours the decibel level is high, but the fresh, creative food is worth the cacaphony.

Bernard's Inn at Ridgefield, 20 West Lane, Ridgefield, CT 06877; (203) 438–8282; www.bernardsinnatridgefield.com; $$$. The Inn at Ridgefield, in a white clapboard house, has been around for decades but

Silvermine Tavern's
New England Clam Chowder

Innkeeper Frank Whitman is willing to share one of his Silvermine Tavern mainstays, his clam chowder. In his atmospheric tavern, we like to think that patriots during the Revolutionary War enjoyed the chowder as much as we do, but it is probably just a romantic notion to think the recipe is that old.

2 cups cherrystone or littleneck clams with their juice*
1 can clam juice
4 strips thick-cut smoked bacon
½ cup diced celery
1 cup diced onion
2½ cups medium all-purpose or Yukon Gold potatoes,

peeled and diced into ½-inch cubes
2 cups water
2 teaspoons salt
1 teaspoon finely chopped fresh thyme
2 cups heavy cream
Salt and pepper to taste

* Fresh chopped clams are available at many fish markets or in some grocery stores and are fine to use. It is also possible to get fresh clams in the shell and shuck your own.

was showing its age when Bernard and Sarah Bouissou took it over in 2000. They not only refurbished it head to toe, but they raised its culinary level spectacularly. It is now so lovely—outside with its plantings, inside with its four airy, impeccably maintained dining rooms—that it is almost a no-brainer choice for special occasion dining. But Bernard's skills in the kitchen (he worked at Le Cirque in New York for years) are

1. Drain clams and save the juice. Strain the juice to remove any bits of shell. Add the canned clam juice to make 1½ cups.
2. In a skillet, cook the bacon until crisp, remove bacon and all but 2 tablespoons of the bacon fat. Drain and chop the cooked bacon. Sauté the celery and onion in the bacon fat until the onion is clear.
3. In a soup pot, cook potatoes in the water with the salt until barely tender. Add the bacon, onion, celery, clam juice, thyme, and chopped clams. Bring to a simmer and cook for 2 minutes. Add the cream and return to a simmer; season to taste with the salt and pepper. The clams should be cooked through, but not overcooked or they will become tough.
4. Serve immediately with New England Common Crackers or oyster crackers.

Silvermine Tavern
284 Silvermine Avenue
Norwalk, CT 06850
(203) 847-4558
www.silverminetavern.com
$$

It is possible to add a pat of butter at the end, but the chowder is rich enough with the heavy cream as is.

Serves 8.

so creative that they make even a regular lunch or dinner special. He splices modern ingredients—often Asian—into a classical French repertoire to create gems like lobster fricassee with snow peas, fiddlehead ferns, taro-root and lotus-root chips, in a lemongrass lobster emulsion. The lengthy wine list has been as thoughtfully selected as each table's floral arrangement, with many well-priced vintages as well as rarer ones.

City Limits Diner, 135 Harvard Avenue, Stamford, CT 06902; (203) 348–7000; $. With its Art Deco decor, oversize booths, and quadruple-lifesize coffee-cup-and-doughnut display, City Limits has a retro look. Surprisingly, it dates only from 2002, and its modern American menu reads like today. There are a few old-timey dishes, like Southern fried chicken, but many others have an Asian touch: steamed bass with fresh ginger and scallions in a wine-soy sauce and crispy crab wontons, for example. An in-house bakery does a variety of sweet rolls, muffins, donuts, pies, cakes, and tortes. Reasonable prices (another touch of yesteryear) make City Limits a tempting place to drop by, especially for breakfast, but also for lunch, snacks, or dinner. Another reason for a visit: It is just plain fun. Surprisingly in a diner, the beer list is exceptional, with many microbrew selections from all over North America and Europe.

Coromandel Cuisine of India, 25 Old King's Highway North, Darien, CT 06820; (203) 662–1213; $–$$. In the past ten years, Indian restaurants have sprouted all over the state, but Coromandel outdistances them all, for its creative variety of South and North Indian dishes and the gracious welcome every guest receives. Mirrors, wall paintings, and colored lights create a festive ambience in limited space. Best value is the mod-

Biggest Dining-Out "Sleeper"

French restaurants of all stripes—haute cuisine, cafes, and bistros—are major landmarks along southwestern Connecticut's culinary landscape. What makes Ondine special is that it delivers first-rate French food in surroundings reminiscent of a French country inn at prices far below many more ordinary non-French restaurants. Though Ondine's a la carte prices are themselves reasonable, the best deal is the prix fixe menu, which offers five courses (soup, salad, a choice among ten appetizers, ten entrees, and ten desserts) and coffee or tea at a price charged by some restaurants for two courses alone. This may sound like too much food, but portions are sensible, not gargantuan. With such dishes as *confit de canard*, billi bi, baked onion soup, salmon filet *aux poivres*, hazelnut soufflé, and tarte Tatin, chef-owner Dieter Thiel sets a pretty table with fresh flowers, candles, Staffordshire china, and comfortable, padded plush chairs. Ondine, in its handsomely appointed, two-tiered dining room, offers *haute* dining at *bas* prices. It's enough to make you hum the *Marseillaise*.

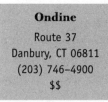

Ondine

Route 37
Danbury, CT 06811
(203) 746–4900
$$

estly priced buffet lunch, consisting of seven or eight hot dishes, breads, sundries, chutneys, salad, and several desserts. As if that isn't plenty, a waiter delivers piping-hot naan bread and fresh-baked, mildly spicy tandoori chicken, as part of the fixed-price buffet. The a la carte menu is not pricey, either. On it you will find chef Anthony's signature lamb chops, sizzling hot and well-seasoned Indian style, and a delightful appetizer

Top Dogs

If you want to start an argument, state *dog*matically that so-and-so's hot dogs are the world's best. We won't bark up *that* tree, because taste is so individual, but we will say that what makes Rawley's *our* top hot dogs—with more bite than bark—are three factors: (1.) the way they cook the Roessler's beef-and-pork wieners, starting them in a fryer, then finishing them off on the grill; (2.) the grilled buns, which add crunchiness to the finished dog; and (3.) "the works," the bacon, mustard, sauerkraut, and raw onions blanketed over the dog in its bun. This is no fast-food delivery:

Rawley's

1886 Post Road
Fairfield, CT 06430
(203) 259-9023
$

Expect to wait five or even ten minutes for your finished dog. Rawley's is supposedly Martha Stewart's favorite hot dog spot, but don't expect anything fancy. The weathered shacklike building on the Post Road has just a few stools at the counter, where you place your order and can watch the cooking process in the open kitchen. Rawley's also sells burgers, tuna melts, and other sandwiches, for take-out and eat-in, but, doggone it, the franks are best-of-show.

called Coromandel's Shamm Savera—small spinach cups filled with farm cheese in a tangy tomato-honey sauce. Whether you like your Indian food mild, moderate, or incendiary, Jose Pullopilly and his staff happily oblige.

Gail's Station House, 378 Main Street, Ridgefield, CT 06877; (203) 438–9775; $–$$. This boisterous local hangout consists of two dining areas with wood floors, pressed-tin ceilings, and wall pegs "wearing" funky vintage hats. The magnet is the food—reasonable, nourishing, and abundant. Gail's shines especially at weekend breakfast, an old-fashioned, high-caloric pig-out. Families drift in and out all morning long to read the newspapers and gorge on eggs and crisp bacon, house-made muffins, scones, and hash browns, along with fresh-squeezed orange juice and coffee with endless refills.

Meigas, 10 Wall Street, Norwalk, CT 06850; (203) 866–8800; $$$. Spanish-born Ignacio Blanco set the standard for fine Spanish cuisine in Connecticut when he opened Meson Galicia in 1985. It has now morphed into Meigas, and the food is even more delicious. Ignacio's emphasis is on fresh seafood, roast game, and veal. We have never tasted octopus this tender; grilled, with bacon, roasted potatoes, garlic, and sherry vinegar sauce, it is perfection. Bravo! Bravo also for the grilled duck breast with mango, pinenuts, and white beans; quail stuffed with shrimp, mushrooms, and sweetbreads; braised short ribs in Rioja red wine and ginger; and braised baby lamb shank. Meigas desserts are superb, especially the *croquetas de chocolate*—almond–covered chocolate balls topped by coconut foam. There is a well-selected Spanish wine list, with some excellent values. Installed on the ground floor of a restored trolley barn, Meigas is like a Spanish country inn, with ladder-back chairs, terra cotta tile floors, well-spaced tables, and impeccable service.

Olé Molé, 1030 High Ridge Road, Stamford, CT 06905; (203) 461–9962; $. You have to see this to believe how limited space has been converted to a visually appealing dining area. Terra-cotta and mustard-yellow walls, Mexican tiles, and artful effects are a backdrop for zesty flautas, enchi-

Brendan Walsh's
Fabulous Indian Pudding

When celebrity chef Brendan Walsh left Arizona 206 in New York to take over the kitchen at The Elms, a historic Ridgefield inn whose pedigree goes back to 1799, he turned away from southwest cooking to devote his skills and imagination to what he calls "Yankee cuisine." One of the pleasures of dining in the pleasantly subdued restaurant or casual tavern at The Elms is to discover how creatively Brendan has "reinvented" some of the mainstays of the Colonial Connecticut kitchen—chowders, roasts, and puddings—while preserving the essence of the originals. His modern adaptation of Indian pudding brings excitement and lightness to a rather stodgy relic of the past. In his version, Brendan retains the molasses flavor without letting its heaviness dominate.

Corn Bread

⅓ cup buttermilk

1 egg

¼ cup sour cream (crème fraîche)

⅓ cup cornmeal

½ cup all-purpose flour

⅓ cup light brown sugar

1 tablespoon baking powder

¼ teaspoon cinnamon

Pinch each of ginger, nutmeg, and salt

4 ounces butter, melted

Vegetable spray

Custard

2 eggs plus 3 yolks

⅓ cup maple syrup

⅓ cup molasses

Pinch of salt

1½ cups milk

1 cup cream

Caramel

2 cups sugar

1 tablespoon lemon juice

1 tablespoon water

For corn bread:

1. Combine buttermilk, egg, and sour cream. Combine all dry ingredients in another bowl. Add wet ingredients to dry ingredients and fold in butter at the end.
2. Coat an 8-by-8-inch pan with vegetable spray. Bake at 350°F for about 20 minutes. Let cool. This can be made a day ahead.

For caramel:

1. In a heavy saucepan combine sugar, water, and lemon juice. Cook over medium heat, stirring occasionally, until caramel turns amber.
2. Pour into 10 4-ounce ramekins. This step can be done in advance.

For custard:

1. Combine eggs, extra yolks, maple syrup, and molasses, and whip lightly.
2. Combine salt, milk, and cream. Bring cream mixture to a simmer. Remove from heat and slowly pour it into egg mixture while whisking. Mix until combined.

To assemble:

1. Crumble corn bread in a bowl. Mix in custard and let the mixture rest so that the corn bread soaks up the liquid. Pour into ramekins over the caramel and bake in a water bath at 325°F for approximately 45 minutes to 1 hour. Can be served hot or cold, but we prefer it warm.

Serves 10.

The Elms Restaurant & Tavern

500 Main Street (Route 35)
Ridgefield, CT 06877
(203) 438-9206
$$$

ladas, and other Mexican dishes. Primarily a take-out place, there are merely eight tables-for-two along one wall. Paper plates, cups, and plastic tableware do not hamper the enjoyment of the chunky guacamole, blue-corn calamari, blue-cornmeal-covered chicken wings, and other favorites. Salsas and molés are the stars, especially molé negro slowly simmered with dried fruit, nuts, dried chilies, tomatoes, onions, cilantro, and various spices. Three olés and a cha-cha-cha for this tiny Mexican gem.

The Restaurant at Rowayton Seafood, Rowayton Avenue, Rowayton, CT 06853; (203) 866–4488; $$. In slightly cramped quarters facing the boats moored at Cavanaugh's Marina, this no-frills restaurant turns out some of the freshest seafood imaginable. And no wonder! It is owned by and down the driveway from a fresh seafood store of the same name. The raw bar features local bluepoint oysters and others from Maine and British Columbia. You might spear also the deep-fried Ipswich clams and oysters (in a light, well-seasoned batter, they are favorites of ours), oyster pan roast, steamed or broiled lobsters, and grilled or pan-roasted fish. The lobster rolls, copiously packed with fresh chunks of tender lobster, celery, and onions lashed together with mayonnaise, are popular at lunch. In warm weather you can enjoy the deck overlooking Five Mile River, but deck seating is first come, first served.

Restaurant Jean-Louis, 61 Lewis Street, Greenwich, CT 06830; (203) 622–8450; www.restaurantjeanlouis.com; $$$. Since it opened in 1985, this petite place has offered one of the state's premier dining

Connecticut's Best
Sunday Brunch Pigout

For the essence of old-time Connecticut, nothing approaches Silvermine Tavern, whose pedigree dates back more than 200 years to the time it was a sawmill. The tavern really jumps at Sunday brunch, a prix fixe all-you-can-eat buffet with scrambled eggs, bacon, and sausage, cheese blintzes, French toast, eggs Benedict, potato pancakes, broccoli-Cheddar soufflé, vegetable lasagna, and corned-beef hash. Pancakes with various fillings and genuine New England maple syrup are made to order as you watch. And there are assorted sweet rolls, fresh-baked muffins, bagels, and the inn's signature sticky buns: big, yeasty caramelized buns rolled in pecans, so popular they are served at lunch and dinner as well. In warm weather, brunch is especially enjoyable on the spacious, sycamore-shaded deck overlooking a millpond, rife with ducks and swans, and the lazy Silvermine River. In winter, a fire burns brightly in one of the cozy dining rooms (as well as the inn parlor), and guests enjoy the old, worn brick floors, walls decorated with Early American weather vanes, farm implements, and antique signs. On special occasions, we have treated ourselves to an overnight in one of the tavern's antiques-filled guest rooms, snuggling into a four-poster bed with fishnet canopy. The Thursday prix-fixe New England buffet dinner is also popular and features live jazz.

Silvermine Tavern

284 Silvermine Avenue
Norwalk, CT 06850
(203) 847–4558
www.silverminetavern.com
$$

experiences, thanks to the expertise of its chef-owner, Jean-Louis Gerin, who apprenticed with three-Michelin-star chef Guy Savoy. Seating a mere forty-five, every detail is perfect, from the superb French food and flawless service to the fresh flowers on the well-spaced tables and the restful, pastel surroundings. The food is "la nouvelle classique," in Jean-Louis's words, lighter than the haute cuisine of old, but based on classic styles, using stocks and reductions rather than the cholesterol-heavy ingredients of yore. The results are full, natural flavors, just as delicious and much healthier. In addition to the regular menu, there is a *prix fixe menu degustation*, with samplings of Jean-Louis's many specialties. He also stages a number of wine dinners throughout the year, one celebrating the new Beaujolais, others featuring various French wineries. Though elegant, Restaurant Jean-Louis is not pretentious. Once inside the doors, you feel you are in a French country inn rather than in downtown Greenwich. *"A bientôt,"* as Jean-Louis would say.

River Cat Grill, 148 Rowayton Avenue, Rowayton, CT 06853; (203) 854–0860; $$. One of our favorite casual restaurants, River Cat Grill offers modern American cooking that is fresh, light and creative, with a menu of salads, thin pizzas with offbeat toppings, burgers, sandwiches, pasta dishes, grilled meats, and fish. Fish-and-chips is a menu staple, as is shepherd's pie, made with a garlic-potato puree crust. Save room for desserts, which are really seductive here, especially the signature black-and-tan crème brûlée, warm Valrhona chocolate cake, and Mr. Shane's ice creams. River Cat is as popular for lunch as for dinner, but with live music Wednesday through Sunday evenings, the bar and com-

Several years ago it might have been difficult to say "who's on first" as deluxe restaurants go. But then chef Thomas Henkelmann and his wife, Theresa, bought the highly regarded Homestead Inn in Greenwich (itself a mecca of fine dining). This rambling 1799 house-and-barn with Victorian additions is a stellar dining establishment, now known as the Thomas Henkelmann. Everything is fine-tuned here, from the valet parking, the greeting at the door and cordial, highly polished service to the gracious surroundings and exquisite French cuisine. There are two intimate dining rooms, the large one with fireplace, wood posts, and exposed wood-beamed ceilings (our favorite room in winter), the other cozy and snug. A third dining room is a glass-enclosed porch, ideal in summer, with views of the lawn and garden. Staffers never hover but they pay attention. If you drop a fork or napkin, someone is instantly at your side to replace it. The same attention is paid to the food, as you will discover in dishes like Dover sole with artichoke chips and truffled mashed potatoes; rack and loin of venison with pureed chestnuts, gnocchi a la Romaine and quince compote; and grenadin of veal on an island of creamy Maine lobster risotto, in a sea of port wine sauce with crisps of Parmesan lace.There is an exceptional wine list to match the food. Of course there is a price for such perfection, but as a splurge experience, it is hard to match. You might even spend the night in one of the inn's nineteen handsomely furnished guest rooms. It is no wonder the inn-cum-restaurant is a member of the esteemed Relais & Châteaux group.

Thomas Henkelmann at Homestead Inn

420 Field Point Road
Greenwich, CT 06830
(203) 869-7500
www.thomashenkelmann.com
$$$

pact dining room can be noisy. In warm weather you can eat outside on a small, fenced-in patio facing the road.

Brewpubs & Microbreweries

Bank Street Brewing Co., 65 Bank Street, Stamford, CT 06901; (203) 975–8728; www.65bankstreet.com; $$$. One sip of the flavorful, English-style ales here may tempt you to make a "run on the bank." This brewpub in a former bank epitomizes the grandeur of Gold Coast high finance in its marble floors and glittering kaleidoscope of stained glass in the overhead dome. Ted Steen and his father (and partner), Jim, bought this historic landmark in 1996 and adapted it with stunning results. The 40-foot-long marble counter where tellers once raked in deposits now is the base for a wooden bar, where patrons happily tap the Bank's liquid assets. On-site brewing is open to view, and up to thirty different recipes flow through the pipes annually, including Lock City (Stamford's industrial nickname) Pale Ale, and a golden (of course) Greenwich lager. Begin with a sampler of four small tastes and your interest may grow. The fruity Banker's Bitter is especially memorable, as is the roasty, semisweet Safecracker Stout. You can also bank on satisfying your appetite with a panoply of well-prepared vittles, including sandwiches, grilled meats and fish, and sundry salads. There is a buffet brunch on Sundays. Bar hours: Monday—Saturday, 11:30 A.M. to 1:00 or 2:00 A.M.; Sunday close, 10:30 P.M.

SBC Downtown Restaurant Brewery,
131 Summer Street, Stamford, CT 06901;
327–2337; $–$$. This offshoot of
Southport Brewing Company opened its
cavernous faux-industrial quarters in
2001. The stacks of barley-malt sacks and
gleaming fermenters near the entrance suggest that SBC
takes beer seriously. Brewer/co-owner Mark da Silva and head chef Dave
Ruligliano had five years of success at Southport Brewing Company
before expanding here. Slightly sweet, somewhat spicy Stamford Red is
one of the more complex-tasting house beers. Don't hesitate to ask for
sample tastes of the others, which might include Rippowam Lager, One
Way IPA, and Bull's Head English pale ale. Chef Ruligliano presides over
the kitchens in both places, with tasty hanger steak, crunchy "brew
fries," and assorted pizzas as reliably satisfying menu items. Thursday
is Karaoke Night and "family time" (with a magician) is Sunday
evening. Hours: Monday to Thursday from 11:30 A.M. to 1:00 A.M., Friday
and Saturday from 11:30 A.M. until 2:00 A.M., Sunday from 2:00 P.M. to
10:00 P.M.

Southport Brewing Co., 2600 Post Road, Southport, CT 06490;
(203) 256–BEER; www.info@southportbrewing.com; $–$$. A loyal clien-
tele has been enjoying the brews and food here since it opened in 1996.
Once past the copper-clad beer tanks by Southport Brewing's entrance,
you are in a large restaurant-cum-brewery where a wide range of estery,
ethereal ales are made. Your best bet is a sample assortment to assess
the talents of brewer/co-owner Mark da Silva, whose fifteen beers on tap

Fusion, but Not Confusin':
A Trio of Top Asian Food Parlors

Ching's Table, Main Street, New Canaan, CT 06840; (203) 972–8550; www.chingsrestaurant.com; $. On a Friday night, it seems as though every family in New Canaan is dining at this small Asian restaurant in the center of town. The place is quieter during the week and at lunch. The strengths are in the Thai and Chinese specialties, served piping hot and consistently well prepared. Our favorites are wild sticky rice dim sum, tempura shrimp with a lemon dip (unlike the Japanese version but excellent in its own way), pad Thai, spicy Indonesian beef sambal, sesame chicken, and Thai curry casserole. What gives Ching's Table such appeal is the freshness of each dish, as well as the pleasing presentation. The celadon-green decor is attractively low-key, with large windows, rattan furnishings, and oriental artifacts.

Tai Pan, 376 Post Road East, Westport, CT 06880; (203) 227-7400; $$. At first you may wonder where you are. Is this a Yangtze riverboat or a jungle path? Why are you walking to your table over a bridge with running water visible beneath the glass floor? And what's with that water-

range from the refreshing Bones Light at the easily quaffed end of the spectrum to nearly opaque, espressolike Black Rock Stout and Fairfield Red, an award-winning deep amber. Seasonals include Old Blue Eyes blueberry ale, Mill Hill pilsener and SouthToberfest. The inviting bar area boasts whimsical trompe-l'oeil brewhouse scenes. Wherever you sit,

fall gushing over a fieldstone wall? Surprisingly, the funky decor works and shouldn't distract you from the very good food, with origins all over Asia. Among our favorites are Indonesian dishes like salad gado-gado, rendang beef, prawns Bali style, and pork a la Bali, along with Panang curries and Szechuan Chinese special-ties. There is a decent microbrewery beer list as well. Tai Pan does a sizable take-out business, with free delivery in the Westport-Weston area.

Wild Ginger Café, 461 Main Street, Ridgefield, CT 06877; (203) 431–4588; $. When a restaurant boasts of too many cuisines, there is always the specter of "Jack of all trades . . ." But in the case of this small storefront cafe, decorated with photographs of the Far East, the chef really has mastered dishes native to Thailand, Malaysia, Japan, Indonesia, and China, thanks partly to the fact that so many of these cuisines share similar ingredients. By limiting the number of dishes from each country, Wild Ginger scores with its noodle dishes, appetizers, and entrees. Japanese tempura, Thai curries, and Asian char-grilled chicken are among many cross-cultural successes here.

remember Southport's strengths are in the three *P's:* pints, pizzas, and porterhouse steaks. The kitchen was voted best brewery-restaurant in the state in a 1999 survey. Early-evening and late-night happy hours on weekdays keep this convivial place humming, with karaoke every Thursday and "family time" with a magician every Sunday evening. Hours: 11:30

A.M. to 1:00 A.M. Monday through Thursday; 11:30 A.M. until 2:00 A.M Friday and Saturday; 11:00 A.M. to 9:00 P.M. Sunday,

Wine Trail

Connecticut Wine Trail, www.ctwine.com, offers three trail plans that show where ten of the state's wineries are located, the best roads to reach them, and important information about each (hours for tastings, tours, picnicking, nearby points of interest). In this area, DiGrazia and McLaughlin are the wineries included in Connecticut Wine Trail, Trip 1, which can be printed out from the Web site (listed above).

DiGrazia Vineyards, 131 Tower Road, Brookfield, CT 06804; (203) 775-1616; www.digrazia.com. Paul and Barbara DiGrazia opened their winery in 1984 with four types of wine. At present they sell twenty-three different wines, based on homegrown French vinifera hybrid grapes, plus inventive combinations of fruit and flavors, and have garnered gold, silver, and bronze medals for their efforts. The DiGrazias have brought to the market wines such as their Blacksmith Ruby Port and Yankee Frost (a white ice wine). Their flavor combinations include "Evangelico" pear dessert wine, "Winterberry" (grape, black currant, and raspberry dessert wine), and "Autumn Spice" (white grapes, pumpkin, and spice). The DiGrazias now produce 7,000 cases each year of their twenty-three wine types, eleven of which have been unique enough to warrant registration of their formulas. The tasting room and gift shop are inside a low-slung contemporary building festooned with flowers. Tours are daily Wednesday through Sunday, 11:00 A.M. to 5:00 P.M., April to December 7; and Saturday or Sunday, 11:00 A.M. to 5:00 P.M., January through March.

McLaughlin Winery, Albert's Hill Road, Sandy Hook, CT 06482; (203) 426–1533; e-mail: mclaughlinwine@snet.net. Morgen McLaughlin Smith is the owner, general manager, and winemaker of the sixteen-acre vineyard that is part of the 160-acre farm her family bought in the 1940s. Since 1979 this fertile Housatonic River valley estate has produced Seyval Blanc, Vidal Blanc, Aurora, Cayuga, Chancellor, Marechal Foch, and Leon Millot grapes on-site and has contracted for Chardonnay, Merlot and Cabernet Franc from the North Fork, of Long Island vineyards and Riesling from wineries in New York's Finger Lakes. In March you can watch maple-syrup-making in the sugarhouse, ride the tractor, cross-country ski, and hike the trails. During summer, visitors can picnic on the grounds or, every other Saturday and Sunday, enjoy a prix-fixe catered lunch at 1:00 P.M. (reservations essential). In July and August there are jazz concerts (call for details), and in fall you are welcome to join the grape harvest. There is even a guest cottage for overnight visitors. New England food products—jams, salad dressings, McLaughlin's own maple syrup, and wines—are for sale in the country store, an adjunct of the tasting room. Open daily June to December 31 from 11:00 A.M. to 5:00 P.M.; January to May, on weekends, from 11:00 A.M. to 5:00 P.M. Winery tours are by appointment only.

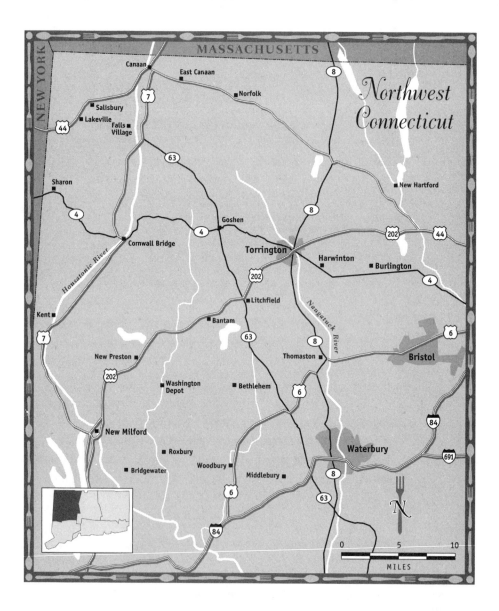

Northwest Connecticut

MASSACHUSETTS

NEW YORK

Canaan
East Canaan
Norfolk
8
7
Salisbury
44
Lakeville
Falls Village
63
Sharon
4
New Hartford
Goshen
8
4
Cornwall Bridge
202
44
Torrington
Harwinton
Burlington
202
Kent
Litchfield
4
Bantam
63
Naugatuck River
7
New Preston
8
Thomaston
6
Bristol
202
Washington Depot
Bethlehem
New Milford
6
Roxbury
Waterbury
84
Woodbury
Middlebury
691
Bridgewater
8
6
84
63

N

0   5   10

MILES

Housatonic River

Northwest Connecticut

This corner of the state encompasses Litchfield County, which has long been known as a weekend vacationland of the rich and famous—the likes of Meryl Streep, Arthur Miller, Tom Brokaw, and Henry Kissinger—who come not to be seen but to escape being seen. It is no wonder that people in pressure-cooker jobs gravitate to this region. It is a serenely beautiful area of undulating hills, placid lakes like Waramaug (which is surrounded by three delightful country inns, known for their excellent dining rooms), trout streams, the meandering Housatonic River, and wooded nature preserves, such as the White Memorial Foundation & Conservation Center, with its 35 miles of hiking and cross-country ski trails just outside Litchfield.

The village of Litchfield is a gem of another kind, with a much-admired green and wide carriageways lined with magnificent eighteenth-century clapboard houses. Don't be deceived: Litchfield may look drowsy, but it has one of the area's most sophisticated restaurants, an up-to-the-minute grocery, and a European gourmet food shop with home-baked German and Dutch breads and pastries. As in so much of this area, pastoral beauty is accompanied by urban comforts.

This is a land of secluded country estates and postcard-pretty villages like Salisbury, Lakeville, and Sharon, with classic steepled churches, scenic greens, and historic inns. The sleepy town of Woodbury is an antiquer's idea of heaven with its many antiques shops tucked into vintage houses along the town's mile-long main thoroughfare, punctuated by several fine restaurants and one of the state's most complete natural-food markets. Kent's main street is bordered by art galleries, craft shops, a great ice-cream parlor, a bakery, a Belgian chocolatier, and other specialty food stores and cafes, as you might expect in such a bustling art center.

The region is also a patchwork quilt of farmlands, with some local farms still worked today by descendants of the families that started them in the 1700s. Through the generations they have raised cattle, sheep, and pigs; used maple trees for sugar; and sold fruits and vegetables. Many still do, at old-fashioned roadside farm stands, which are sometimes untended, operating on the honor system. The woods and back roads offer wide-angle vistas of hillsides dappled with old orchards and new vineyards. A surprising number of independent food entrepreneurs—butchers, bakers, and candlestick makers; producers of smoked meats and game, cakes and candy, ice cream, chocolates, pork products, cheese—have their homes and plants here, in villages and hamlets tucked among wildflower meadows, woods, and fields. You will find them in these pages.

This tranquil area appeals to many people because of what it doesn't have: no superhighways, casinos, blinking neons, huge resort hotels, ubiquitous advertising signs, excess of fast-fooderies, chain hotels, strip malls, or theme parks. These omissions are seen as positives by those people who live or spend time here. Among them are semiretired, high-powered New Yorkers and others seeking getaway weekend homes and ultraprivate retreats. There are nature lovers and sportsmen who fish, canoe, and go tubing in the Housatonic, balloon high above Mohawk Mountain, and hike to the summit of Mount Tom near Bantam. Whether sportsmen, movie, television and stage stars, fashion designers, famous musicians and artists, authors, politicians, diplomats, or CEOs, they all have chosen this north-by-northwest area for its restful pleasures, an important one of which is good food, which your taste buds will appreciate.

Made or Grown Here

Bear Pond Farm, 25 Cook Street, Washington Depot, CT 06794; (860) 868–7036; www.bearpondfarm.com. Returning to his family's farm after years of roaming, Craig Colvin began to grow vegetables and herbs organically. He now concentrates on converting his fresh herbs into pungent pestos. Among his nut-free pestos are basil (made with Genoese basil), cilantro, lemon, mintucha (an oregano-like Sicilian herb and mint), oregano, watercress, and perennial scallion. With the herbs, he uses Pecorino Romano cheese from sheep's milk. Craig sells his pestos direct mail and at farmers' markets in southwestern Connecticut

and New York City's greenmarkets. He also makes and sells several herbal salad dressings and a pasta sauce that combines Heirloom tomatoes, mintucha, honey, nutmeg, and apple-cider vinegar. His latest creation is a raisin-dotted, rhubarb-based barbecue sauce called Rhubarbesque, which has a cayenne edge and is especially well mated with pork, beef tenderloin, and chicken.

The Egg & I Pork Farm, 355 Chestnutland Road (Route 109), New Milford, CT 06776; (860) 354-0820; www.eggandiporkfarm.com. "The secret of flavorful pork," says Jim Dougherty, proprietor of a five-acre, 200-year-old pig farm, "is to process quickly. If we kill Friday, the meat is in the smokehouse Saturday and in the store by the next Friday."

Why the name, The Egg and I, for a pig farm? Jim explained, "It just appealed to me because, like the people in the book of that name, farming wasn't my first occupation. They raised chickens; I went for pigs. I was a union steamfitter in Bayside, Queens, and then found a run-down farm here and moved in on New Year's Eve 1977, starting with chickens and two pigs. It's been a work-in-progress ever since." Jim now processes twenty to twenty-five pigs a week and sells to retailers and restaurants in the area, such as The Pantry and Mayflower Inn in Washington Depot and Bull Bridge Inn in Kent, as well as to the Williams-Sonoma catalog. Ham steaks, spiral sliced hams, bone-in, bone-out hams, old-fashioned daisy hams, loin chops, smoked bacon, kielbasa, Italian sausage, and bratwurst are all sold in the attractive, spacious shop Jim has opened on the farm. "We sell everything but the squeal," he jokes. Best-sellers are the smoked bone-in hams and pork loins. We're partial to the smoked bacon and pork chops and love to

Jim Dougherty's Easy One-Dish Pork and Peppers

6 ounces flat noodles
1 pound pork tenderloin
3 tablespoons soy sauce
½ cup orange juice
2 tablespoons balsamic vinegar
1 tablespoon honey
2 teaspoons cornstarch

¼ teaspoon freshly ground
pepper
Vegetable cooking spray
1½ cups strips of red bell
pepper
1½ cups strips of yellow bell
peppers cut into same size
as red-pepper strips

1. Cook noodles in boiling water; drain and set aside.
2. Cut pork into medallions and combine in large bowl with 1 tablespoon of soy sauce. Set aside.
3. Combine remaining soy sauce, orange juice, vinegar, honey, cornstarch, and ground pepper.
4. Coat a nonstick skillet with vegetable spray and stir-fry the pork until brown. Remove pork from the skillet. Add red and yellow peppers to the skillet and stir-fry for 2 minutes.
5. Return pork to the skillet, add juice mixture, and bring to a boil. Add noodles and cook until noodles are heated. Serve immediately.

Serves 4.

The Egg & I Pork Farm

355 Chestnutland Road (Route 109)
New Milford, CT 06776
(860) 354–0820
www.eggandiporkfarm.com

visit the shop to get ideas from his "recipe corner" and browse at the works by local artists he displays on his walls.

Matthews 1812 House, 250 Kent Road (Route 7), Cornwall Bridge, CT 06754; (860) 672–0149; www.matthews1812house.com. What began in 1978 in the kitchen of Deanna Matthews's 1812 farmhouse with a few brandied apricots and fruit-nut cakes is now a flourishing line of cakes, candies, cookies, and dessert sauces and toppings, sold via the company Web site and by catalog (175,000 printed each year) all over the state and around the United States and directly in a compact shop on the factory grounds. Fresh, all-natural ingredients are used, and everything is hand-baked. New products are added regularly. Our current favorites are the marzipan cake and shortbread. A good way to get acquainted with the line is the 1812 Cake Sampler of four loaf cakes (country spice, chocolate-raspberry liqueur, chocolate rum, and lemon-rum sunshine).

Nodine's Smokehouse, North Street (Route 63), Goshen, CT 06756; (860) 491–4009; www.nodinesmokehouse.com. You name it, Nodine's (pronounced no-dine) seems to smoke it: sausages (venison, chorizo, kielbasa, beef, maple, chicken with sun-dried tomatoes and with green peppercorns), whole game (Cornish game hen, pheasant, turkey, geese, duck, chicken), fish (bluefish, mackerel, trout, salmon), meats (pork and beef), and various Cajun-spiced items (andouille sausage, tasso ham, bayou bacon), as well as New England cured ham in spiral cut and boneless ham. Then there are the smoked cheeses (cheddar, provolone, Gruyère, Swiss, Pepper Jack). In business since 1986, Johanne and Robert Nodine and their son Calvin sell to shops (like Carbone's Market

From a repertoire of 180 flavors—sixteen available on any given day—Stosh's has served luxuriously rich ice cream (with 16 percent butterfat) daily from April 1 to the end of October since 1983. The locale has changed recently. Still in Kent, Stosh's is now situated in a 1700s house (once a stagecoach stop) with post-and-beam construction and a beamed ceiling. Folks stop by for the incredibly rich ice cream and for Stosh's other specialty, the Dazzle Dog, a one-quarter-pound all-beef skinless hot dog wrapped in a hand-rolled bun made on the premises. It is the ice cream, though, that is pivotal. Proprietor

Stosh's Ice Cream
Main Street (Route 7)
at Maple
Kent, CT 06757
(860) 927–4495

Robert Natale credits Stosh's popularity to the fact that he uses no preservatives, no extenders, no emulsifiers, and no stabilizers. "We don't use food coloring," he explains, "that's why the pistachio is white. We don't cut corners by cutting the cream content, and all our ingredients are top-notch." He uses pure coffee extract, Madagascar pure vanilla (called Bourbon vanilla), and Royal Dutch cocoa for his chocolate. A special treat is the waffle cone, dipped in imported French chocolate. Some of the current "cool" flavors are Turtle (vanilla ice cream, chocolate drops, pecans, and caramel in five layers), Chocolate-Chocolate (as decadently rich as chocolate mousse), and Mudslide. There are also sundaes: Total Eclipse (a house-made brownie with two scoops of Chocolate-Chocolate ice cream, hot fudge, and chocolate sprinkles) or Partial Eclipse (with vanilla instead of chocolate ice cream). A group feast is the Dippodopolus, which consists of sixteen scoops of ice cream, banana halves, rivers of toppings, hot fudge, nuts, and whipped cream—a hit with the students at nearby Kent School. Chaiwalla and Hopkins Inn are among other area outlets for this silky-smooth product.

and Hannah's Bakery in Torrington) and restaurants throughout Connecticut and in New York City. Check the company Web site or mail-order catalog for the whole line. A modest shop (with the rather high-falutin name "Nodine's Gourmet Shop") is inside an old dairy barn on the ten-acre property. The shop, crammed with smoked goods, as well as New England–made crackers, jams, and jellies, is always busy. People stop by for soup and sandwiches (noted on a giant blackboard) with as many trimmings as a delicatessen and giant homemade cookies (delicious!). The beef barbecue on sesame-seeded bun is really special. Smoking was originally done in the barn, but now is in Torrington; factory tours can be arranged by calling (860) 489–3213.

Specialty Stores & Markets

Bantam Bread Company, 853 Bantam Road (Route 202), Bantam, CT 06750; (860) 567–2737. In the rear lower level of an old clapboard house is a little bakery where Niles Golvin's fresh-from-the-oven bread is sold. The aromas are so intoxicating that we can rarely leave without a loaf of Kalamata-olive sourdough clutched in our hands. Other compelling choices include sunny flax sourdough, semolina, traditional peasant, and caraway rye. There are focaccias with five different toppings, pound cakes, pumpkin-walnut bread, five kinds of cookies, and certain breads baked only on a specific day of the week, like wheat-free spelt bread on Wednesday, Irish soda bread on Thursday, challah on Friday, and raisin on Saturday. The pies—like the latticed raspberry and other fresh berry pies

and pumpkin-pecan tarts—
are equally seductive, with
wonderful crisp and flaky

crusts. In limited space, jams, vinaigrettes, Brook View Sugar House
maple syrup (made in nearby Morris), and imported dried pastas are sold
as well.

Belgique Patisserie & Chocolatier, 1 Bridge Street (corner of
Routes 7 and 341), Kent, CT 06757; (860) 927–3681. This charming
shop, in a Victorian carriage house, is as beautiful as a European patisserie, which isn't surprising, as the owner, Pierre Gilissen, is Belgian.
His handmade chocolate candies (traditional Belgian pralines, chocolates, and truffles), cakes, tortes, and pastries are in the elegant
Belgian style and are made on the premises without preservatives.
Pierre uses the premier Belgian-made and imported Callebaut because
it is 100 percent cocoa butter, without any vegetable oils. *Arlequin,
Javanais,* raspberry *Bavaroise,* chocolate hazelnut *dacquoise,* and fruit
mousse cakes are a few of the cakes, along with cookies, fruit tarts,
breakfast pastries, and delicious Belgian hot chocolate. In warm
weather Pierre and his wife, Susan, make refreshing ice creams in
unusual flavors (in addition, of course, to chocolate)—toasted almond
and fig, for example—and sorbets, like lime and pear. Also for sale are
a number of imported Belgian treats: pralines, truffles, marzipan, *pâtes
de fruit,* and Callebaut chocolate for baking. Belgique has recently
opened an elegant Salon de Thé in the pristine 1898 Victorian house
on the same grounds, where tea and lunch—and dinner on weekends—
are served.

Belgique's Tarte Tatin

Pierre Gilissen, Belgian chocolatier, is also a master baker and pastry maker. He was willing to share his recipe for a French/Belgian version of apple pie, using one of Connecticut's favorite crops.

2 cups plus 2 tablespoons
  granulated sugar
¼ cup water
1 cup unsalted butter (at room
  temperature), cut into
  pieces

8–10 apples (Granny Smith,
  Red or Golden Delicious)
6 ounces (1 sheet) puff pastry
1 egg, beaten

1. Place 2 cups sugar plus the water in a deep saucepan and slowly bring to a boil for approximately 15–20 minutes, or until the mixture turns golden brown.
2. Remove from heat and *carefully* add the pieces of butter a little at a time, stirring gently until dissolved. (Use extreme caution as the mixture will be very, very hot. A deep pan is needed, as the mixture boils

The Dutch Epicure Shop, 491 Bantam Road (Route 202), Litchfield, CT 06759; (860) 567–5586; www.alldutchfood.com. German-born pastry chef Wolfgang Joas and his Dutch wife, Betsy, emigrated to the United States in 1968 and took over a simple Dutch bakery. With their daughter Wilma, they have made it a gallimaufry of Dutch and German cakes, cookies, and breads, all baked by Wolfgang. He also

up when the butter is added.) Immediately pour into a 9-inch glass pie plate. This will be the base of the tart.

3. Peel, core, and cut apples in half lengthwise. Pack them close together, with the halves upside down (flat side up) over the caramel mixture in the pie plate.

4. Cover apples with the puff-pastry sheet, tucking in the dough between the apples and the side of the plate. Brush the puff pastry with a little of the beaten-egg mixture to make the pastry shine. Sprinkle the 2 tablespoons of sugar over the top.

5. Place the pie plate on a baking pan to prevent spills and bake in a 375°F oven for about 30 minutes or until puff pastry is cooked. Remove the pie plate from the oven and cool the tart until the caramelized sugar has thickened to syrup consistency—about 10–15 minutes.

6. Place a serving plate or platter on top of the tart and turn upside down to unmold.

7. The tart is best served warm, preferably with vanilla ice cream or crème fraîche.

Serves 6–8.

Belgique Patisserie & Chocolatier
1 Bridge Street (corner of Routes 7 and 341)
Kent, CT 06757
(860) 927–3681

makes seasonal specialties: New Year's Eve *berliner*, Easter eggs filled with house-made truffles, Christmas stollen and Dutch chocolate letters, and more than fifteen types of cookies. This well-stocked European outpost also disperses eight different kinds of Gouda, Dutch hard goat cheese, other Dutch and European cheeses, sausages and meats (supplied by a German butcher in New Jersey), jams, jellies, Dutch licorice, condiments, *stroopwafels*, *speculaas* spice cookies, Droste pastilles, *pannekoeken* mixes, Indonesian sambals, *kafferlime* leaves, spices, and seasonings. A freezer bulges with fresh-made soups, casseroles, and *spätzle* (all made on the premises). There are a few nonfood items as well: Delftware, German soaps, 4711 cologne, and the like. If you can't make it to Litchfield, the Web site sells a number of Dutch Epicure products.

Harney and Sons Fine Teas, 11 Brook Street, off Route 44, Salisbury, CT 06068; (860) 435–5051 (shop) or (800) 832–8463 (factory, for a catalog); www.harney.com. The Harneys have been selling tea since 1983. In addition to a wholesale, mail-order, and Internet business, with teas shipped all over the United States, this handsome shop/tasting room, with its wide pine floorboards, retails Harney teas, special tea gift assortments, and tea samplers, as well as tea-related items: assorted teapots, tea cozies, cast-iron trivets, Japanese cast-iron teapots, sets of Japanese ceramic cups, silver-plated tea strainers, and books about tea. You are invited to sample several of the 200+ varieties of tea in smart black canisters with gold labels that line the shelves and cabinets. Among the selections are black, green, and white teas (including a delicate Winter White Earl Grey, new to the line), organic teas, herbals, decaffeinated teas, floral and holiday teas, and iced teas. Also for sale are English scone mixes, shortbreads, honey, and crispy Brittany crepes coated in dark chocolate and wrapped in foil, among a number of upscale products. It's enough to turn anyone into a tea-totaler. Tours of the factory require an appointment.

The Kent Coffee and Chocolate Company, 8 Main Street, Kent, CT 06757; (860) 927–1445; www.kentcoffeeandchocolate.com. More than the life-size, overstuffed black gorilla seated near the entrance, the heady aromas of chocolate and coffee have lured visitors to this shop-cafe since it opened in 1991. We can't think of a better place to stop, between browsing at Kent's many art galleries, for a cup of fresh-roasted coffee or tea and a nibble of fudge or hand-dipped truffles. Or even for a game of chess, which is set up at a rear table. The coffees (fine-quality Arabica beans from around the world) are roasted in small batches to ensure maximum flavor and aroma. Most popular are the French roast, house blend, and breakfast blend.

It is difficult to play favorites with the handmade chocolates, but the most popular are the truffles, pecan turtles, and chocolate-dipped pretzels. Kent's rich, thick, old-fashioned fudge comes in six seductive flavors, including chocolate peanut butter, penuche, mudslide fudge, and Heath bar fudge. Available by mail order or via the store's Web site are some thirty-three coffee blends and twenty-four chocolate assortments, fudge, and several attractively packaged gift items—maple syrup miniatures, King Ludwig's Bavarian nuts, and four flavors of tea jams.

Litchfield Gourmet, 33 West Street, Litchfield, CT 06759; (860) 567–4882. Just across from the Litchfield Green, this specialty store has the rambling ambience of an old-fashioned grocery, which it is, but it is also much more. Yes, it has fresh grade-A produce, fresh seafood delivered four or five times a week from the Boston dock, and certified fresh-cut Angus beef. But it is also a delicatessen, with a big assortment of imported cheeses, cold cuts and sausages, salads, and

take-away items. Owner Renee Giumarro is justi-
fiably proud of the store's new look, with an
espresso bar that serves a variety of European
coffees and a cafe that offers hot breakfasts
and lunches, with almost everything made on the premises,
from the omelets, frittatas, four or five hot soups daily, and sandwiches to an array of baked goods that include breads, muffins, coffee
cakes, and desserts. During the cafe's season—from Memorial Day
through fall-foliage weekends—big stars are the ice creams, sorbets,
and granitas made especially for the store.

The Monastic Art Shop at the Abbey of Regina Laudis,
273 Flanders Road, Bethlehem, CT 06751; (203) 266–7637; www.
abbeyofreginalaudis. In a small shop on the grounds of this clois-
tered convent snuggled into the hills are many products made by the
Benedictine community. The boutique French-style cheeses are first
rate (the discerning West Street Grill in Litchfield features them).
You will also find honey, herbs for seasonings, vinegar, and hot mustards here. Other products include woven and knitted scarves, stoles,
and sweaters made from Abbey sheep wool, cards, books, religious
art objects, and compact discs of Abbey chants. Call ahead for hours.

New Morning Natural and Organic Foods, Middle Quarter Mall,
Route 6, Woodbury, CT 06798; (203) 263–4868; e-mail: newmorn@wtco.net.
Shoppers partial to organic and natural foods may be awestruck, as we
were on our first visit, by the magnitude of this family-owned supermarket. If it is missing anything, we can't think what it might be. Fresh

fruits and vegetables, chicken, fish, cereals, breads, all kinds of packaged natural-food products, herbs and spices, teas, soy and organic milk, organic cheeses, soy products, pastas, ice creams, and a section of packaged frozen meals (vegetarian and organic) are all here. There are bins with beans and lentils (including black turtle beans, adzuki, and black-eyed cowpeas), dried fruits, nuts (including five different types of cashews), seeds (flax, brown sesame, and Hungarian pumpkin among them), rice, couscous, hulled barley, quinoa, whole wheat, and organic coffees. Help yourself to fresh soup from three big black cauldrons in a small soup corner. A deli case offers take-out salads, salmon cakes, and other entrees, and there is a separate room with homeopathic medicines and vitamins. This store is definitely worth a detour.

Nine Main Bakery & Deli, 9 Main Street, New Preston, CT 06777; (860) 868–1879. Just off New Preston's town center, Nine Main is a welcome addition to this part of the Litchfield Hills landscape. The inspiration of owner Liz Johnson, the tidy shop, with its mere twelve tables, glistens. Salads and entrees in the take-out display cases are presented in handsome bowls as attractive as the dishes themselves. Cookies, scones, and muffins are oven-fresh from the kitchen. The muffins come in twenty-seven different flavors—lemon raspberry, blueberry, banana, peanut butter, pumpkin cheesecake, butterscotch pecan, and chocolate chip & peanut butter, among them. Two soups are available each day, and there is a small selection of Connecticut-made preserves, chutneys, and salsas for sale.

The Pantry, Titus Square, Washington Depot, CT 06794; (860) 868–0258. A combination cafe, gourmet food, and culinary-supplies shop, The Pantry, since it opened in 1978, has been a meeting place for locals, who congregate for lunch, coffee, sweets, and specialty food shopping. There are twelve tables in the center of the store, surrounded by racks and shelves chock-a-block with tempting packaged delicacies, herbs, spices, various olive oils, mustards, jams, and goodies like Chocolate Lace and imported Niedereggen Lübeck pralines, marzipan, and truffles, as well as Portuguese pottery, a wealth of baskets, Le Creuset pots, and other cookware. A refrigerated display case features English and French cheeses. People come from miles away to enjoy the baked ham and other made-to-order sandwiches, fresh-baked breads, brioches, muffins, and mouthwatering pastries, all made on the premises.

The Silo Store, Upland Road, New Milford, CT 06776; (860) 355–0300; www.thesilo.com. The largest section of this interesting store, which is part of the Ruth and Skitch Henderson farm, is devoted to high-end culinary tools, pots, pans, casseroles, cookware, glassware, barware, utensils, appliances, linens, gadgets, and other accoutrements. There is a section in which made-in-Connecticut nonperishable food products are sold, like Middlesex Farms glazes and Candlewood Apiary honey (made in Brookfield), along with other nonstate products—jams, raspberry-wasabi dipping mustard, olives and condiments, and gourmet mixes. Despite its remote location, the store (with a notable cooking school) has been going strong since 1972. Hours change with the seasons, so it is best to call ahead.

Stroble's, 14 North Main Street, Kent, CT 06757; (860) 927–4073. Unpretentious as it is, Stroble's is the tasty blossom that visitor bees hover around. Not for its cramped, down-to-earth looks, but for the breads, cakes, tarts, cookies, and oversize cupcakes that beckon in the glass display cases. The individual carrot-cake cupcakes (with a frosting carrot on the top of each), garden-party cupcakes in three-color icing, chocolate-mousse-bonbon cupcakes, and the oversize pie-of-the-day are especially inviting. Stroble's also does a steady business in breakfasts, take-out lunches, sandwiches, wraps, and salads. But the cakes and cookies are the nectar.

Sweet Maria's, 159 Manor Avenue, Waterbury, CT 06705; (203) 755–3804; www.sweet-marias.com. Since 1990 Maria Sanchez has been whipping up delicious cakes and cookies in her well-named bakery, which is the fulfillment of a childhood dream. As a teenager, she worked in a neighborhood bakery. After earning a marketing degree in college, she joined an advertising agency but baked cakes at night as a hobby. Finally she opened her own bakery in her old neighborhood, with her motto: "More than just another pretty cake." Now her huge repertoire includes layer cakes, loaf cakes, tea cakes, cheesecakes, carrot cakes, apricot/strawberry/pineapple mousse cakes, amd special creations like Maria's Booze Crooze (yellow cake with rum, coconut, and pineapple). Her frostings are just as imaginative: cherry nutter (cherry with buttercream), chocolate Heath bar crunch, and rocky road (chocolate buttercream with chocolate chips, walnuts, and marshmallows), as well as the standard flavors. Many cakes are special order. The bakery also sells, via its Web site and mail order, loaf and Bundt cakes, biscotti in six flavors, at least fifteen different cookies, and Maria's four cookbooks. As Jackie Gleason might say, "How sweet it is."

Thyme-Enz Harvest, 10 Academy Street, Salisbury, CT 06068; (860) 435–9733. Ensconced in an old clapboard house on a tiny lane off Salisbury's long Main Street is this popular hangout. There are merely five tables, a small serve-yourself coffee bar, and a display case packed with salads, a dozen to-go entrees, and several hams for sandwiches. Danish pastries, muffins, and cookies are made on the premises.

Farmers' Markets

For up-to-the-minute information about dates and times, call Connecticut Department of Agriculture at (860) 713–2503, visit the Web site at www.state.ct.us/doag/, or e-mail at ctdeptag@po.state.ct.us.

Bristol Farmers' Market, Stock's Playground, Middle Street, Bristol. Saturdays from 10:00 A.M. to 1:00 P.M., first week of July through October.

Kent Farmers' Market, Kent Green, Kent. Saturdays from 9:00 A.M. to noon, early May through October.

New Milford Farmers' Market, Town Green, Main Street, New Milford. Saturdays from 9:00 A.M. to noon, mid-May through October.

Thomaston Farmers' Market, Town Green, Main Street, Thomaston. Thursdays from 3:00 to 6:00 P.M., second week of July through October.

Torrington Farmers' Market, Torrington Plaza (across from the Green), Torrington. Tuesdays from 3:00 to 6:00 P.M., and Saturdays from 10:00 A.M. to 1:00 P.M., mid-June through October.

Waterbury Farmers' Market, Grace Baptist Church, 65 Kingsbury Street, Waterbury. Fridays from 3:00 to 6:00 P.M., July through October.

Waterbury II Farmers' Market, Brass City Mall, Sears Automotive parking lot, Waterbury. Thursdays from 2:00 to 6:00 P.M., second week of July through October.

Farm Stands

Averill Farm, 250 Calhoun Street, Washington Depot, CT 06794; (860) 868-2777. Nine generations of the Averill family have farmed these 200 hilltop acres since 1746. Some of the buildings, the 1830 house, and the barn date back to the early 1800s. In 1990 Sam and Susan Averill, with their two children, took over the farm, where they grow dozens of apple varieties and twelve types of pears, all available for picking-your-own. The Averill farm stand also offers honey, cider, maple syrup, pumpkins, and cut flowers. Open August to December, daily, from 9:00 A.M. to 5:00 P.M.

Clark Farm, Flanders Road at Flanders Nature Center, Woodbury, CT 06798; (203) 263–5801; www.clarkfarm.org. John Clark has leased farmland from the Flanders Nature Center since 1992. He grows organically more than fifty kinds of vegetables, thirty different herbs, and many cut flowers. His farm stand, located under shady maple trees in the Flanders Nature Center parking lot, sells his vegetables (including garlic), herbs, seeds, flowers, and bedding plants, but the Clark Farm has many other seasonal activities. Every month in spring, summer, and fall, the farm hosts a bring-your-own pondside picnic (no charge) and workshop walks and classes (with recipes provided) on wild grasses, edible plants, and subjects related to organic and sustainable agriculture. On a night with a full moon, John hosts a pondside tea. Guests bring their own refreshments (he provides the tea), guitars, and other musical instruments, and all enjoy the moon and a hike through the fields. The farm stand is open July to October on Wednesdays from 3:00 to 7:00 P.M. and on Saturdays from 1:30 P.M. to dusk.

Ellsworth Hill Orchard & Berry Farm, 461 Cornwall Bridge Road (Route 4), Sharon, CT 06069; (860) 364–0025; www.ellsworthfarm.com. Michael Bozzi and his family cultivate their seventy-acre farm's 3,000 plum and apple trees (eighteen apple varieties including Ozark Gold, Macoun, Cortland, Empire, and Red Delicious), blueberries, strawberries, raspberries, and pumpkins. June through November is pick-your-own time for raspberries, strawberries, apples, pumpkins, and gourds. In the big farm store near the road, you can buy Bozzi's cider, home-baked cider doughnuts, pies, and pastries, as well as all the fresh fruit in season. The Bozzis planted Australian pumpkins one year and came up with a pink one that became nationally famous. They're trying for a Down Under repeat! They welcome visitors to roam their fields and enjoy the hills, woods, and views of buildings that date back to the 1700s. You can also fish for trout in the pond and even take a hayride. Open daily from 10:00 A.M. to 5:00 P.M. from June to November.

Freund's Farm Market and Bakery, Route 44, East Canaan, CT 06024; (860) 824–0650. In a huge barn-red building next to a large greenhouse, Theresa Freund sells fruit, corn, and other vegetables, maple syrup, honey, cut flowers, and bedding plants from the family farm. In a full kitchen on the second floor, Theresa and helpers bake whole-grain breads and baguettes, pies, cakes, cookies, and doughnuts. Pies are a big specialty, with some two dozen types (some are seasonal and must be ordered ahead) and even sugar-free pie. Theresa bakes bite-size holiday cookies, which can be ordered in three-pound assort-ments in 12-inch dome platters. Also for sale are Theresa's own jellies and authentic salsas (made by a Mexican helper), along with Cabot and McCam cheeses and Guida ice cream. Freund's also does catering; orders are especially heavy during the Christmas holidays. The roadside farm store and greenhouse garden center are part of a 225-cow dairy farm, which Theresa's husband, Matthew, runs. "This all started," he says, "way back when my mother sold her corn under a maple tree by the side of the road."

Lamothe's Sugar House, 89 Stone Road, R.F.D. 3, Burlington, CT 06013; (860) 675–5043; www.lamothesugarhouse.com. On 350 acres, this working farm has grown from seven taps for maple sugar to its present 3,000 taps. From mid-February to the end of March on Saturdays and Sundays, visitors can watch the maple-sugar-making process. The store sells maple sugar products year-round, from soup to nuts, or rather from maple syrup to maple-sugar-coated nuts. That includes maple candy, maple cream, maple taffy, maple-walnut caramels, maple sugar, granulated maple sugar (like brown sugar but drier), even maple vinegar. What began as a hobby is now a full-time family business, as Lamothe's also wholesales and mail-orders its products. You can order via the farm Web site.

Maple Bank Farm, 53 Church Street (Route 317), Roxbury, CT 06783; (860) 354–7038; e-mail: bronsonch@aol.com. This venerable property has been in the Hurlbut family since 1730, when John Hurlbut was granted six acres by the King of England. The foundation of John's original house is still visible, within 100 feet of the current farm stand. Cows, sheep, and pigs were the first mainstays, but over generations, fruit and vegetable crops were added. Cathy Hurlbut and her husband, Howie Bronson, have been living in the old

1830 farmhouse since 1980. At their farm stand (new in 1986), they sell apples for eating and baking, along with potatoes, carrots, garlic, onions, fresh herbs, jams, apple cider, maple syrup, pies, pastries, and breads. Cows and sheep grazing on the nearby hillsides often poke their noses through the split-rail fence, hoping for snacks of apples or carrots. The Bronsons invite you to pick your own blueberries. Open from March to December 22, Tuesday through Sunday, from 10:00 A.M. to 5:00 P.M.

Maple View Farm, 276 Locust Road, Harwinton, CT 06791; (860) 485–0815; e-mail: mgauger@snet.net. Mark and Carole Gauger grow a variety of small organic fruits and vegetables, which they sell at farmers' markets. The small farm stand—really a cart on wheels—at the end of their driveway displays their overstock. The stand operates on the honor system. Select your organic tomatoes, cucumbers, peppers, onions, potatoes, and blueberries, and put your payment in the small cash box on the cart.

March Farm, 160 Munger Lane, Bethlehem, CT 06751; (203) 266–7721; e-mail: mafluff@aol.com. Tom March's fresh-fruit harvests begin in July with blueberries, continue with greenhouse tomatoes, pick up with thirteen varieties of apples, then peaches, sweet corn, and pumpkins, continuing right into October. Pick-your-owns include blueberries, apples, and pumpkins. At the farm stand (which is open March to late November from 10:00 A.M. to 6:00 P.M.), Sue March offers honey, maple syrup, mulled cider (from the March mill), jams, jellies, and fresh cider doughnuts, pies, and cookies from the on-site bakery.

Roberts Orchard, 125 Hill Street, Bristol, CT 06010; (860) 582–5314; e-mail: e.ferrier@att.net. If you want more than an apple a day, Roberts is happy to oblige—with Macoun, McIntosh, Cortland, Honeycrisp, Jonagold, Mutsu, and Red Delicious. The Apple House farm store is ensconced in a big red barn, along with the bakery and cider-making and storage facility. There you can buy fresh cider, apple butter, apple cakes, mini-cider-doughnuts (freshly made on Saturdays and Sundays), and apple crumb pies (a specialty), along with fresh apple, cranberry apple, pecan, mince, and pumpkin pies, oven-fresh pumpkin bread, honeywheat bread, a variety of homemade muffins, and Roberts's own homemade jams and jellies (made from the peaches, raspberries, and other fruit grown on the seventy-acre farm). A wall tap in the store enables you to draw your own cider in a jug, and you may place an advance order for your favorite Thanksgiving pies. In addition, there are hayrides and a Pumpkin House (open weekends, with a narrated story with life-size characters). Open after Labor Day through Thanksgiving, Monday through Saturday from 9:00 A.M. to 5:30 P.M., Sunday from 10:00 A.M. to 5:30 P.M.

Rustling Wind Creamery, 148 Canaan Mountain Road, Falls Village, CT 06031; (860) 824–7084; www.cheeseatrustlingwind.com. In a minuscule shop attached to the cheese-making facilities, Joan Lamothe sells—on the honor system—all kinds of products made on her 233-acre farm, from honey, jellies, jams, chutneys, herbed vinegars, oils, and maple syrup to goat's milk fudge (from the farm's thirty-two goats), goat's-milk soap, and sweaters, scarves, mittens, and gloves made from the wool of the farm's fourteen sheep. The big draw is the English-style cheeses: Cheshire, blue, sage, Wensleydale (including three special herbed Wensleydales), and a soft, herbed, goat-cheese spread. During summer Joan also sells her cheeses at farmers' markets in Kent, Canaan, and Sheffield. Open year-round from 10:00 A.M. to 6:00 P.M.

Schaghticoke, 191 Northrop Street, Bridgewater, CT 06752; (860) 355–8085. Rick Dembeck grows a wide variety of certified organic vegetables, as well as herbs and flowers. Pick your own pumpkins and corn maize in the fall. For sale year-round are nonorganic goat cheeses, goat's milk, and free-range eggs. The farm stand is open daily from 9:00 A.M. to 6:00 P.M. in season. Rick also sells his fresh wares in farmers' markets in Greenwich and New Canaan during the growing season.

Starberry Farm, 81 Kielwasser Road, Washington Depot, CT 06776; (860) 868–2863; e-mail: starberry@snet.net. For twenty-five years Sally and Bob Futh have been leading a fruitful (ahem) existence on their twenty-five-acre farm, growing eighteen types of apples, five types of peaches and plums, and four each of nectarines, apricots, and cherries. They invite you to pick your own, from cherry time in June to the end of October. They also sell homemade pies, jams, jellies, and fresh-peach ice cream (in season). Stop by from June to Thanksgiving (even later if the weather cooperates, but it is wise to call ahead), 10:00 A.M. to 5:00 P.M.

Tonn's Orchard, 418 Milford Street, Burlington, CT 06013; (860) 675-3707. Herbert Tonn and family take their produce to several farmers' markets during the week and spend weekends from August to October at their peach-and-apple farm or in-town fruit stand. At the farm on Preston Road, you can pick your own on weekends from noon to 5:00 P.M., starting with peaches in August, and apple varieties (Paula Red and McIntosh, among others) as they ripen, until October. Meanwhile, Tonn's Milford Street fruit stand sells fresh sweet corn, tomatoes, blueberries, raspberries, and cucumbers daily, from July through October, 10:00 A.M. to 7:00 P.M.

Windy Hill Farm, 164 Hillhouse Road, Goshen, CT 06756; (860) 491-3021. The Allens have been providing freshly harvested vegetables on their farm for the past twenty years. Throughout the growing season Marianne and Doug supply sweet corn, tomatoes, potatoes, cucumbers, pumpkins, and other veggies, as well as their own maple syrup and fresh eggs. These are available at various times of the season (call ahead for specific times) from mid-July to mid-October, daily from 9:00 A.M. to dusk.

Food Happenings

March: **Maple-Syrup Making Demonstrations,** Flanders Nature Center, Flanders Road, Woodbury, CT 06798; (203) 263-3711; www.flandersnaturecenter.org. Demonstrations are on weekends in March. Check for times.

April: **Hotter Than Heck Festival,** Waterbury area; (203) 573–0264 or (203) 754–7552; www.waterburyyouthservices.org. Things get devilishly hot around Waterbury at this festival, which benefits the nonprofit Waterbury Youth Services, which helps 5,000 local children and families. It has been such a sellout that larger quarters are required in the future. The theme remains the same: hot, hot, REALLY HOT food. Some twenty-eight restaurateurs, caterers, and specialty food vendors gleefully turn up the heat, with offerings like volcanic wings, fiery salsas, and chocolate chile-pepper cookies, all fierce enough to get you crying in your beer (or beverage of choice). An admission ticket gives you access to a vast array of hellishly incendiary appetizers, entrees, and desserts, as well as live entertainment and an auction featuring gift certificates for fine dining. Timid tastebuds are welcome, too, as there are some dishes for the faint-of-palate. Check for date and new locale.

June: **A Taste of Litchfield Hills,** Haight Vineyard, Chestnut Hill, Litchfield, CT 06759; (860) 567–4045. A magnet for 5,000 visitors, this fête at the Haight Vineyard property guarantees a weekend of fine New England and international foods and wines prepared by local restaurant chefs, culinary demonstrations, ice carving, upscale shopping, live music, winery tours, and vineyard hayrides. Dates are either the third or fourth Saturday and Sunday in the month, held rain or shine. Check with Haight to be sure of the dates. Hours: 11:00 A.M. to 8:00 P.M. Saturday, 11:00 A.M. to 5:00 P.M. Sunday.

December: **Gingerbread House Festival,** St. George's Episcopal Church, Tucker Hill Road at Route 188, Middlebury, CT

06762; (203) 758–2165. Since 1972 this bazaar and fair run by church volunteers has been going strong and, beginning the first Saturday in December, it lasts through the next Saturday, with all proceeds going to the church. Houses, trees, animals, and people made of gingerbread are displayed in fifty or more miniature scenes (all sold after the final Saturday). Not everything at the fair is gingerbread, though there are homemade ginger cookies for sale (5,000 of these were sold in 2002 at $1.00 apiece); for sale also are handmade knitted scarves, hats, and gloves, and wooden decorations and tree ornaments. A casserole and salad luncheon is served on opening Saturday. Check for hours.

Learn to Cook

Rustling Wind Creamery & Stables, 148 Canaan Mountain Road, Falls Village, CT 06031; (860) 824–7084; www.cheeseatrustlingwind.com. For four to six weeks in spring, cheesemaker Florence Brocklehurst comes from England to teach cheese-making classes. For dates and details, check Rustling Wind's Web site.

The Silo Cooking School at Hunt Hill Farm, Upland Road, New Milford, CT 06776; (860) 355–0300 or (800) 353–SILO; e-mail: cooking@thesilo.com. This comprehensive cooking school was begun by Ruth and Skitch Henderson in 1972 on their farm in the rolling hills outside New Milford. Classes, which are conducted by famous chefs, cookbook authors, restaurateurs, and noted nutritionists, cover a wide range of gastronomic interests, skills, and age groups. The Silo Web site provides detailed descriptions of upcoming classes, as long as four months ahead, and you may register on-line. Courses usually consist of a single class of about three hours, mostly offered Saturdays and Sundays, but occasionally classes are held on Thursdays and Friday evenings. Ruth, author of several cookbooks, and Skitch, former orchestra leader and food enthusiast, sometimes teach classes themselves.

Landmark Eateries

The Cannery, 85 Main Street, Canaan, CT 06018; (860) 824–7333; $$. This storefront restaurant in the center of town doesn't look exceptional. Its pressed-tin ceiling, vintage wall sconces, and booths along one wall suggest a homey old-fashionedness, but wait until the food arrives. Under chef-owner William O'Meara's tutelage, everything we have eaten in this "American-style bistro" is first-rate. The menu changes often, but we recommend the *haricots verts* and roasted tomato salad tossed with pesto, the velvety puree of carrot-and-turnip soup, followed by sautéed duck breast with beet glaze or veal medallions in lemon-chive butter. The O'Meara touch is subtle, not ostentatious, and there are enough surprising aspects to pique your interest, like the fennel vinaigrette with the warm calamari salad. Prices for the high quality are surprisingly moderate.

Adrienne's Roasted Apple and Pumpkin Soup

Every fall the Connecticut landscape is weighted down in pumpkins, or "pompions," as colonial cookbooks called them. Inventive chefs now use this autumn bounty in such dishes as pumpkin gnocchi, pumpkin-seed biscotti, pumpkin hash, even almond-raisin pumpkin bread. Adrienne Sussman, chef-owner of the popular Adrienne restaurant in New Milford, hits all the right notes in her modern American menu. She likes to follow the seasons and does so admirably in this delicious soup, suitable for a chilly fall or winter day.

6 Granny Smith apples

2 tablespoons olive oil

½ onion, diced

1 small stalk celery, diced

1 small carrot, diced

1 small leek, chopped

2 cloves garlic, chopped

1 shallot, chopped

2 cups dry white wine

2 cups apple cider

2 bay leaves

1 cinnamon stick

3 cloves

3 cups vegetable or chicken broth

1–1½ cups solid-packed canned pumpkin (not pie filling)

Pinch of salt

1 Granny Smith apple, diced and sautéed

Cinnamon-flavored sour cream

Carol Peck's Good News Café, 694 Main Street South (Route 6), Woodbury, CT 06798; (203) 266–4663; e-mail: carolepeck@good-news-café.com; $$. What we like best about this sunny, informal place, with its roomy booths, original art on the walls, and taped classical music,

1. Core and quarter the apples (do not remove the skin). Place in a preheated 425°F oven and roast until soft and golden. Remove and set aside.
2. In a large saucepan over medium heat, sauté in olive oil the onion, celery, carrot, leek, garlic, and shallot until softened.
3. Add the wine, cider, bay leaves, cinnamon stick, cloves, and the roasted apples (from step 1) to the saucepan and cook to reduce until *almost* dry.
4. Add the broth and the pumpkin to the mixture and simmer for approximately 15 minutes. Remove the bay leaves, cinnamon stick, and cloves. Remove the mixture from heat and cool slightly.
5. Puree the mixture in a food processor or blender until smooth. Adjust seasoning with salt, if necessary. Serve hot, garnished with sautéed diced apple and cinnamon-flavored sour cream.

Makes 12–15 generous servings.

Adrienne

218 Kent Road (Route 7)
New Milford, CT 06776
(860) 354–6001
$$

is the way chef-proprietor Carol Peck combines disparate ingredients to come up with so many winners. Dishes like lobster chunks and Swiss chard in baked macaroni with provolone cheese and truffle oil, and Jack's pecan-crusted fresh oysters with cherry, jicama, tomatillo salsa,

The Cannery's Eggplant Ravioli

Pasta dishes have become as ubiquitously American as pizza pie, as chef William O'Meara demonstrates in his popular ravioli variation.

Filling

1 eggplant

2 small onions

2 teaspoons olive oil

1 cup toasted walnuts

6 leaves fresh basil

Pinch of sugar

Pinch of cayenne pepper

Salt and pepper to taste

Fresh Pasta

3 cups flour

4 eggs

Water

Tomato Butter Sauce

1 cup pureed fresh tomatoes

4 ounces unsalted butter

Salt and pepper

For filling:

Cut eggplant in half and roast in 350°F oven until tender. Slice onions thinly and caramelize in sauté pan with olive oil until nicely brown. Place eggplant, onions, walnuts, basil, sugar, cayenne, and salt and pepper in food processor. Process until smooth. Set aside.

and chili aioli all come to mind. A pioneer in using local organic, seasonal farm foods, Carol remains ahead of the curve in many of her imaginative renderings. Becky Vermilyea, the pastry chef, performs magic with her Mile High coconut layer cake with mango and raspberry sauce and her pumpkin cheesecake with dates, toasted coconut, and spiced pumpkin seeds. Carol's rounds of country peasant breads are available

For pasta:
1. Place flour in bowl of food processor, along with eggs and 1 teaspoon water. Process until dough gathers. It should feel slightly sticky to the touch. Using a pasta rolling machine, roll the dough into sheets, to desired thickness. This will probably be to about #8.
2. Lay out half the sheets and place 1 tablespoon of eggplant filling at 2-inch intervals to fill each sheet. Using a pastry brush, wash the borders of each filled sheet to allow a top sheet to adhere to the bottom sheet. Pinch the dough all around each square of filling. Cut with a pastry wheel or a knife. This should make about 24 large raviolis.
3. When ready to serve, cook raviolis in boiling salted water. When cooked, place in a large bowl and cover with sauce.

For tomato butter sauce:
Heat tomatoes in saucepan and slowly whisk in butter to emulsify. Season to taste.

Serves 6.

The Cannery

85 Main Street
Canaan, CT 06018
(860) 824–7333
$$

for purchase, and a display case with Bridgewater Chocolates is an added temptation.

Chaiwalla, 1 Main Street, Salisbury, CT 06068; (860) 435–9758; e-mail: chaiwalla@snet.net; $. Inside a little clapboard house set back from the road in the center of town, this charming tearoom is a wee oasis for breakfast, tiffin, lunch, and leisurely afternoon tea five days a week. Freshly made salads, quiches, and sandwiches are standard offerings, as are the delicious house-made tarts, pies, and cakes, like whiskey cake, carrot cake, and strawberry-rhubarb cobbler. You can count on loose brewed tea here, as Mary O'Reilly, Chaiwalla's owner, is a tea enthusiast. She also does a retail and mail-order business selling fine and rare teas, which she collects from China, Japan, India, Morocco, and elsewhere in the tea-growing world. Among her selections are Sherpa, the Himalayan climbers' tea, five types of Darjeeling, Nilgiri, Terai, China Keemun, several Assams, fine green Kashmir Kawab from North India, and rare white tea. According to Mary, the name *Chaiwalla* means "tea bearer" in Hindi and Sanskrit.

Hopkins Inn, Hopkins Road, New Preston, CT 06777; (860) 868–7295; www.thehopkinsinn.com; $$. A touch of the Tyrol on a hillside overlooking Lake Waramaug—that is just the beginning of the Hopkins Inn story. Under the ownership of Beth and Franz Schober, the inn has been going strong since 1977 (with a winter break for the restaurant each year during the slow season, January through March). Chef Franz brings his classical Austrian culinary training to modern versions of *wiener schnitzel,* sweetbreads Viennese, *backhendl* (made with free-range chicken and lingonberries), *kalbsrahmgulasch* (veal in paprika–sour-cream sauce), and *bauernsalat* (farmer's salad: potato salad with bacon and herb dressing), among many other delectable, hearty dishes. Beth runs the inn, with its eleven guest rooms and two apartments, in a comfortable, restored 1847 frame house. With their son Toby's recent

Chaiwalla's Famous Tomato Pie

This delicious, easy-to-make pie is a signature luncheon dish at Chaiwalla, a cozy tearoom in Salisbury.

2 cups flour
4 teaspoons baking powder
¼ cup butter
⅔ cup milk (approximately)
10–12 plum tomatoes, peeled and halved

2 tablespoons torn fresh basil leaves
1 tablespoon chopped chives
1½ cups grated sharp cheddar
⅓ cup mayonnaise

1. Preheat oven to 400°F.
2. To make biscuit crust, combine flour and baking powder in a bowl and cut in butter until mixture becomes coarse. Add enough milk to make the dough medium-soft.
3. Place half the dough on a floured board and roll it to fit a 9-inch pie pan. Arrange the dough in the pie pan and cover with the tomato slices. Sprinkle the basil and chives over the tomatoes. Top with half the cheese and coat thinly with mayonnaise. Add the remaining cheese.
4. Roll the remaining dough thin enough to fit over the top of the pie and pinch closed. Bake until brown on top, about 20 minutes. If you prefer more seasoning, add ¼ teaspoon coarsely ground black pepper.

Serves 6.

Chaiwalla
1 Main Street
Salisbury, CT 06068
(860) 435-9758
e-mail: chaiwalla@snet.net
$

involvement, a second generation now helps manage the inn. There are two alpine-style dining rooms, one with a fireplace, both with *gemütlich* Austrian touches. In summertime you may dine under a giant horse-chestnut tree on the flagstone terrace overlooking the lake. There are many extra-value touches here, which is why the Hopkins Inn has such a loyal clientele: A small loaf of warm, crusty bread is served with the appetizers, followed by a crispy-fresh house salad, and entrees are accompanied by a fresh vegetable and rice or potatoes. Desserts are traditional gems: peach Melba, strawberries Romanoff, Grand Marnier soufflé glacé, Toblerone sundae, and pear Hélène. The Schobers also bottle their popular Hopkins Inn House Salad Dressing and Hopkins Inn Caesar Salad Dressing, which they sell at the inn and at markets throughout western Connecticut.

The Mayflower Inn, Route 47, Washington Depot, CT 06794; (860) 868-9466; $$$. Despite the Early American name, this is the most sophisticated inn in Connecticut, rebuilt by Adriana and Robert Mnuchin in 1992, on the site of a onetime private school. It is furnished in English-country-house style, with fireplaces, a book-filled library, and luxurious lounges. The kitchen is devoted to American and continental specialties, often with an Asian twist. On a menu that changes seasonally, pastas are homemade, breads and pastries are from the inn's own bakery, produce and organic herbs are from the inn's gardens, salmon is house-smoked, and game sausage made in-house. The extensive, original wine cellar has won a *Wine Spectator*'s Award of Excellence. Dining in any of the three dining rooms is a special experience—worth its priciness—with such accoutrements as Limoges china, fine crystal, and silver. In warm weather, you may eat on the open deck overlooking the well-kept grounds and gardens. The Mayflower is a member of the prestigious Relais & Châteaux, which is no surprise.

Oliva, Route 45, New Preston, CT 06777; (860) 868–1787; $–$$. What this minuscule cafe lacks in size—it seats a mere thirty-two—it more than makes up for in the quality and originality of its food. Chef-owner Riad Aamar formerly worked at Doc's, a pizzeria-plus down the road, so he has Italian and Mediterranean food down pat. Just as delicious and more unusual are his North African dishes, like appetizers of Moroccan eggplant with mint, mixed Moroccan spices, pecans and lemon and grilled stuffed calamari with mixed nuts, spices, prunes, and lemon. Just thinking of his spice-scented entrees makes us hungry. Moroccan lamb shank with rosemary, cumin, mushrooms, white beans, and tomato and roasted Tunisian chicken with rosemary, ginger, saffron, Mandarin oranges, apricots, and pine nuts come quickly to mind. Seductive aromas, spices, and combinations give this Mediterranean restaurant distinction. For the adventurous palate, this is "definitely worth a detour."

West Main Restaurant, 8 Holley Street, Lakeville, CT 06039; (860) 435–1450; $$. The locale has changed from Sharon to Lakeville, and so has the street (from Main to Holley), but that didn't deter Susan Miller, owner, and Matthew Fahrner, chef, of this handsome restaurant, whose name remains resolutely West Main, Holley be darned. In moving to a renovated Revolutionary War arsenal, West Main now is considerably

Hopkins Inn Rösti Potatoes

Nutmeggers can never find too many recipes for potatoes, a staple crop here. Austrian chef Franz Schober serves his rösti potatoes with many of his Hopkins Inn Austrian and Swiss specialties.

4 small red potatoes or 2 large ones
¼ cup diced white onions
¼ cup diced bacon slices
Salt and pepper to taste
2 tablespoons melted butter

1. Wash and boil the red potatoes until tender but not soft. Cool in refrigerator; then peel and shred with a large grater.
2. In a saucepan, sauté the onions and bacon until golden brown. Drain the bacon fat. Add the mixture to the shredded potatoes and season to taste with salt and pepper.
3. Sauté mixture with the melted butter in a nonstick skillet at moderately high heat. Do not stir or mix. Flip the rösti potatoes over when you see the steam rising. If you cannot, then cover them with a plate, turn them onto the plate, and slide them back, sautéed side up, into the skillet.
4. When you see the steam again, potatoes should be thoroughly cooked. Both sides should have a golden-brown color. Serve piping hot.

Serves 4.

Hopkins Inn Tiroler Gröstl

For a delicious breakfast or luncheon entree, combine Franz Schober's rösti potatoes with ham and bacon slices. This popular Hopkins Inn dish is easy to make and very festive.

¼ rösti mixture (uncooked)

2 slices ham, cut into small
    strips

2 tablespoons melted butter

4 slices bacon

2 eggs

1 slice toast

1. Mix the rösti ingredients with the ham.
2. Heat a nonstick pan, add melted butter, and spread out the bacon slices. Spread the rösti-ham mixture on top of the bacon slices. Sauté at moderately high heat until you see the steam rising. Do not stir.
3. Flip the mixture or cover pan with a plate and turn the mixture onto the plate; then slide them, sautéed side up, back into the pan. When the steam rises again, both sides should be golden brown in color.
4. In a separate nonstick skillet, cook the two eggs, either scrambled or plain fried, over medium heat until lightly cooked. Place the bacon-rösti-ham mixture on a large plate, with the fried or scrambled eggs on top of them, and serve with toast.

Serves 1.

Hopkins Inn

22 Hopkins Road
New Preston, CT 06777
(860) 868-7295
$$

more spacious, with three dining areas and a separate bar for displaying vivid abstract paintings behind well-separated tables. We like the world-wide range of the menu, with its Asian and Mediterranean influences, and the fact that the kitchen is able to produce everything the menu promises, from spicy pork dumplings and sea-salt-sprinkled house *frites* to rice-paper-wrapped "wild" striped bass, grilled tamarind-glazed salmon, and house-made ice creams. Mostly we just like being here, leisurely sipping the last of our wine, listening to the live music (available Thursday through Saturday), and winding down from a busy week. Open for dinner only.

West Street Grill, West Street, Litchfield, CT 06759; (860) 567–3885; $$$. In a stylish, L-shaped dining room, hung with mirrors and vibrant paintings by local artists, some of the area's most consistently fine cooking can be found. Proprietor James O'Shea is a genial host and was an innovator in combining fresh ingredients in creative ways. Many of Connecticut's finest farm-grown products—sweet corn, Heirloom tomatoes, and basil—as well as eggs from free-range chickens amd cheeses from seven statewide cheesemakers, can be found here. Many of James's chefs have graduated to restaurants of their own all over the northwest corner, but he trains each replacement well, as consistency seems to be an O'Shea fetish (which may explain his success). There are many pleasing details here; note especially the sprightly Quimper faïence service plates. Part of the fun—aside from the terrific food—is checking out some of your fellow diners, often famous New Yorkers (Tom Brokaw and Henry Kissinger come to mind) who have weekend homes nearby. Such "names" can often be found at table 21 and the other tables in the row down the center of the restaurant (considered prime seating to whom such distinctions matter).

Wood's Pit B*B*Q & Mexican Café, 123 Bantam Lake Road, Route 209, Bantam, CT 06750; (860) 567-9869; $. Like any authentic barbecue joint, Wood's is as plain as toast. The proof is in the eating, and at Wood's you will find some of the best barbecue in Connecticut. Wood's has a culinary split personality, serving both down-and-rustic barbecue food and Mexican specialties. Stick to the barbecue side of the menu and concentrate on what Wood's does best: ribs, ribs, and more ribs (we are not, uh, ribbing you). Best-sellers, we were told, are the platters of pork ribs, which are lean, meaty, and full of the rich, deep-down flavor that comes from slow pit cooking and the use of green, not dry, hickory, oak, and apple woods. The Rib Tickler is another winner: lean St. Louis–style pork ribs, richly smoked. Other meat triumphs are the melt-in-the-mouth tender sliced beef brisket and the pulled pork (pork shoulder smoked for eighteen hours, then shredded and seasoned with spices and sauces). Onion rings—thick pinwheels in a shroud of batter—are served in a novel way, on a wooden spindle.

The sides are tasty here, especially the ranch-baked beans and jalapeño corn bread. Oh yes, the barbecue sauce—a blend of ketchup, vinegar, brown sugar, and a secret cache of spices—is lip-smacking zesty, not overly sweet.

West Street Grill's Brandade of Salt Cod

We used to disdain cod, this native swimmer in New England's Atlantic waters, but after trying this recipe of James O'Shea of Litchfield's West Street Grill, we have been converted.

2 pounds salted codfish, boneless and skinless, soaked in cold water for 2 to 3 days, changing the water at least 3 times daily

2 medium red onions, cut into thin slices

3 fresh bay leaves or 3 fresh Kaffir lime leaves

1 fresh red chile pepper (mild), seeds and stems removed

½ bunch fresh cilantro or Italian parsley

2 cups milk

1 cup heavy cream

1 cup olive oil (preferably French)

2½ tablespoons fresh, finely minced garlic (minced by hand with a pinch of salt until a paste forms)

1 pound russet Burbank potatoes, peeled and cut into thick cubes

Freshly ground white pepper

Fresh sea salt to taste

White truffle oil (optional), chervil, diced chives (for garnish)

6–10 paper-thin discs of bread

1. Place drained codfish in a single layer in a large pan. Cover with cold water, the onion slices, bay or Kaffir lime leaves, chile pepper,

and cilantro or parsley. Bring mixture to boil, immediately lower heat, and simmer for 2–3 minutes. Turn stove off and allow fish to remain in water for 5–6 minutes. Drain well and discard the water. Remove any bones and skin. Flake the fish well.

2. Blend milk and cream and warm in a saucepan over low heat.

3. Warm olive oil and garlic in a separate pan.

4. Meanwhile, boil the potato chunks. Drain, then steam for 2–3 minutes to slightly dry. Pass them through a ricer. Place warm riced potatoes in a mixing bowl and beat at low speed. Add flaked cod and beat at high speed. Alternately add small amounts of warm milk-cream mixture and warm garlic until all are used. Do not overbeat, but be sure mixture is well blended.

5. Season with white pepper. Taste and add a little sea salt if needed; do not add until mixture is thoroughly tasted.

6. If you wish to serve the brandade immediately, place small mounds in 3-inch rings in the center of plates, drizzle with truffle oil and garnish with chervil and diced chives. Drizzle crostini with truffle oil and serve on a separate plate to accompany the brandade.

7. If you wish to serve the dish later, divide portions into small gratin dishes and broil until pale golden brown. Drizzle with truffle oil, garnish with chervil and chives, and serve with crostini.

Serves 6 as an entree,
8–10 as an appetizer.

West Street Grill
West Street
Litchfield, CT 06759
(860) 567–3885
$$$

Connecticut Wine Trail, www.ctwine.com. Its Trail 1, with map and winery details, can be printed out from the Web site and includes Haight and Hopkins wineries. (At this printing, Jerram and Strawberry Ridge wineries have not yet been included on the map or in the literature.)

Haight Vineyard, Chestnut Hill, Litchfield, CT 06759; (800) 577–9463; www.haightvineyards.com. You will know you have arrived at this oldest of the state's wineries (1978) when you see the huge wooden wine tun at the entrance. At the sprawling building in the center are the works, where the grapes are converted and aged. Currently, Sherman Haight grows or imports from Chile Chardonnay, Seyval Blanc, Riesling, Merlot, and Maréchal Foch grapes or concentrates and produces nine wines (three of them have added fruit or honey). In the spacious upstairs tasting room/showroom of the main building, you may sample Haight's range of wines. Self-guided tours are simple, following the Vineyard Walk; in summer, there is an outdoor cafe where food, wine, and beer are available.

Haight hosts several annual events: an Olde Fashioned Winter Celebration in mid-February; Barrel New Vintage Tasting in March and April (when guests sample and comment on the new wines, helping the vintners determine preferences for the new vintages); A Taste of Litchfield Hills in June (see Food Happenings); and the Old-fashioned Harvest Festival in late September, a crescendo of live music, grape-stomping contests, hayrides, pony rides for the kids, and artisans creating and selling their crafts. (Call ahead for dates and times.) The tasting room is open from Monday through Saturday from 10:00 A.M. to 6:00 P.M., Sunday from noon to 5:00 P.M.

Hopkins Vineyard, 25 Hopkins Road, New Preston, CT 06777; (860) 868–7954; www.hopkinsvineyard.com. High above Lake Waramaug, and across the road from the Hopkins Inn (no relation), is the farmland settled by Elijah Hopkins upon his return from the Revolutionary War. Over the years his descendants have grown tobacco and grain crops and have raised sheep, race horses, and dairy cattle, but since 1979 William and Judith Hopkins have grown grapes and produced wines. Among their wines are Chardonnay, Seyval Blanc, Cabernet Franc, and Pinot Noir, some of which have won awards in national and international competitions. Their huge nineteenth-century barn is now a winery, with the wine bar and showroom tucked into the old hayloft. Relax here over wine, along with cheese, fresh bread, and pâtés, while enjoying the striking views of the lake and countryside below. Hopkins is open for tastings and tours from May through December, Monday through Saturday, from 10:00 A.M. to 5:00 P.M., Sunday from 11:00 A.M. to 5:00 P.M. The rest of the year it is open on a more limited schedule: call for hours and days.

Jerram Winery, 535 Town Hill Road, New Hartford, CT 06057; (860) 379–8749; www.jerramwinery.com. One of Connecticut's newest wineries, Jerram occupies a four-acre spread, in the aptly named Town Hill district of a small town that was settled in the early 1700s. To develop the winery, owner James Jerram drew on his

It may take a heap of living to make a house a home, but it only takes a savvy Englishman to turn a bar into a real pub. That is what David Davis has done here. Driving into Norfolk, you can't miss the large brick building that dominates the tiny commercial center of town. Its sign says THE PUB AND RESTAURANT WHERE SOCIABILITY IS PRONOUNCED. With stained glass, vintage photographs of old Norfolk buildings on the knotty pine and brick walls, and a chair at one table whose back and seat are made of bleached moose antlers (talk about the prime seat in the house!), the funky display is cozy enough to make even strangers feel at home. David, who was once co-owner of a posh inn in Fairfield County (Stonehenge), has created a pub ambience where comforting pub grub is served along with 130 different beers, including some from Belgium, England, Germany, and France. In addition to regular burgers, there are lamb burgers, tuna burgers, black-bean burgers, and portobello burgers, as well as chili with corn bread and English fish-and-chips and a ploughman's lunch. Dinner specials sometimes include spa and/or Atkins diet items.

The Pub & Restaurant

Route 44
Norfolk, CT 06058
(860) 542–5716
$

agriculture studies at Rutgers University, operations management at Rensselaer Polytechnic, and years in the food and beverage industries. He began his winery in 1999 with six grape varieties, including Chardonnay, Maréchal Foch, Seyval Blanc, Aurora, and Cabernet Franc. He now offers six wines, which include "Gentle Shepherd, "S'il Vous Plait," and "White Frost." Winery hours for tastings are from 11:00 A.M.

to 5:00 P.M., Wednesday through Sunday, but from January through March the hours are limited to weekends.

Strawberry Ridge Vineyards, P.O. Box 242M, New Preston, CT 06777; (860) 868–0730. In 1990 New Yorkers Susan and Robert Summer bought land just north of the Hopkins Inn above Lake Waramaug and cleared five acres for grapevines. With professional advice and experienced management, they planted Chardonnay vines from Alsace in 1992. By 1996 the grapes yielded the first wine. The following year the Summers bottled their first Ascot Reserve wine, which had been fermented in imported oak barrels. Three years later Ascot Reserve won a bronze in the American Wine Society's 2000 competition and an 83 (of 100) rating from *Wine Spectator*. Of more importance to wine lovers, Ascot Reserve is now found on wine lists at elite restaurants such as Nobu, Circo, Scottsdale's Café Blue, and the Beverly Hills Peninsula. In Connecticut, it is available at nearby Boulders Inn on Lake Waramaug, West Street Grill in Litchfield, and Washington Depot's Mayflower Inn. You will have to try Ascot Reserve at one of these restaurants (or others that may have been added) because the winery itself is private (sorry, no samples and no tours).

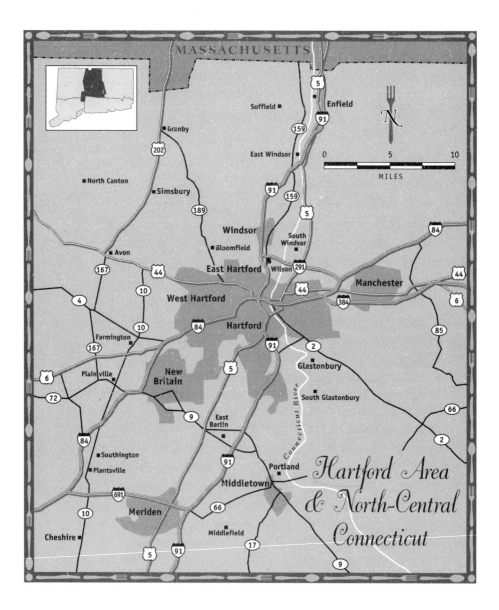

MASSACHUSETTS

Suffield ■ Enfield

Granby ■

East Windsor ■

North Canton ■

Simsbury ■

Windsor

Bloomfield ■ South Windsor ■

Avon ■

East Hartford Wilson ■

West Hartford Manchester

Hartford

Farmington ■

Plainville ■ New Britain Glastonbury

South Glastonbury ■

East Berlin ■

Southington ■ Portland ■

Plantsville ■ Middletown

Meriden

Middlefield ■

Cheshire ■

Connecticut River

N

0   5   10
MILES

*Hartford Area
& North-Central
Connecticut*

Hartford Area and North-Central Connecticut

Hartford, as the state capital, is a centripetal force that has brought to its center all kinds of artistic, cultural, political, ethnic, and culinary forces. These include a steady stream of new restaurants, ethnic grocery stores and bakeries, specialty food shops, and an influx of people from diverse ethnic backgrounds (including Vietnamese and Afghans) to enjoy them. Mark Twain, who lived in the city for twenty years, called Hartford "the best built and handsomest town I have ever seen" and would have marveled at the variety and spiciness of the city at present.

During the last century, Hartford's major culinary happenings, fiestas, and shopping took place along Franklin Avenue, the Italian neighborhood salt-and-peppered with restaurants, bakeries, Italian delis, food importers, and mom-and-pop food shops, many of which are still in their original locales. One of our favorite Hartford food events is the seasonal downtown farmers' market held within the gates of the splendid Old State House, the oldest state house in the country, designed by Charles Bulfinch in the Georgian style in 1796.

Hartford spills over into leafy, suburban West Hartford, which is a smaller potpourri of diverse restaurants, cafes, coffeehouses, and specialty food shops. Three of the largest international ethnic grocery markets in the area are within its town limits.

Radiating out from Hartford in all directions are many of the state's oldest towns, like Windsor and Suffield to the north and sleepy Old Wethersfield to the south, with all its stately eighteenth-century houses locked in time. On the east side of the Connecticut River is Glastonbury, which manages to be both sophisticated and rural at the same time, and whose well-groomed vintage houses are home to many Hartford "movers and shakers." The town is tucked among orchards and farms that are some of the oldest and most productive in the state. Just north is Manchester, with one of the best Italian restaurants in a state that prides itself on many excellent ones.

What makes this entire terrain around Hartford so appealing is that it is still so agricultural, dappled with historic little towns that are surrounded by wooded hillsides, cultivated fields, and valleys. The Connecticut River runs south from Massachusetts, squiggling through the middle of this area. Its fertile banks have made this a productive farmland for generations. The number of small family-run farms (up to 500 acres) in this area is the largest in the state. These family enterprises produce gigantic salad baskets of fresh vegetables and fruits that are sold from their own farm stands and at farmers' markets all around the area. Many of the area farms invite you to pick your own berries, apples, and other crops.

An especially beautiful town is Farmington, one of Hartford's upscale suburbs, with many handsome houses, smart restaurants and food shops, and a prime location along the restless Farmington River. In neatly manicured, sedately rural Simsbury, you will find good restaurants, gourmet shops, and a producer of cheese, milk, and delicious ice cream.

South of Hartford in New Britain is an enclave so full of Polish groceries, meat markets, and restaurants, with signs written in Polish, that you may think you have landed in Warsaw. Middletown now caters to its Wesleyan University clientele, with a notable diner, vegetarian restaurant, and assorted ethnic eateries—a big change from its decades as a mill town. The surrounding countryside blossoms in spring with flowering orchards. One of the biggest, at Middlefield, has the largest indoor farm market in the state. You will read about it and others below.

Made or Grown Here

Arugula, 953 Farmington Avenue, West Hartford, CT 06127; (860) 561–4888; e-mail:cgehami@aol.com. Christiane Gehami began making and selling her surefire scone mixes two years before she opened Arugula, a Mediterranean bistro, in 1996, but now you can buy the scones at the bistro (or order them via e-mail). They come in four flavors: chocolate cappuccino, apricot, whole-wheat currant, and streusel (nut combination). A few specialty stores, like Marlborough Country Barn in Marlborough, also handle the mixes.

Desserts by David Glass, 1280 Blue Hills Avenue, Bloomfield, CT 06002; (860) 525–0345 or (800) DAVID–99; www.davidglass.com. Best known of David Glass's many scrumptious desserts is the Ultimate Chocolate Truffle Cake, a dense chocolate cake that sends chocophiles straight to nirvana. It is one of twenty heavenly desserts made by this twenty-year-old company. Others—all dubbed The Ultimate—include New York Cheesecake, Chocolate-covered Banana Cheesecake, and Key Lime Pie. If there is a Glass dessert more superlative than the Ultimate Luscious Italian Almond Cake, it is probably the Ultimate Chocolate-covered Luscious Italian Almond Cake. The desserts are made in Bloomfield (the company moved in 2003 from Hartford's historic Colt factory) and can be bought there ("seconds" are sold too), as well as on the Web site, by direct mail, or through retail stores. Wild Oats in West Hartford and Lyman Orchards in Middlefield carry the line. The factory offers free tastings Wednesday, Thursday, and Friday before major holidays (check for days) from 11:00 A.M. to 3:30 P.M.

Giff's Original, Box 1212, Cheshire, CT 06410; (203) 699–8605; www.giffsoriginal.com. For the tang of New England in your cooking, there is nothing quite like the Cranberry Pepper Relish and Cranberry Ginger Chutney made by Marie "Giff" Hirschfeld of Giff's Original. Marie began concocting relishes and salsas in her kitchen and now sells her five all-natural, no-fat, low-salt kosher products at specialty food shops all over the state, including Bon Appetit in Hamden, Nine Main in New Preston, and the Old State House in Hartford. In the line as well are Mango Spice Salsa, which won an award from the Specialty Foods Association, Grill & Marinade Sauce, and the original Pepper Relish. Marie also sells through her Web site, shipping via parcel post or UPS.

Gloria's Gourmet, 161 Woodford Avenue, #45, Plainville, CT 06062; (860) 747–0496. An interest in herbs and spices led Gloria McCarthy to create her imaginative line of dip mixes, which she sells in dry packets (to add to sour cream for dips and spreads) to small and large markets in the state. You may find her garlic-bread topping, garlic dip, bagel spreads, and oil infusions at Gardiner's Market in South Glastonbury and Santilli's Epicure Market in Farmington, among other outlets.

Gluten Free Pantry, Inc., 182 Oakwood Drive, P.O. Box 840, Glastonbury, CT 06033; (860) 633–3826; www.glutenfree.com. When food writer Beth Hillson was diagnosed with celiac disease, the gluten-allergic disease, she didn't realize it would lead to a new business. Before long she was creating a whole panoply (or pantry) of gluten-free and wheat-free bread mixes, pancake mixes, and brownie and cookie mixes, some of which have won taste awards in competition with non-allergy-free products. Ten years and 300 to 400 products later, Beth has a thriving Internet business, selling her products all over the United States. Customer favorites are her brownie mix, chocolate-cake mix, and Favorite Sandwich bread mix. You will find them in their cheerful multicolored packets at Wild Oats in Granby, Garden of Light in Glastonbury, and

Today's Market Natural Foods in Avon, among many outlets throughout Connecticut.

Gulf Shrimp Seafood Company LLC, 240 Atwater Street, Plantsville, CT 06479; (860) 628–8399; www.gulfshrimp.info. Forget the idea of Gulf shrimp. Chad Simoneaux, proprietor, was honoring his home state of Louisiana when he set up his wholesale seafood business in 1991, but the reams of seafood he buys fresh daily, five days a week, in Boston have nothing to do with the Gulf. In his enormous 18,000-square-foot plant, Chad has fish and shellfish so fresh that the many restaurants and retailers he sells to (like Metro Bis in Simsbury, Hopkins Inn in New Preston, and Star Fish Market in Guilford) swear by his wares. Wholesale delivery six days a week is made within twelve hours of the catch. In late April and May, he gets Connecticut River shad and shad roe, and from mid-May to September, he stocks fresh soft-shell crabs. Retail orders, via Fed Ex, get overnight delivery. Chad also has retail space in his plant, where he sells to the public his fresh seafood and fully prepared fresh-frozen items, including stuffed shrimp, clams casino, seafood chowders, soups, fried whole-belly clams, and seafood egg rolls.

Krystyna's Specialties Inc., 88 Commerce Street, East Berlin, CT 06023; (860) 829–6558. Krystyna's Pierogi Priest label was designed by Father Nadolny of St. Stanislaus Church in Meriden, and the priest's charitable Good News Fund receives 5 percent of the proceeds from the pierogies sold by Krystyna's, which began producing these stuffed dumplings in 1994. Krystyna's sells four types of pierogies: cabbage, cabbage and mushrooms, potatoes and cheese, and plain farmer's cheese. According to manager Rob Kataneksza, the best-selling pierogi is the potato and cheese. Mostly, Krystyna's sells to distributors, but you can find these popular Polish dumplings at Lyman Orchards in Middlefield, Geissler's in East Windsor, and the Gnazzo Food Center in Kensington, as well as at Shop Rite stores throughout the state.

Omar Coffee Company, 555 Franklin Avenue, Hartford, CT 06106; (800) 394-OMAR; www.omarcoffeecompany.com. Since 1937 the Cocola family has been importing some eighty kinds of green coffees from all over the world and slow-roasting them to sell retail and wholesale to such outlets as Carbone's in Hartford and Windsor Donut in Windsor. Omar's factory has just moved to Newington, but its spacious Hartford store is an attractive stop for fresh coffee, one of Omar's elaborate coffee gift baskets, a cup of one of the five daily coffee specials, and/or a biscotti or pastry to nibble on as you sip and relax in the shop's comfortable living-room-like lounge. In 1994 Omar's established a scholarship program at the University of Connecticut; the newest coffee, Husky Blend, was created to aid the program and seems to be sold ubiquitously all over central and eastern Connecticut.

Sally's Specialty Products, 350 Asylum Street, Hartford, CT 06103; (860) 278-RIBS; www.blackeyedsallys.com. Barbecue and blues, an irresistible combination. That is probably why Black Eyed Sally's BBQ & Blues restaurant began marketing its popular barbecue sauces—Cajun Beer BBQ, Black Jack Molasses, Mardi Gras, and the Original Habañero—

and soon added other products: Black-eyed Sally's Rib Rub and Cajun Spice, as well as T-shirts, denim shirts, caps, and other memorabilia. You will find Sally's sauces at most Stop & Shops, or you can order them directly on-line from Sally's Web site or pick them up at the restaurant. Sally's says "our pigs do fly" and also sells the restaurant's famous smoked pork, BBQ rib dinner and ribs-to-go, ready to heat and eat. They are shipped every Monday with a two-to-three-day delivery anywhere in the United States.

Sassy Sauces, P.O. Box 535, Avon, CT 06001; (860) 677–2818; www. sassysauce.com. As executive chef at Avon Old Farms Inn, Charles Simmons created and now markets three sharp sauces, all of which make great marinades or glazes for meat or fish. Mouthful-O-Mango Barbecue Sauce, Sweet-N-Tangy Balsamic Vinaigrette, and Spicy Citrus Sauce are all used in the Old Farms Inn kitchens and can be purchased at the inn. They are also available by mail order or his Web site.

The Thompson Candy Company, 80 South Vine Street, Meriden, CT 06451; (203) 235–2541. You may not know Thompson by name, though the company's origins go back to the nineteenth century, making it one of the oldest, if not *the* oldest, chocolate-candy producer in Connecticut. Chances are you have seen Thompson's chocolate bunnies, Easter eggs, Santas, cigars, and other chocolate novelty molds. They are all made in Meriden and sold at Three Cheers Hallmark in Meriden, at Village Chocolatiers in Guilford, and elsewhere in the state and United States. A small shop attached to the factory displays the range of Thompson's creative designs in milk, bitter, and white chocolate, molded into seasonal shapes. Special orders can be placed through the shop, which also sells solid, filled, and boxed chocolates by other producers.

Town Farm Dairy, 73 Wolcott Road, Simsbury, CT 06070; (860) 658–5362. Bill Walsh's twenty-to-thirty Jersey cows on his seventy-five-acre farm must be well-fed, happy critters, for they produce some of the richest, creamiest milk around. This is evident to anyone stopping by the pint-size store (behind the white farmhouse, in front of the red barn) for milk or the many milk products Bill makes in small quantity: two kinds of yogurt, sour cream, cream cheese, and three kinds of hard, handcrafted cheese (Colby, stirred-curd cheddar, and a salty, flavorful Almshouse). Every other week the dairy makes what Bill calls "adult ice cream," meaning it is not overly sweet, with flavors like espresso, pecan caramel, and, in the fall cranberry season, cranberry-orange-walnut. Delicious! The store is open daily except Sundays and Tuesdays. In summer, Bill also sells his milk products at the West Hartford Farmers' Market and at the Pickin' Patch farm stand in Avon.

Specialty Stores & Markets

A Dong Supermarket, 160 Shield Street, Hartford, CT 06110; (860) 953–8903. In a profligate 32,000-square-foot space, Phuong and Khiem Tran, a Vietnamese couple, have fulfilled an Asian immigrant's wildest food dream: a market with every conceivable type of comfort food from home, and then some. At first glance, A Dong looks like any big American supermarket, but then peer at the products: fresh, canned, baked, dried, pickled, and frozen foods from Vietnam, Laos, Cambodia, Thailand, China, the Philippines, Korea, and Japan, all impeccably organized and displayed. Fresh-roasted, lacquer-colored whole ducks and suckling pigs hang from hooks. A bakery section has Banh sandwiches and bean cakes; there are fresh-produce and frozen-foods sections and even a vast department full of oriental china, pots, cooking utensils, and imported gift items. If you are an Asian food aficionado, A Dong's is a one-stop, *must*-stop shopping center for sure.

Connecticut Product Store, 765 Asylum Avenue, Hartford, CT 06105; (860) 713–2569. Located on the second floor of the Department of Agriculture building, this compact shop is a showcase for made-in-Connecticut food products, which cover every inch of counter space wall to wall. A visit is a delightful way to grasp the wide range of products available and to buy a sampling for yourself or as gifts. The beautifully displayed and packaged jams, condiments, sauces, spices, oils, candies, and mixes make you want to swoop them all up. As the store is open on a limited schedule, only nonperishable goods are available. Call for hours.

Crown Super Market, 2471 Albany Avenue, West Hartford, CT 06117; (860) 236–1965. Picture a New York–style Jewish delicatessen enlarged to supermarket size and you have an idea what Crown Super Market is like, with every imaginable type of kosher food, including a wide assortment of baked goods, poultry, and meats. Although predominantly kosher, there are some other foods as well, mainly natural and organic.

Daybreak Coffee Roasters, 2377 Main Street, Glastonbury, CT 06033; (800) 882–5282; www.daybreakcoffee.com. Tom Clark's shop is more than just a place to have a terrific cuppa. He has forty different types of fresh, high-quality, unroasted green coffee beans from around the world for sale, which he roasts before your eyes. While you sip a latte, an espresso, a cappuccino, or one of Tom's special aromatic roasts, either in the shop or outdoors in warm weather, you may munch on a scone, muffin, turnover or cookie, freshly baked right at Daybreak. This is a good source of gifts, too, with one hundred gift baskets to choose from and all kinds of food items, many made by other Connecticut food producers, like Bridgewater Chocolates. In addition to the shop, Tom sells his superior coffees wholesale. You will find them at Say Cheese! in Simsbury and Lyman Orchards in Middlefield, among many places.

DiBacco's Food Imports, 553 Franklin Avenue, Hartford, CT 06114; (860) 296–7365; www.dibaccosfoodimports.com. Like so many of the Italian stores along Franklin Avenue, DiBacco's, after twenty-eight years in business, has extremely loyal customers, who come for the wide array of imported Italian foods—an incredible variety of dried pastas, olive oils, cheeses, coffees, and packaged, canned, and dried goods. Then there are Mario and Angela DiBacco's fresh-baked Italian breads and pizzas, store-made Italian sausages (which are also sold to restaurants and distributors), soups, and grinders made daily for lunch take-outs.

Mozzicato De Pasquale Bakery & Pastry Shop, 329 Franklin Avenue, Hartford, CT 06106; (860) 296-0426; www.mozzicatobakery.com. De Pasquale's bread shop has been in this location since 1908, but when Gino Mozzicato bought it in 1975 and combined it with his pastry shop, the spacious, immaculate quarters became the best of two worlds: marvelous breads (Italian, Sicilian, Tuscan, rye, pumpernickel) and rolls and heaven-sent cakes (rum cake, tiramisu, Torta al Cappuccino, lemon and raspberry mousse cakes, hazelnut, Napoleon cake, almond tortes, Italian cherry nut, wedding, Easter, Christmas, special-occasion cakes) and delectable cookies (biscotti, pignoli, amaretti, taralli, crescents). Mozzicato also makes Italian-style gelatos in twelve luscious flavors and, in warm weather, lemon granita as tartly refreshing as any you'd find on the streets of Napoli. Next door, through a separate entrance, is **The Mozzicato Caffè,** a large room seating forty, where you can enjoy an espresso, a cappuccino, or a latte with a Mozzicato pastry and perhaps a cordial. Franklin Avenue, the historic Italian district, has undergone many ethnic changes in recent times, but Mozzicato De Pasquale continues to thrive, a favorite of Italians and newer arrivals alike.

Say Cheese!, Simsburytown Shops, 924 Hopmeadow Street, Simsbury, CT 06070; (860) 658-6742 or (888) 243-3373; www.Saycheese.com. Yes, emphatically, say cheese—more than 125 varieties of imported cheeses, as well as forty flavors of coffee beans, French and English jams, assorted vinegars, oils, sauces, syrups and mustards, teas, cookies, candies and crackers, and chocolates. All are on display at this elegant gourmet cheese shop, which styles itself *"la grande pantrie"* and also specializes in fancy, imaginative gift baskets packed with goodies. China and high-end cooking utensils are also for sale here. A second shop, **Say Cheese Too!,** is now open at 968C Farmington Avenue in West Hartford (860–233–7309), with a similar inventory.

Scandinavian Foods of Farmington, 244 Main Street, Farmington, CT 06032; (860) 677–1881; www. Scandiafood.com. This all-Scandinavian all-the-time store looks from the outside like a modified dairy barn. Inside, the dairy products are all kinds of cheeses, mostly from Sweden (Västerbotten, Prästost, Gräddost) and Norway (Jarlsberg, Norvegia, Gjetost). There are also whole Julskinka hams, Danish Leverpastej, and frozen Swedish meatballs, as well as a large assortment of crisp and flat breads, crackers, gingersnaps and other cookies, candies, jams, and condiments. The shop is especially festive around Christmastime, with colorful straw and wood tree elves, trolls, and ornaments, candlesticks, flags, calendars, wool sweaters, caps, and other gift items, all imported from the four Scandinavian countries.

Scott's Jamaican Bakery, 1344 Albany Avenue, Hartford, CT 06112; (860) 247–3855. Small and bustling, Scott's, located on the corner of Kent, is a mecca of West Indian baked goods, with fresh-baked corn bread, cinnamon bread and rolls, plantain and coconut tarts, and a host of other Caribbean pastries. A small freezer contains Scott's famous

AN INTERNATIONAL BAZAAR ON FARMINGTON AVENUE

On 2 blocks of Farmington Avenue in West Hartford, near the Hartford line, is a trio of ethnic food markets catering to an international clientele, chock-full of imported foods to delight, attract, and appeal to adventurous home cooks.

Cosmos International, 770 Farmington Avenue, West Hartford, CT 06119; (860) 232-6600. A veritable supermarket of mostly Indian and Pakistani foodstuffs, Cosmos sells huge sacks of rice, dried fruits, nuts, spices, jars of hot sauces, pickles, chutneys, pappadum mixes, chappati flour, a variety of teas, curry pastes, butter ghees, cooking oils, and spicy mixes. There is a produce section with Indian eggplant, okra and fiery chiles, and even a deli case with Indian specialties prepared by a Cosmos chef—lamb vindaloo, chicken tika masala, fresh-made cheese—ready for takeout. There are foods from Israel and the Middle East as well.

Delicacy Market, 774 Farmington Avenue, West Hartford, CT 06119; (860) 236-7100; www.delicacymarket.com. Two doors down from Cosmos, Delicacy Market is crammed with Russian, Ukrainian, and other East European favorites. They include Estonian, German, Russian, and Polish sausages; twenty-nine salamis from all over and cold cuts; forty-six types of smoked fish; Lithuanian and Latvian breads; seventeen imported cheeses, including Swedish; grains, lentils, and beans; Ukrainian and Russian hard candies;

Russian teas; dried fruits, nuts, and seeds; jars and cans of pickled vegetables; store-made pierogies, blintzes, and raviolis; and yogurts and butters from Israel, Latvia, and Poland. There are also fresh fruits and vegetables and hot meals for take-out, such as pierogies, potato pancakes, and stuffed cabbage.

Tangiers International, 668 Farmington Avenue, West Hartford, CT 06119; (860) 233-8168. Though this huge store, on the corner of Prospect, might more aptly be named Athens, for all the Greek products it contains, there is something for every Middle Eastern food fancier here, whether North African, Jewish, Turkish, Armenian, Syrian, Egyptian, or Bulgarian. Some foods are premises-made, like hummus, babba ghanoush, stuffed grape leaves, kibbe, tabbouleh, and spanakopita. Others are imported: jars of Bulgarian eggplant and spiced whole tomatoes, tubes of harissa (the spicy North African seasoning), herb teas, Greek olives in brine, Lebanese berry syrups, all kinds of grains, dried lentils and beans, sumac and other herbs, cheeses from Greece and Bulgaria, Jordan almonds, Turkish delights, even a well-stocked frozen-food section. What first caught our eyes was the vast refrigerated case full of baklava and other honey-accented Middle Eastern pastries and sweets. A lunch counter in the rear is a gathering place for coffee and daily specials like a lamb gyro or falafel sandwich, to eat there or take home. Pause a minute to enjoy the Babel of languages.

Jamaican beef patties, shaped like empanadas, ready to take home for a quick meal.

Farmers' Markets

For up-to-the-minute information about dates and times, call Connecticut Department of Agriculture at (860) 713–2503, visit the Web site at www.state.ct.us/doag/, or e-mail at ctdeptag@po.state.ct.us.

Avon Farmers' Market, Old Avon Village parking lot (between Double Down Grill and Blumen Laden), Avon. Saturdays from 9:00 A.M. to 1:00 P.M., mid-July through October.

Bloomfield Farmers' Market, Bloomfield Town Hall, 800 Bloomfield Avenue, Bloomfield. Saturdays from 9:00 A.M. to 1:00 P.M., early July through October.

East Hartford Farmers' Market, Raymond Memorial Library, 840 Main Street, East Hartford. Fridays from 9:00 A.M. to 1:00 P.M., early July through October.

Hartford Asylum Hill Farmers' Market, Asylum Hill Congregational Church, Hartford. Wednesdays from 11:00 A.M. to 2:00 P.M., mid-July through October.

Hartford Downtown Farmers' Market, Old State House, Main Street entrance, Hartford. Mondays, Wednesdays, and Fridays from 10:00 A.M. to 2:00 P.M., June through November.

Hartford Park Street Farmers' Market, Walgreen's parking lot (corner of Park and Washington Streets), Hartford. Mondays from 10:00 A.M. to 1:00 P.M., July through October.

Hartford Regional Market, exit 27 off I–91, Hartford. Open year-round from 5:00 A.M. to noon; the largest food-distribution terminal between New York and Boston.

Manchester Farmers' Market, town parking lot, Main and Forest Streets, Manchester. Saturdays from 8:00 A.M. to 12:30 P.M., early July through October.

Meriden Farmers' Market, Butler Street parking lot (corner of West Main and Grove Streets), Meriden. Saturdays from 8:30 A.M. to noon, mid-July through October.

Middletown Farmers' Market, South Green on Old Church Street, Middletown. Tuesdays and Thursdays from 8:00 A.M. to noon, mid-July through October.

New Britain Farmers' Market, St. Ann's Church, 109 North Street, New Britain. Thursdays from 11:00 A.M. to 2:00 P.M., second week of July through October.

New Britain/Urban Oaks Farmers' Market, 225 Oak Street, New Britain. Fridays from 2:00 to 6:00 P.M., and Saturdays from 9:00 A.M. to 1:00 P.M., mid-May through October.

South Windsor Farmers' Market, Wapping Shopping Plaza, Oakland Road (Route 30), South Windsor. Sundays from 11:00 A.M. to 2:00 P.M., mid-July to October.

Suffield Farmers' Market, Town Green, Main Street, Suffield. Saturdays from 9:00 A.M. to noon, July through October.

West Hartford Farmers' Market, LaSalle Road Public Parking, West Hartford. Tuesdays and Saturdays from 9:30 A.M. to 1:30 P.M., Thursdays from noon to 4:00 P.M., May through October.

Wilson/Windsor Farmers' Market, Connecticut Service for the Blind, 184 Windsor Avenue, Windsor. Tuesdays from 3:00 to 6:00 P.M., July through mid-November.

Wilson/Windsor II Farmers' Market, 321 Windsor Avenue (next to Dairy Bar), Windsor. Fridays from 3:00 to 6:00 P.M., mid-July through October.

Oatmeal Zucchini Bread

Zucchini in summer and fall are as common in Connecticut as wildflowers. Those who grow them usually have such bumper crops that they bestow their bounty on their friends, and almost every restaurant serves zucchini in some combination or another. We adapted this recipe from the booklet From the Farm to the Table, *produced by the Cooperative Extension System of the University of Connecticut. It is delicious served with afternoon tea or coffee.*

3 eggs
1 cup sugar
⅔ cup vegetable oil
1 teaspoon vanilla
1¾ cups all-purpose flour
1 cup raw oats
1 tablespoon baking powder
½ teaspoon salt
2 teaspoons ground cinnamon

½ teaspoon ground ginger
1 teaspoon ground nutmeg
2–3 cups peeled and shredded or grated zucchini
⅓ cup raisins
⅓ cup coarsely chopped walnuts

1. Preheat oven to 350°F. Grease bottoms of two 8-by-4-inch loaf pans.
2. In a large bowl, beat together eggs, sugar, oil, and vanilla. Add flour, oats, baking powder, salt, and spices. Mix lightly until dry ingredients are moist. Stir in zucchini, raisins, and nuts.
3. Spoon the batter into loaf pans. Bake about 45 minutes or until a knife or toothpick inserted in the center comes out dry. Cool 10 minutes on a wire rack. Remove from pans and cool completely before slicing.

Makes 2 loaves.

Arisco Farms, 1583 Marion Road, Cheshire, CT 06410; (203) 271–0549. At Alex and Beverly Arisco's fifteen-acre farm, you are welcome to pick your own sweet corn, eggplants, tomatoes, and peppers or buy from their farm stand. The Ariscos have farmed here since the late 1950s. You will find them at their stand between 9:00 A.M. and 5:00 P.M. every day from mid-July to the end of September.

Arlow's Sugar Shack, 101 Bushy Hill Road, Granby, CT 06035; (860) 653–3270. Doris and Arlow Case, here for forty years, call their self-service farm stand the Sugar Shack, where they sell a wide range of seasonal vegetables, including cucumbers, peppers, pumpkins, summer and winter squash, zucchini and tomatoes, produce from other farms, and their own homemade maple syrup and sugar (which is available year-round). Stand hours: July through September, Monday through Saturday from 9:00 A.M. to 5:00 P.M.

Belltown Hill Orchards & Farm Market, 483 Matson Hill Road, South Glastonbury, CT 06073; (860) 633–2789; www.belltownhill orchards.com. The Perelli family has farmed in the rolling hills around Glastonbury since 1910. Donna and her sons Don and Mike are the current owners. They follow the CORE Values approach, which means following ecologically balanced growing practices and Connecticut State Pest Management techniques for ecologically based agriculture. They welcome you to pick your own berries, pears, peaches, sweet and tart cherries, apples, pumpkins, and tomatoes. Relatively new are their twelve varieties of red, green, and blue grapes (ready in mid-August). They also have bakery goods. Open from the end of June through January, Monday through Friday 9:00 A.M. to 6:00 P.M., Saturday and Sunday from 8:00 A.M. to 6:00 P.M.

Botticello Farms, 209 Hillstown Road, Manchester, CT 06040; (860) 649–2462; e-mail: millybo@aol.com. According to Shelly Oeschsler of Botticello Farms, "If it is Connecticut-grown (and tastes good), we try to make it available to the consumer." With more than 50,000 square feet of greenhouse space, planting begins as early as January. At the farm stand, veggies make the world go round, the likes of squash (zucchini, summer, acorn, butternut, buttercup, spaghetti, and Hubbard), peppers (bells, cubanelles, long hots, habañeros, jalapeños, Thai hots, Hungarian hots, and Italian sweets), onions, cucumbers, tomatoes, corn, pickles, sugar pumpkins and jack-o'-lanterns, gourds, and Indian corn. Also for sale, by the pound, basket, or bushel, are seasonal fruits from other local farms and orchards. These include strawberries, raspberries, blueberries, peaches, nectarines, many kinds of apples and plums, several pear varieties, and potatoes (Green Mountain, Yukon Gold, Chefs, and red). You may also pick your own vegetables in a season that runs from April to December, daily from 8:00 A.M. to 7:00 P.M.

Bushy Hill Orchard & Cider Mill, 29 Bushy Hill Road, Granby, CT 06035; (860) 653–4022; www.bushyhill.com. Nora and Hal Law bought Bushy Hill in 1976 and now have 15,000 trees. The apple trees are all limited to 6-foot heights, and the peaches are on trellises up to 7 feet, making it easy for pick-your-own efforts. To pollinate apple blooms, Nora and Hal have thirty-two beehives, but bears persist in sneaking their honey! Their bakery turns out dough-

nuts, cookies, Amaretto muffins, apple, blueberry, and pumpkin pies, even puff pastry Bavarian strudel—and the record shows that nary one of these has been snagged by bears (yet). Call for hours and days.

Deercrest Farm, 3499 Hebron Avenue, Glastonbury, CT 06033; (860) 644–4407. The Bronzi brothers, Huchinson and Jonathan, and their wives are turning out a cornucopia of fresh fruit and vegetables at their Deercrest Farm each year. At their farm stand they sell twenty kinds of apples, eight types of pears, apricots (which Jonathan calls "fussy and delicate"), beans, peas, three types of peppers, eggplants, broccoli, cauliflower, summer squash, zucchini, and six other squash types, including acorn and turban. The brothers plan to add white nectarines next. The stand is open from April into December from 9:00 A.M. to 6:00 P.M. daily.

Dondero Orchard Farm Stand & Bakery, 529 Woodland Street, South Glastonbury, CT 06073; (860) 659–0294; www.dondero orchards.com. The Dondero family has had practice farming; they started in 1911 and are still going strong, with twelve types of apples, three of pears, plus fruit and vegetables. They close the bakery and farm stand Christmas Eve (after all the holiday pies and gift baskets have been carried away). Each spring they reopen when their strawberries are ripe for sale and when rhubarb, cherries and lettuce, peas, asparagus and squash are coming on. The apples, nectarines, pears, corn, blackberries, raspberries, cabbage, turnips, onions, winter squash, and pumpkins appear later. Then there are the homemade fruit pies, tea breads, strawberry shortcakes, caramel apples, and, for dog lovers, Fat Paw Homemade Dog Biscuits. Open June to December, daily from 8:00 A.M. to 6:00 P.M.

Easy Picken's, 46 Bailey Road, Enfield, CT 06082; (860) 763-3276. For Francis and Linda Kelliher, farming their fifty-three acres since 1950 has been a family affair. They get by with a lot of help from son Bryan, while another son and two daughters and their families live nearby and help, too. The harvest for sale consists of tomatoes, peppers, eggplant, Spanish onions, leeks, beans, cabbage, cauliflower and beets. You may cut your own herbs (basil, cilantro, dill, parsley, and others) and pick your own apples (Macoun, Gala, Jonagold, Kinsei, Rubinette, Sayaka, and a dozen more varieties), Japanese and prune plums, yellow and white peaches, raspberries, blueberries, and pumpkins—in their seasons. The Kellihers offer Sunday wagon rides after Labor Day at 2:00, 3:00, and 4:00 P.M., and on an early Sunday in October there is an annual Gourd Hunt. Open July to November, Friday through Sunday from 9:00 A.M. to 5:00 P.M. and Monday through Thursday from 9:00 A.M. to noon.

Gigi's Native Produce, 48 Shaker Road, Enfield, CT 06082; (860) 881–8297. Gina (Gigi), Ron, and daughter Olivia Veser invite you to pick your own vegetables and fruit on their twenty-five-acre farm. For the picking are strawberries, sweet corn, tomatoes, peppers, squash, pole beans, cucumbers, native potatoes (Red Bliss and Yukon Gold), and melons in season. There are also herbs, homemade pies, and fresh flowers available beneath the large awning-shaded cart, from May to October, daily from 9:00 A.M. to 6:00 P.M.

Gotta's Farm, 661 Glastonbury Turnpike (Route 17 south), Portland, CT 06480; (860) 342–1844. It is pick-your-own time when the apples ripen at Richard Gotta's from August onward. There is fresh cider, too. But you are welcome to visit the farm stand earlier for the sweet corn, tomatoes, peppers, squash and melons, which ripen at various times. Check it out from May to October, daily from 9:00 A.M. to 6:00 P.M.

Hickory Hill Orchard, 170 Fleming Road, Meriden, CT 06450; (203) 272–3824 or (860) 828–5016. Lynn and Fred Kudish have had busy times at their farm for the past twenty years, keeping up with the sales of their own and other local produce. Their pick-your-own fruits, available after mid-August, include four of the ten types of apples they produce (McIntosh, Macoun, Red and Golden Delicious, Ida Red, Rome, Fuji, Mutsu, Winesap, and Cortland), Bosc pears (they also grow Bartlett and Seckel), peaches, and nectarines. They sell flowers from local nurseries through December. Open mid-August through December, from 10:00 A.M. to 5:30 P.M. daily.

High Hill Orchard, 170 Fleming Road, Meriden, CT 06450; (203) 294-0376. Wayne Young, the manager of High Hill Orchard, runs a busy farm from August through December, selling the tomatoes, onions, corn, peppers, beans, eggplants, pumpkins, peaches, apples, pears, and flowers grown here. Peaches, Bosc pears, and four of the twelve apple varieties are yours for picking. Open August through December, Saturday and Sunday from 10:00 A.M. to 5:00 P.M., and from September, Tuesday to Friday as well, noon to 6:00 P.M.; closed Mondays.

Karabin Farms, 894 Andrews Street, Southington, CT 06489; (860) 621-6363; e-mail: farmingct@cox.net. If you seek variety in pick-your-owns, visit Diane and Michael Karabin's fifty-acre farm, which they have been running since 1984. They offer four types of apples, six of peaches, as well as pumpkins, and, in December, Christmas trees. Their farm store sells all these as well as maple syrup, honey, and flowers (raised in two attached greenhouses). You can also picnic on the grounds, and, at the end of the year, there are hayrides. Open daily from August to the end of October, 9:00 A.M. to 5:00 P.M.

Lyman Orchards, junction of Routes 147 and 157, Middlefield, CT 06455; (860) 349-1793; www.lymanorchards.com. The Lyman family spread goes back to 1741 and now covers 1,100 acres, with 300 acres of berries, apples, peaches, pears, and pump-kins. Lyman Orchards now includes a golf course and club and the state's largest indoor farm market, the Apple Barrel Farm Market, which is to farm stands what a

With the charm and insouciance of a French bistro—banquettes, antique hutch, and wall of mirrors—Metro Bis serves contemporary American food with some Asian spins, at surprisingly affordable prices. After the first moments of our first visit, we knew we were in good hands when delicious sesame-seed–crusted Italian bread arrived along with a spread of red-pepper hummus. There are Thai, Korean, and Middle Eastern touches, mostly in the appetizers, that add to the pizzazz of the intriguing menu. Chef Christopher Prosperi, who owns the bistro with his wife, Courtney, is an enthusiastic booster of Connecticut products, which grace all aspects of his stylish cuisine. House-smoked salmon, grilled tandoori marinated leg of lamb, and chile-seared, farm-raised catfish with curried split-green peas and Serrano ham are a few of our memorable choices, though the menu changes often. Don't forget to pick up some of Chris's own bottled salad dressings as you leave. There are three: Caesar, Tomato Ginger, and Balsamic, all deliciously tangy. Metro Bis also hosts cookbook authors and wine dinners from time to time.

Metro Bis

7B Simsburytown Shops
928 Hopmeadow Street
Simsbury, CT 06070
(860) 651-1908
e-mail: mail@metrobis.com
$$

Humvee is to a Geo—humongous. There, year-round, you will find the orchard's fruit, cider, cider doughnuts (and holes), pies, other bakery goods, preserves, vinegars, salsas, apple sauce, and condiments, as well as many other Connecticut-made food products. The orchards are open for farm tours, and pick-your-own apples, peaches, pears, blueberries, strawberries, and raspberries are available from June to October. Lyman's calendar is packed with events: an Easter Apple Hunt, summer Music Festival, Food Expo, Blueberry Bake-off, Apple Pie Baking Contest, and Winterfest Celebration; check for dates. Also notable is the Lyman Homestead, a handsome building on the National Registry of Historic Places. The orchards and market are open daily except Tuesday year-round, from 10:00 A.M. to 6:00 P.M.

Ogre Farm, 180 Old Farms Road, Simsbury, CT 06070; (860) 658–9297; e-mail: georgehallogre@aol.com. George Hall, who comes from a long farming line, calls himself the daddy of all Connecticut's organic farmers, with an eleven-and-a-half-acre spread that has been organic since 1967 and certified for twenty-some years. At his roadside farm stand, he sells all the produce he grows, except for that sold at the farmers' markets in West Hartford and at the Old State House in Hartford. George's seasonal produce—everything is picked fresh daily— includes lettuce, carrots, beets, parsley, potatoes, tomatoes, sugar pumpkins, corn, spinach, herbs, cabbage, and cauliflower. George also sells honey from his twelve hives, free-range eggs (from one hundred chickens, fed on nonmedicated grain), and large jack-o'-lantern-size pumpkins that are not organic. Open from the first week of July to Halloween.

Peter Draghi Farm, 379 Scantic Road, East Windsor, CT 06088; (860) 282–9063. The winters of 2001 and 2002 were chilling experiences for Phyllis and Peter Draghi: Freezing weather finished their fruit crops. Undaunted, they continue to tend their apple, peach, plum, and

Sandi Rose's
Microwave Raspberry Cobbler

Sandi Rose provided us with this recipe, which we have modified slightly. It is a treat to make during raspberry season.

¾ cup flour
½ teaspoon baking powder
Pinch of salt (optional)
3 tablespoons butter, softened
¼ cup sugar
⅓ cup milk

1 cup fresh raspberries
⅓ cup orange juice
3 tablespoons sugar
¼ teaspoon ground cinnamon
⅛ teaspoon ground nutmeg

1. Stir together flour, baking powder and salt (if you use salt). Set aside.
2. In a small mixing bowl, beat butter in a blender for 30 seconds. Add ¼ cup sugar and beat again. Then add the dry ingredients alternately with milk, beating after each addition until a soft dough forms.
3. Spread the dough evenly over a 1¾-quart microwave-safe dish.
4. Stir together raspberries, orange juice, 3 tablespoons of sugar, cinnamon, and nutmeg. Pour over the dough.
5. Cook, uncovered, at 100 percent power for 7–9 minutes, or until the berry mixture is bubbly and the dough is cooked and springs back when lightly touched. Serve warm, topped with vanilla ice cream or whipped cream.

Serves 4–6.

Rose's Berry Farm

295 Matson Hill Road
South Glastonbury, CT 06073
(860) 633–7467
www.roseberryfarm.com

nectarine trees and expect to welcome pick-your-own-ers to luscious, healthy fruit. Their crops will be available mid-July through October. Call ahead for days and hours.

The Pickin' Patch, Nod Road, Avon, CT 06001; (860) 677–9552. The name may sound whimsical, but farming is serious business to Janet and Donald Carville. Janet's grandfather was the seventeenth generation of Woodfords who originally settled this property, which once totaled 500 acres and is still one of the state's ten oldest farms (and Avon's oldest business). The Carvilles specialize in small fruits—blueberries, raspberries and melons—and peas, beans, spinach, lettuce, squash, beets, tomatoes, peppers, sweet corn, and, in October, pumpkins. From their thirteen greenhouses they sell cut flowers and potted vegetable plants. Their farm stand is open daily, June through October from 8:00 A.M. to 6:00 P.M.

Rogers Orchards—Main Farm, Long Bottom Road and Meriden-Waterbury Turnpike, Southington, CT 06489; (860) 229–4240, and **Rogers Orchards—Sunnymount Farm,** Meriden-Waterbury Road (Route 322), Southington, CT 06489; (203) 879–1206. Seven generations of Rogers have farmed here since 1809, and presently Frank and his son John harvest 250 acres. Between them, they claim to be Connecticut's largest apple grower, each year harvesting twenty varieties, the most popular being McIntosh, Macoun, Cortland, and Empire. You may pick your own on weekends, after they begin to ripen. Available at both Rogers farm stands are peaches, pears, vegetables, apple cider, doughnuts, honey, and apple and other fruit pies. Both stands are open daily from the end of July to just after Mother's Day in May the following year. Hours at the Main Farm stand are 8:00 A.M. to 5:00 P.M. and at Sunnymount Farm stand 9:00 A.M. to 6:00 P.M.

Rose's Berry Farm, 295 Matson Hill Road, South Glastonbury, CT 06073; and **Rose's Berry Farm at Wickham Hill,** 1200 Hebron Avenue, Glastonbury, CT 06033; (860) 633-7467; www.rosesberryfarm.com. The Rose family operation has been going on since 1910, and its apple trees and berry patches now cover one hundred acres of rolling hills. The South Glastonbury farm is a beautiful property where you may pick your own apples, strawberries, blueberries, raspberries, and pumpkins and also enjoy Sunday breakfast (the last Sunday of May through October) on the deck while overlooking apple orchards, ponds, and scenic vistas. The farm store stocks farm-fresh cider, six types of homemade pies, muffins, jams, and fruit vinegars. At the greenhouse you may buy blueberry plants and, in season, Christmas trees. Summer hours at the farm are Monday to Thursday from 8:00 A.M. to 8:00 P.M., Friday and Saturday from 8:00 A.M. to 6:00 P.M., and Sunday from 9:00 A.M. to 5:00 P.M. Rose's farm stand is not on the farm but is situated few miles north in Glastonbury on Wickham Hill, where most of the same farm produce and comestibles are for sale from May to October, Monday to Friday from 10:00 A.M. to 6:00 P.M. and Saturday and Sunday from 9:00 A.M. to 5:00 P.M.

Scott's Orchard & Nursery, 1838 New London Turnpike, Glastonbury, CT 06033; (860) 633-8681; www.scottsorchardandnursery.com. Woody and JoAnn Scott welcome you to Apple Hill from mid-March through December 24. Their pick-your-own fruits include eight varieties

HARTFORD—HOME OF THE FIRST AMERICAN COOKBOOK

Until 1796, when Amelia Simmons, about whom little is known, had her "receipts" published in Hartford, most Americans relied on English cookery books, but the different climate, crops, and facilities begged for a book indigenous to America. Her forty-seven-page paperback, entitled *American Cookery*, included foods unheard of in Europe: cranberry sauce, pumpkin and mince pies, Rye 'n' Injun (a dark bread made with molasses, yeast, and white corn), spruce beer, watermelon-rind pickles, and five recipes using cornmeal. For the next thirty-five years, her recipes were reprinted, often without credit to the source.

of peaches (ripening in August through September), three of plums (into October), pears (September through October), and nine varieties of apple, including Cortland, Macoun, Empire, McIntosh, and Winesap (August through October). Check their Web site for the pick-your-own schedule and preview of events and times.

Udderly Wooly Acres, 581 Thompson Street, Glastonbury, CT 06033; (860) 633–4503; e-mail: t-jkemble@erols.com. Tom and Joan Kemble sell organic vegetables, salad greens, garlic, and "super sweet" corn (in July and August). Organic eggs and fresh herbs are added reasons to stop, and pick-your-own raspberries in July and August may be an even stronger attraction. Why the name? The Kembles raise and sell lambs to restaurants and food stores. Call ahead for open times.

Urban Oaks Organic Farm, 225 Oak Street, New Britain, CT 06051; (860) 223–6200. If you expect a conventional farm, Urban Oaks will surprise you. It consists of four large greenhouses on a city street. There, certified organic farming is done under climatic and atmospheric control, with strict supervision of all aspects of the process by managers Mike Kandefer and Tony Norris. Urban Oaks is a nonprofit farm project that sells primarily to restaurants and retail stores. Public access is limited to Fridays from 2:00 to 6:00 P.M. and Saturdays from 9:00 A.M. to 1:00 P.M., when you may buy fresh greens (lettuce, kale, and chard), carrots, herbs, peppers, zucchinis, apples, pears, and produce from eight other certified organic farms in Connecticut and other states. On the Saturday before Labor Day, Urban Oaks hosts an Annual Tomato Sandwich Contest, with prizes for the most creative sandwich made with the farm's tomatoes, plus as many other ingredients as a contestant wishes to pile on. The only caveat: You have to be able to eat the sandwich by hand, not with implements.

Woodland Farm, 575 Woodland Street, South Glastonbury, CT 06073; (860) 633–2742. Arden and Harold Teveris have been farming here since 1963. Now, with their third son, Peter, and his wife, Nancy, plus a bevy of visiting grandchildren, they tend their thirty-acre farm and produce fruit jams and fresh cider for sale at their farm stand, along with summer and late-harvest apples, freestone peaches, red and yellow plums, nectarines, sweet and sour cherries, blueberries, raspberries, and strawberries. Open daily from August through December, 9:00 A.M. to 6:00 P.M.

 Food Happenings

April: **Wine on Ice,** Hartford, CT; (800) 287–2788; e-mail: special events@cptv.org. Connecticut Public Television's annual wine auction has become a tradition, with 200 lots of fine and rare wines up for bid. Starting off the gala event is a champagne reception, followed by dinner with fine wines and then the auction. Proceeds go to the educational programming on CPTV and WNPR. The site changes from year to year, so call for current dates and locale.

May: **Dionysos Greek Festival,** St. George Greek Orthodox Church, 301 West Main Street, New Britain, CT 06052; (860) 229–0055. This annual four-day event begins on the Friday of Memorial Day weekend and ends Monday at 8:00 P.M. In between you can feast on homemade Greek foods—the likes of spanakopita, gyros, shish kebab, and baklava, fresh from the church kitchen. In addition, you will find Greek jewelry and handcrafts, Greek music, dancing, and entertainment. A Dionysian happening for sure. Opa!

June: **Taste of Hartford,** Main Street downtown, Hartford, CT; (860) 920–5337 or (860) 728–3089. A four-day event, this spotlights the food of more than fifty restaurants in the Hartford area. Along with good food, there is continuous, nonstop entertainment. Call for dates and details.

Mid-June: **North Canton Strawberry Festival,** Community United Methodist Church, 3 Case Street (corner of Route 179), North Canton, CT 06019; (860) 693-4589. Going strong every June since 1951, this strawberry celebration includes bake and tag sales, a plant booth, and activities for children. The festival is most famous for its towering super-duper strawberry shortcake, made with homemade biscuits, butter, strawberries, and yards of fresh whipped cream.

Mid-June: **Old-Fashioned Strawberry Festival,** Plantsville Congregational Church, 109 Church Street, Plantsville, CT 06479; (860) 276-1045. Since 1993 this daylong Friday (always on Friday) festival, which lasts from 5:00 to 8:00 P.M., has been a celebration of the strawberry. Centerpieces are luscious strawberry shortcakes, but visitors—usually about 500 of them—also enjoy hot dogs and nostalgic music, the work of the Bristol Old Time Fiddlers.

July: **Tchicken & Tchaikovsky,** Hubbard Park, West Main Street, Meriden, CT 06450; (203) 238-7784. Since 1995—usually on the evening of July 2 or 3—music and food have been a winning duet for Meriden residents. The mood is mellow, as people congregate under Hubbard Park's sheltering trees to listen to a free concert by the Meriden Symphony Orchestra, while munching on barbecued chicken, fresh-baked corn bread,

FOOD LOVERS' TIP

If it's an authentic Italian meal you crave, you can be sure to find one on Franklin Avenue, historically Hartford's old-time Italian neighborhood. In just 4 long blocks, from 318 Franklin to 624 Franklin, you'll find eleven Italian restaurants, including these well-known ones: Sorrento at 371; Casa Mia at 381; Chef Eugene at 428; Corvo at 494; Ficara's Ristorante at 577; Carbone's at 588; and Capriccio at 624. Buon appetito!

corn-on-the-cob, potato salad, and drinks, all provided by a licensed caterer. The finale is Tchaikovsky's *1812 Overture,* accompanied by fireworks, which winds up the occasion with a bang. Literally.

Mid-September: **Celebration of Connecticut Farms,** (860) 296–9325; www.hartfordfood.org. Usually held on a Sunday in mid-month, this moveable feast changes venue every year. Contact is Elizabeth Wheeler, director of Agricultural Programs, Hartford Food System, 509 Wethersfield Avenue, Hartford, CT 06114. This annual outdoor fund-raising event—usually a sellout weeks ahead—benefits the Connecticut Farmland Trust, which protects the state's dwindling farmlands. The celebration is co-chaired by a big name (Meryl Streep has done the honors twice in recent years) and leading chef (like Jacques Pépin) and features twenty-five-to-thirty of the state's best chefs, who prepare dishes from Connecticut-made food products. There are cheese

Hartford Election Cake

This rich, fruity cake was first publicized in Amelia Simmons's American Cookery *book. Because the book was published in Hartford, the cake became known as Hartford Election Cake. It was popular throughout New England and was served after town meetings. Later its fame spread all over the country, reaching its zenith in the 1830s. Today it is virtually unknown, even in the city that gave it its name, but it is still a rich, tasty fruitcake, even in this modernized version.*

2¾ cups all-purpose flour
¼ teaspoon salt
1 package active dry yeast
¼ teaspoon ground nutmeg
¼ teaspoon ground ginger
¼ teaspoon ground allspice
¼ teaspoon ground
   cinnamon
¼ teaspoon ground coriander
1 teaspoon minced orange zest
1 cup lukewarm milk
¼ cup unsalted butter

¼ cup tightly packed brown
   sugar
⅓ cup granulated sugar
1 egg
1 teaspoon orange flower
   water
¼ cup rum
½ cup raisins (preferably
   golden sultanas)
½ cup currants
1 cup coarsely chopped
   pecans

1. In a large mixing bowl, combine 1 cup of the flour, salt, yeast, nutmeg, ginger, allspice, cinnamon, coriander, and orange zest.

2. In a saucepan over medium heat, warm the milk, butter, brown sugar, and granulated sugar until barely warm, stirring constantly to prevent burning. Pour the mixture into the dry ingredients and mix well.

3. Beat egg lightly and add it to the bowl along with the orange flower water and rum. Using an electric mixer, beat the mixture at low speed for a half minute, scraping the sides of the bowl often to mix thoroughly. Then beat at high speed for 3 minutes.

4. Stir the remaining 1¾ cups of flour into the mixture by hand. Stir in the raisins, currants, and pecans until well mixed.

5. Cover and set aside in a warm place for about 1½ hours or until doubled in size.

6. Grease well the bottom and sides of a 9-by-5-by-3-inch bread loaf pan. Spoon the mixture into the pan and let it rise again for approximately 1 hour or until doubled again.

7. Preheat oven to 350°F. Bake the cake for about 40–50 minutes or until a toothpick inserted in the center comes out dry. Remove the pan from the oven when the cake is done and cool it on a rack before turning it out. You can put a simple sugar-water glaze over the cake, but it is rich enough without.

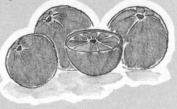

Makes 1 loaf cake.

artisans, local vintners, ice-cream makers, and other food producers, as well as music, art, and tours. For food lovers, this is a "must" happening.

Third Weekend in September: **Cheshire Fall Festival and Marketplace,** Bartlem Park (Route 10), Cheshire, CT 06410; (203) 272–2345; www.cheshirechamber.com. An annual one-day event since 1991, sponsored by the Junior Chamber of Commerce and Kiwanis Club, this becomes more popular as the years go by. There is live entertainment and booths galore, with some eighty displays by the town's civic organizations. Between six and ten booths are sponsored by local restaurants, dispensing—among other tasty treats—chowder, fried dough, sandwiches, and the famous Blackie's hot dogs. Parking is free, but there is a fee for the festival.

October: **Apple Harvest Festival,** Town Green, Main Steet, Southington, CT 06489; (860) 628–8036; www.appleharvestfestival.com. A road race at 8:00 A.M. the first Saturday in October leads off this lively festival, going strong annually for more than thirty-four years! The carnival kicks off at noon on the town green, with a parade at 1:00 P.M. a crowning of the queen, a street fair, and live music until 8:00 P.M., with apples and apple products stars of the food booths. The celebration resumes the following Thursday through Sunday. Hours vary on different days; call the phone number or check the Web site for details.

Mid-October: **Apple Harvest,** Welles Street, Glastonbury, CT 06033; (860) 659–3587. Right after Columbus Day, you can depend on this free, annual two-

Best Barbecue Ribs

At Black-eyed Sally's BBQ & Blues in Hartford, the midnight-blue, tin-tiled walls and ceiling provide a funky backdrop for some of the best barbecue to be found in the Nutmeg State, as well as Cajun and Creole specialties. Add colorful paintings of Muddy Waters and other blues greats, and live entertainment Wednesday through Saturday evenings, beginning at 9:00 P.M., and the setting is perfect for the mighty eats at Sally's. James and Dara Varano opened Sally's in 1995 and have made it the jumpingest blues joint around. Headline acts have included Johnny Rawls and Sonny Rhodes Blues Band. As for the slow-smoked ribs, Sally's forte, we recommend the BBQ Rib Sampler: four meaty, falling-off-the-bone tender pork ribs in a peppy bourbon-and-molasses sauce. If you like your ribs more incendiary, rub on some of Sally's red-hot Cajun beer barbecue sauce. Dynamite! Though ribs rule the roost, we often begin a meal with Cajun popcorn, nubbins of deep-fried Louisiana crawfish tails in a zesty Tennessee tartar sauce. And for a finale, there's sweet-potato pie, Mississippi mud pie, or oven-warmed peach and berry crisp with vanilla ice cream. As you leave, you will probably want to pick up a bottle or two of Sally's devilishly good sauces.

Black-eyed Sally's BBQ & Blues

350 Asylum Street
Hartford, CT 06103
(860) 278–RIBS
www.blackeyedsallys.com
$–$$

Best Ballpark Food

There are three minor-league baseball parks in Connecticut—homes of the New Haven Ravens, the Norwich Navigators, and the New Britain Rock Cats—and a team from the independent Atlantic League, the Bridgeport Bluefish. They all offer variations on the usual ballpark food. It is fast food, of course, but there is fast food and Fast Food; in baseball terms, New Britain's homey Willowbrook Park is the culinary champion, especially its Sam Adams Rooftop Grill. You will relish (oh-oh) the creamy New England chowder, packed with clams, onions, and potatoes, the crisp, waffle-cut french fries with a garlic edge, mozzarella cheese sticks, kielbasa sausages with sauerkraut, Italian sausages with peppers and onions on a grinder roll, and grilled hot dogs with a choice of mustard—Gulden's spicy brown or Dijon. Rosol's, a local meat market, supplies mildly spiced all-beef franks, as well as the kielbasa and Italian sausages. The food displays, the work of Centerplate, offer wide assortments and choices. Though none of the other ballparks strikes out, New Britain clearly has the highest batting average, with enough gustatory home runs to keep fans cheering all season long.

New Britain Rock Cats

Willowbrook Park
230 John Karbonic Way
New Britain, CT 06051
(860) 224–8383
www.rockcats.fanlink.com

day harvest event to be apple-polished, as it has been for nearly thirty years. Expect to find apple pies, puddings, cakes, and other apple-centered delicacies provided by local and international food vendors, along with farm trucks piled high with shiny fresh apples. Other foods include old standbys: soups, stuffed potatoes, and ice-cream sandwiches. A noon parade from town hall is followed by carnival rides, singing groups, and, of course, apples galore, all from 9:00 A.M. to 5:00 P.M. both days. Call for specific dates.

***November:* Star Chefs Auction of Greater Hartford,** Hartford Windsor Marriott, 28 Day Hill Road, Windsor, CT 06095. Each year sometime during the first week in November, acclaimed chefs and caterers gather at a gala event: a money raiser for the March of Dimes. A chefs' reception and cocktails are followed by samplings of great foods and beverages and a silent auction, then a live auction and dessert. High points at the live auction (with a celebrity master of ceremony), are the packages, offered by chefs and vendors, which might be a dinner party prepared by a renowned chef, a romantic weekend escape at a country inn, a chance to spend a day in the kitchen of a famous restaurant, or dinner for two at a prime new restaurant. For tickets or specifics, call Suzanne Galotti, March of Dimes, at (860) 290–5440, extension 306.

Learn to Cook

Ann Howard Apricots, 1593 Farmington Avenue, Farmington, CT 06032; (860) 673–5405. During winter months, Ann Howard, noted restaurateur and baker, gives a series of luncheon demonstrations and evening cooking classes with her executive chef, Jeff Gantkin, at the restaurant. Plans are underway for "hands-on" classes to be held at Ann Howard's home. Call for schedule, details, and prices.

Learn about Wine

CPTV Wine Forums, (800) 287–2788; www.CPTV.org. A series of wine forums, seminars, and tutored tastings are held each year, usually in April, May, and June at different locations, mostly in the Hartford–North Central area, to benefit CPTV (Connecticut Public Broadcasting System). Each forum includes a buffet dinner and appropriate wines, presented classroom-style by experts. The forums usually begin at 6:30 P.M. and last two hours and are priced by the series or per individual forum. Past forums have had themes of "California Gems," "An American in Burgundy," and "Five Continents of Fine Wine." For specific information, dates, and prices each year, contact CPTV by phone or e-mail.

Spiritus Hartford, 367 Main Street, Hartford, CT 06106; (800) 499–9463 or (860) 247–5431 and **Spiritus West Hartford,** 984 Farmington Avenue, West Hartford, CT 06107; (860) 236–3515; www.spiritus.com for both. In 2002 Martin and Barrie Robbins-Pianka celebrated the twentieth anniversary of Spiritus, their Hartford wine store. Based on their background in the Boston wine trade, they built their business by showcasing little-known wine. Over the years, they have educated the palates of thousands of wine enthusiasts by "training session" classes twice a year, teaching, as Martin says, "how

Best Parisien Brasserie and Wine Bar

In decor, this large, attractive restaurant in downtown Hartford resembles a real *belle époque* Parisien brasserie, with wide mirrors, zinc-topped bar, dark woodwork, bentwood chairs, wall sconces, and chandeliers. In menu, Paris also comes to life, what with hearty brasserie dishes like onion soup gratinée "Les Halles" style, steamed mussels frites, coq au vin, cassoulet with duck confit, braised lamb shank, and braised beef short rib, all prepared with a certain *je ne sais quoi*, a real French touch. We mustn't forget to mention some of the yummy desserts like lemon tart, maple crème brûlée, and freshly made profiteroles filled with mint ice cream. Pastis offers more than just a touch of Paris; every time we are there, we feel transported. A regional French wine list is well matched to the food, and an appealing liqueur menu includes at least four anise-flavored drinks. Talk about a Toulouse-Lautrec moment!

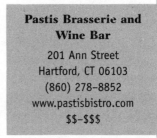

Pastis Brasserie and Wine Bar

201 Ann Street
Hartford, CT 06103
(860) 278-8852
www.pastisbistro.com
$$–$$$

to evaluate what is in the glass, without regard to label, vintage, or hype." Their *Spirit Writings* newsletter goes to some 7,000 wine aficionados each month. Barrie and Martin also keep up with wine enthusiasts through their interactive Web site, which has a Q&A section, wine and travel information, plus their catalog of current wines, which can be ordered directly and delivered anywhere in Connecticut. They have monthly tastings of timely wines at both stores (call for dates and

In a state where Italians are a major immigrant group whose roots here go back to the nineteenth century, it is a little like Russian roulette to select a single restaurant from the hundreds of good ones all over the state. Every town has an Italian eatery that locals swear is the very best Italian food ever. In singling out Cavey's, we like its variety; year-in year-out consistency; warm, friendly atmosphere; and the imaginative way Italian cooking is interpreted. Cavey's was started by the Cavagnaro family in 1933, and its two ground-floor dining rooms, in a free-standing building, are as airily inviting as an

Cavey's

45 East Center Street
Manchester, CT 06040
(860) 643-2751
$$

Italian country house. House-made, very fresh pastas are a special treat here, and we especially like tonnarelli, with oven-dried grapes, walnuts, and Umbriaco; pennette alla Bolognese; and the robust pappardelle, with Cavey's own fennel sausage, broccoli rabe, and caramelized garlic. In truth, all eight pasta dishes are superb. The veal dishes, like the osso buco with soft polenta, are among other Cavey's specialties. Almost everything the kitchen turns out is a winner in our view. Cavey's is actually two restaurants. On the ground floor is Cavey's Italian. Below the stairs in the same building is Cavey's fancier, pricier, and more formal French restaurant, with a separate staff and kitchen. The French is wonderful, too, but Viva Italia! Both restaurants are open for dinner only.

times) and at restaurants (check the newsletter or Web site), and quarterly they organize carefully matched food/wine dinners at specific restaurants in the area.

Landmark Eateries

Ambassador of India, 2333 Main Street, Glastonbury, CT 06033; (860) 659–2529; www.ambassadorofindia.com; $–$$. There is so much we like about this large, comfortable Indian restaurant, it is hard to decide where to begin. Mostly we appreciate the emphasis on North India cuisine, especially the nine dishes cooked in the traditional charcoal-fired clay tandoor oven. We have rarely tasted salmon as moist as the tandoori version here. Navrattan korma (a medley of veggies in a creamy cashew-almond sauce) and chana pindi (chick peas, onion, garlic, and ginger in a spicy tomato sauce) are among many lovely vegetarian dishes. The surroundings—brightly decorated with Indian color and flair—and the solicitous service add to the pleasurable experience of a lunch buffet or leisurely dinner here.

Ann Howard Apricots, 1593 Farmington Avenue (Route 4), Farmington, CT 06032; (860) 673–5405; pub $, restaurant $$$. With a terrace where lunch is served overlooking the surging Farmington River, Ann Howard Apricots is a delightful place for lunch or dinner. At one time a trolley barn, the two-story building

Boneless Veal Breast

This easy-to-make succulent dish is a favorite of Ann Howard and her executive chef at Apricots, Jeff Gantkin.

4 tablespoons olive oil	Coarse salt and pepper
7 cloves garlic, thinly sliced	½ pound sliced pancetta
1 pound Swiss chard, coarsely chopped	2 cups Burgundy wine
	2 sprigs rosemary, chopped
7-pound boneless veal breast	½ gallon veal stock

1. Heat a large roasting pan (large enough to accommodate rolled veal) over medium-high heat. Add 2 tablespoons of the olive oil and all of the garlic. Cook until the garlic is light golden-brown. Add the Swiss chard and stir-fry until soft. Remove the chard and garlic from the pan and cool to room temperature.
2. Trim excess fat from the veal and season with salt and pepper. Lay the veal flat on a cutting board and cover one side of the veal with

has had a significant overhaul. It now boasts three separate dining rooms on the second floor, a pub on the ground floor with its own full menu and more casual fare, and a terrace. From the upstairs windows, you have a wonderful view of the river. Stylish but unpretentious—with delicate apricots painted on the walls and some exposed brick walls—describes both the decor and the modern American cooking. Apricots

the pancetta. Place the Swiss chard down the center. Roll up the veal, tie it with butcher's twine, and set aside.

3. Preheat oven to 275° F. Heat the remaining 2 tablespoons of olive oil in the roasting pan over medium-high heat. Add the veal and brown well on all sides. Deglaze the pan with the wine. Add the rosemary and veal stock and bring to a simmer.

4. Cover the veal with foil and place the pan in the oven. Cook 2 hours; then remove the foil and cook 1 hour more. Turn veal over and cook 1 more hour. Remove the pan from the oven and transfer the veal to serving platter.

5. Heat the liquid in the roasting pan to a boil on top of the stove and cook for 10 minutes, or until the stock coats a spoon. Strain the stock and pour it over the veal. Serve with creamy polenta and broccoli rabe.

Serves 8.

Ann Howard Apricots

1593 Farmington Avenue (Route 4)
Farmington, CT 06032
(860) 673–5405
$$$

was one of the state's first restaurants to emphasize using only the freshest of ingredients. It continues to appeal because of its informal setting and consistently fine food, like grilled Jamaican jerk pork tenderloin with a plantain flan, sautéed sea scallops with fresh asparagus risotto, and pan-seared breast of Long Island duck with creamy polenta. And the awards keep piling up.

Cracovia, 60 Broad Street, New Britain, CT 06053; (860) 223–4443; $. In a small city where Polish seems like the second language, this cafe is one of four Polish restaurants in town and is considered the best. At first sight, what sets Cracovia (named for Crakow, or Krakow, Poland's second city) apart from an ordinary luncheonette is the beautifully executed mural on the wall behind the long lunch counter: a Polish knight in armor on horseback wielding a lance. Another knight graces the rear wall. Nothing else here is fancy, but it is a clean, neat, and tidy local hangout in what is predominantly a Polish neighborhood. If you want a crash course in Polish cooking, try the roast pork stuffed with plums, goulash with dumplings, rolled pork, or potato pancakes. You might sample one of six Polish beers to go with your meal. Cracovia also does a hearty breakfast with French toast, omelets, and egg sandwiches with ham, bacon, or Polish sausage. Fair warning: Portions are humongous.

It's Only Natural, 386 Main Street, Middletown, CT 06457; (860) 346–9210; $. You don't have to be a vegetarian or vegan to enjoy the many creative dishes at this simple but unconventional place. In winning scores of awards as the best vegetarian restaurant in the state, chef-owner Mark Shandle has borrowed from many cultures—hummus platters, spicy Cajun tempeh cutlets, Indonesian gado-gado, Indian somosas, Mediterranean pasta, and dim sum platters. He personalizes as he goes, serving potato-spinach pierogies with caramelized onions, apple butter, sautéed garlic greens, and tofu sour cream, as one example. Success has brought It's Only Natural to a new, larger location on the same street, with three dining areas and an outdoor patio. Portions are still gargantuan, and the easygoing spirit of the old place

Metro Bis Pear Panna Cotta

Chef Christopher Prosperi, who likes using local products when available, makes his Metro Bis delicious pear panna cotta with a Pear William eau-de-vie from Westford Hill.

5½ cups milk
2½ cups cream
1 cup sugar
Pinch of salt
2 tablespoons gelatin
¼ cup water
½ cup Pear William eau-de-vie (pear liqueur)

1 cup pureed poached pears (canned pears can be used and work well)
1–2 pears for garnish, optional

1. Simmer the milk, cream, sugar, and salt together for 10 minutes on low heat.
2. Sprinkle the gelatin over the water and Pear William in a bowl and dissolve.
3. Remove the milk/cream mixture from the heat and stir in dissolved gelatin.
4. Pour the mixture into molds (6-ounce soup cups work well) and refrigerate, covered, for 24 hours.
5. Turn out the pudding from the molds, garnish with poached pear slices, and serve cold.

Makes 10–12 servings.

remains the same. There is live jazz every Sunday, and Tuesday is open-mike night.

Main & Hopewell, 2 Hopewell Road, Glastonbury, CT 06033; (860) 633–8698; www.mainandhopewell.com; $$. With discreet professional service, welcoming ambience, and superb food, Main & Hopewell (named for its corner location) is the kind of place that comes to mind for special-occasion dining, yet its prices warrant eating there much more often than that. In three candlelit dining rooms (we prefer the one with wainscoting and post-and-beam construction for its coziness), the modern American menu has enough variety to please most tastes. We like the way a familiar starter like fried calamari is given the twist of jalapeños and mixed greens and chicken breast is stuffed with sun-dried tomatoes, spinach, and mushrooms and served with risotto and veal gravy. Touches like house-made sourdough rolls, fresh-made apple-butter spread, and house-made ice creams help to make each meal special, whether dinner or lunch.

Max Downtown, City Place, Asylum Street, Hartford, CT 06103; (860) 522–2530; $$$. There are four Max's in the Hartford area, and each is different. Our favorite is Max Downtown, the flagship of the group. The Maxes are not really a chain, but a mini-empire created by Richard Rosenthal, who seems to have a gift for knowing what people like and a flair for matching very good food with a pleasing environment and friendly service. At Max Downtown, we like the bold good looks with a vibrant mural on the upper walls, the buzz and bustle of business diners,

The wonderful, sweet, slightly molasses-tasting Swedish whole grain bread served at the **Dakota** restaurants (225 West Main Street in Avon and 1651 Post Road in Milford) is sold retail by the five-pound and ten-pound loaf in both Dakota locations. We lug a ten-pounder home whenever we are in the neighborhood.

and the robust menu with such items as crispy calamari salad, spicy shrimp firecrackers with a mango sweet chile glaze, and grilled pork chop with sunburst papaya salsa. The chophouse steaks are legendary, as are the five sauce options that go with them. Check out the excellent, globally diverse wine list, with some two dozen wines by the glass. Other Maxes are Max Amore in Glastonbury, Max a Mia in Avon, and Max's Oyster Bar in West Hartford, each with a different look and emphasis.

Peppercorn's Grill, 357 Main Street, Hartford, CT 06106; (860) 547-1714; $$–$$$. Much more polished and sophisticated than its name suggests, this stylish restaurant near the Wadsworth Atheneum exists on two levels and has become a hangout for a youngish, thirty-something crowd. Peppercorn's also attracts Italian food mavens, who consider it, as we do, among the best Italian restaurants in a city full of good ones. We come for the calamari fritti, wonderfully crisp salads (we love the one with grilled asparagus, Vidalia onion, walnuts, and Gorgonzola in a roasted garlic–lemon vinaigrette), various risottos, osso buco, and char-grilled, spice-rubbed free-range chicken diavola. All the pastas are luscious, and even the desserts, not usually an Italian

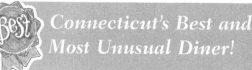

O'Rourke's Diner has won so many awards for its breakfast, lunch, and Sunday brunch that it may be as much visited as Wesleyan University up the road in Middletown. Brian O'Rourke, who bought the restaurant from his uncle (who opened the diner in 1941), has turned this cramped, modest-looking, old-fashioned spot into a veritable Versailles of diners—not in looks, but in the variety and high quality of breakfast and lunch treats he dishes out to students, faculty, local politicos, and discerning tourists who schedule a trip to Middletown just to visit O'Rourke's. This isn't simply an "eggs-over-easy" place; it offers comfort food of a high level. O'Rourke's menu is five pages long, fea-

O'Rourke's Diner

728 Main Street

Middletown, CT 06457

(860) 346–6101

turing thirty-three different omelets, including the Portobello (with

roasted mushrooms, Brie, and roasted plum tomatoes, topped with hollandaise sauce), and such surprises (for a diner) as banana bread French toast and Irish Galway (poached eggs over grilled brown bread with smoked salmon, bacon, hollandaise, and home fries). Holidays like St. Patrick's Day and Easter bring specials, such as Real Men Eat My Quiche (roasted duck with broccoli and Gruyère cheese over vegetable hash). Lunch choices include pasta 'n pesto, andouille cutlet, and Creole chicken.

restaurant strong suit, are superb, especially the warm chocolate Valrhona cake, chocolate bread pudding, and *gianduia pot de crème*.

Shady Glen, 840 East Middle Turnpike, Manchester, CT 06040; (860) 649–4245; $. Local fans swear by the ice cream, which is made on the floor below the diner here, and it is certainly among the best in a state that excels in independent ice-cream producers. There are thirty flavors, mostly using natural flavorings, including chocolate Almond Joy and chocolate peanut butter. Notice the charming mural along one long wall of elves and pixies picnicking on ice cream in a—surprise!—shady glen. The cheeseburgers are popular here, too, made with fried cheese on top, but for us it's the ice cream *über alles*.

Timothy's, 243 Zion Street, Hartford, CT 06106; (860) 728–9822; $. Any qualms you may have about Timothy's from its grungy-looking store-front facade are quickly dissipated once you enter and are seated for lunch at a table in the small, homey dining room, with its black pressed-tin ceiling and lace cafe curtains at the windows. Though it is located in a depressed neighborhood, the stately peaks of Trinity College overlook it from a hilltop across the street. Most of your fellow diners look like escapees from the ivy halls. What gives Timothy's its character are the fresh-made, wholesome dishes, the house-baked multigrain breads, and the house-made desserts. Walking through the bar to the dining room, you might notice fresh-from-the-oven cakes cooling on the bar counter. Service is slow, but the food is worth it, especially sandwiches like grilled eggplant, grilled chicken, and Cuban pork. Sour-cream lime pie, black-magic cake, and fresh-fruit crisp are among the delicious desserts.

City Steam Brewery Cafe, 942 Main Street, Hartford, CT 06103; (860) 525–1600; www.citysteam.com; $$. The imposing building in which this brewery is housed was designed by architect H. H. Richardson in the 1870s. An awesome Romanesque three-story brownstone structure, occupied for decades by Brown Thomson and Company, the state's largest department store, it was completely renovated in 1979. The City Steam Brewery's cavernous premises also include the Brew Ha Ha Comedy Club (with shows Thursday, Friday, and Saturday, featuring comedians from far and near), the Brewery Café (on seven levels, with dining room, open all week), and the Pool Room (which features Irish Jam Session with jigs and hornpipes). Brewmaster Ron Page is in charge of the handcrafted beers. His current brews include Colt Light Lager (named for gun-maker Samuel Colt, a Hartford native), Naughty Nurse Pale Ale (a sunset-hued best-seller), and Original City Steam (an English-type brown ale). Seasonal specialties include Moonglow German-style lager, Black Silk (oatmeal) Stout and Flower of Edinburgh, a high octane "winter warmer." Bar hours: Monday through Thursday from 11:30 A.M. to 1:00 A.M., Friday and Saturday from 11:30 A.M. to 12:30 A.M., and Sunday from noon to 10:00 P.M.

John Harvard's Brew House, 1487 Pleasant Valley Road, Manchester, CT 06040; (860) 644–2739; $$. From platters of satisfying burgers and fries to the juicy New York strip steaks, the food at this brewpub, part of a small Boston-based group, is solid, if unspectacular.

Similarly, the semi-institutional atmosphere is unlikely to win many awards. The beers are something else, so much so that a fair number have been recognized nationally for their excellence. One medal winner is the deep amber Manchester Alt, which has a caramel fruitiness. Others to savor are the flagship John Harvard's Pale Ale, the Munich Light, Black Widow Lager, Old Willy's IPA, and a rich, velvety oatmeal stout called Wild Style. Hours are daily from 11:30 A.M. to 12:30 A.M., but closing at 1:30 A.M. Friday and Saturday.

Trout Brook Grill & Brewhouse, 45 Bartholomew Avenue, Hartford, CT 06106; (860) 951–BREW; restaurant, (860) 951–1680; $$. This brewpub was once the factory that made chains for Harleys, but the only roar today is one of contentment from patrons bathing their bicuspids in pints of beer. The brews freshly made on the premises include the fruity, mildly bitter Thomas Hooker Ale, Trout Brook Blond Ale, a hoppy India Pale Ale, and a rich, chocolatey Porter, along with an ever-changing list of seasonals such as Irish Red. The grill is open for lunch and dinner, with meat and seafood for all seasons. Both pub and grill are open all week from 11:30 A.M. to midnight, but on Saturday from noon and Sunday from 2:00 P.M.

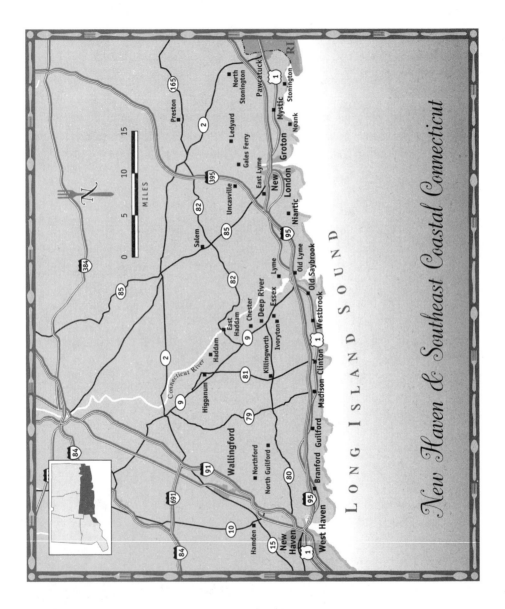

New Haven & Southeast Coastal Connecticut

New Haven and Southeast Coastal Connecticut

So much is happening in New Haven that it could fill an entire chapter in itself, considering the city's amazing gastronomic variety—Japanese, Chinese, Malaysian, Thai, Vietnamese, Korean, Turkish, Ethiopian, Lebanese, French, and Italian restaurants—and the special flavor of Wooster Street, the old Italian neighborhood of tiny stores, *gelato* parlors, pastry shops, restaurants, and pizzerias. The city's sixteen-acre green is the scene of music concerts and arts festivals, so it seems only natural it would be the site each summer of another local celebration: the Great American Pizza Fest. There are so many pizzerias in Greater New Haven it is no surprise that the city considers itself the pizza capital of America.

New Haven is the cultural magnet of this Long Island Sound coastline—with Yale University, museums, three theaters, symphonies, lectures, and arts events. But the entire southeast area of Connecticut has much to offer visitors who love good food and the good life. Just following the shore can keep you in seafaring and seafood nirvana, with stops at the picturesque seaside towns of Branford, Guilford, Madison, Clinton, and Westbrook along the way. Favorite summer habitats of vacationing New Yorkers, these towns have as their heritage beaches (including the expansive Hammonasett Beach State Park), inlets, points, and coves for fishing, swimming, and boating, as well as grassy New England greens and colonial houses (the 1639 Whitfield House in Guilford is believed to be the oldest stone building in New England). Equally appealing to visitors are the many opportunities for terrific food at clam and lobster shacks, ice-cream parlors, delis, coffeehouses, and restaurants with water views.

The entire southeast coast is scalloped with appealing shore villages that are popular fishing and boating centers: Niantic, Waterford, Groton, and Noank. Of special nautical interest are New London, at one time a whaling center and now home to the U.S. Coast Guard Academy, and Mystic, with Mystic Seaport, the reconstructed nineteenth-century New England whaling village (where parts of the movie *Moby Dick* were filmed). Pristine Stonington, almost too perfect to be real, with its old lighthouse and long, narrow Water Street, is a source of fresh-caught sea scallops, red shrimp, and other seafood and has cozy restaurants for enjoying them.

Inland a few miles at North Stonington is an eighteenth-century farmhouse inn that serves meals cooked over the hearth, from recipes dating back to colonial times. Nearby, also, are Connecticut's two Indian casinos, Foxwoods and Mohegan Sun, whose prime interest to food lovers is not the gaming but the fifty-eight eateries they boast between them, two of which are upscale ones run by famous Boston chefs Todd English and Jasper White. No more than a few miles in from this easternmost shore are orchards, fields of vegetables, and dairy and cattle farms.

The Great Pizza War . . . and the Winner Is—

In New Haven, which considers itself the pizza capital of the world, the heated contest between Frank Pepe's Pizzeria and Sally's Apizza has extended far beyond the confines of the old Italian neighborhood of Wooster Street. Fans (as in fanatics) of each are ready to fight (or eat) to the last savory bite. Pepe's is older, dating back to 1925, Sally's merely to 1938. Both serve thin-crusted, crispy-edged, smoky-flavored pies baked in authentic coal-fired brick pizza ovens, stoked with long-handled wooden peels. Both feature a New Haven creation: white clam pie, made with fresh-shucked clams, garlic, oregano, olive oil, and grated pecorino cheese. The owner of Sally's once worked at Pepe's. We cast our vote—and palates—for Pepe's, smitten with its particularly paper-thin crusts, fine-flavored ingredients, and the option of a dozen or more different toppings. We enjoy watching the Rhode Island littleneck clams being shucked for the white clam pizzas, the pared-down basics of the pizza parlor itself, with its modest booths, plain metal trays lined with white butcher paper on which the pies are served, and the pitchers of beer. The focus is on the pies; nothing else matters. We like it that way. To see if you agree, check out Sally's, too, which is also on Wooster Street, which in our book is Pizza Plaza, USA.

Frank Pepe's Pizzeria

157 Wooster Street
New Haven, CT 06511
(203) 865-5762
$

Add to the litany of the area's prime attractions a clutch of delightful Connecticut River towns with four distinguished village inns among them, all noted for fine food. At East Haddam is Goodspeed Opera House, with a landmark restaurant next door. Gillette Castle, a wealthy actor's fantasy house-fortress, roosts high above the river; its ample grounds are a state park, which welcomes picnickers and hikers. Essex, with its photogenic marina and vintage steam train that runs 12 miles along the river, is celebrated for its strict zoning code (no neon signs) and even more so for the fabulous Sunday brunch at its village inn. The river itself is the habitat of Connecticut's official state fish, the native shad; along the riverbanks you will see an occasional shad shack, where you can purchase this seasonal fish and its delicious roe.

Linking all the towns in the southeastern part of the state is an awakened commitment to fine food. Superb fresh seafood is a long time "given," but in recent years there has been a flowering of new restaurants: Indian, Mexican, Thai, Vietnamese, and the like. They have been accompanied by excellent gourmet markets, delis, cheese shops, and bakeries that did not exist here twenty years ago. The discoveries awaiting you are many. Enjoy.

Made or Grown Here

The Cookie Connection, 62 Center Street, Wallingford, CT 06492; (203) 294-9240; www.Thecookieconnection.net. Deborah Lovejoy has a novel idea: making oversize two-ounce cookies, attaching each to a stick, putting several cookies into a "bouquet" or basket filled with silk flowers or other paraphernalia and selling it as a birthday, anniversary, office party, or other special-occasion treat. Her shop is small, but Deborah's enthusiasm is infectious. She takes orders via e-mail (cookiequeen@aol.com) or her Web site and ships UPS. Cookie types are chocolate chip, oatmeal raisin, peanut butter, butter sugar, and double and triple chocolate chip.

Dr. Lankin's Specialty Foods, LLC, 76 Brookshaven Road, Groton, CT 06340; (860) 445–4433; www.awesomealmond.com. For a primary care physician to develop a side business selling almonds may sound slightly, um, nutty, but these almonds are for real. So is Dr. Ken Lankin. Studying almonds for a college thesis on nutrition gave him a desire to experiment roasting and flavoring these tasty nuts. Eventually this led to his creation of Awesome Almonds in three flavors: orange-vanilla, cinnamon-vanilla, and cocoa-java. According to the good doctor, the California-grown almonds are good for cholesterol, heart disease, obesity, and a host of other health problems. You can buy the Awesomes directly from the firm's Web site or at Mystic Sweets & Ice Cream Shoppe in Mystic, Lee's Oriental Market in New London, and Seaport Coffee Roasters in Groton, among many shops in this area. The nuts have no preservatives, salt, cholesterol, or added oils and are a kosher product.

Fabled Foods, 500 South Main Street, Deep River, CT 06417; (860) 526–2666. Not only are the foods fabled but so is the story. This thriving artisan bakery began in 2000 in Deep River (having moved from New Milford, where Ina Laber and her late husband, Austin, ran a restaurant and bakery) and now wholesales its fabulous breads to upscale restaurants, markets, and shops all over the state. Austin was a self-taught baker (until his untimely death in 2002), and Ina is the spark plug of this fast-growing enterprise. With a talented bake staff, she produces a best-selling sourdough bread, sourdough olive and rosemary, sourdough pecan raisin, several Italian rustic breads (pugliese and ciabatta), rye, pumpernickel, multigrain (with twelve grains), 12-grain cranberry walnut, classic country, challah (Fridays only), and classic Kaiser rolls, onion rolls,

plus others and brioche. Look for these crusty, flavorful breads and rolls at Olive Oyl's in Essex and at restaurants like River Tavern in Chester and the Griswold Inn in Essex, among other outlets. We knew the Labers' wonderful breads from their restaurant days and wondered what had happened to them. Presto! Now we know!

Mohegan Aqua Culture LLC, 72 Water Street, Stonington, CT 06378; (860) 535-9279; e-mail: gcrowder@mohegansun.com. Managed by aquaculturist Paul Maugle, this new business (started in 1992 to supply shellfish to Mohegan Sun) grows oysters, bay scallops, and quahog clams in cages (safe from parasites) off the bottom of the ocean floor in the clear, clean waters off Stonington. Their much-prized 3½-inch Wamphassuc Mohegan oysters are briny, plump, and crunchy. In addition to the Mohegan Sun Casino restaurants, they are sold to

Noah's in Stonington and to Anthony J's Bistro in Mystic as well as other area restaurants. On Fridays from 8:30 A.M. to 5:00 P.M., the facility sells directly to the public. Just ring the ship's bell and someone will greet you and take your order.

Old Lyme Gourmet Company, 3 Strawberry Lane, Old Lyme, CT 06371; www.oldlymegourmetcompany.com. In 2002 Jim Goldberg began doodling with popcorn recipes, and soon Roasted Pecan Caramel Popcorn was born. In a short time, he has created two additional products: Vermont Sharp White Cheddar Cheese Popcorn and County Fair Maple Kettlecorn. All come with an attractive package design of a gigantic-wheeled, old-fashioned bicyclist. It isn't corny to tell you that the various popcorns are sold at Bishop's Orchard in Guilford, Our Daily Bread in Deep River, and Olive Oyl in Essex. It is also possible to order from his company Web site.

Palmieri Food Products, Inc., 145 Hamilton Street, New Haven, CT 06511; (800) 845–5447; e-mail: sales@palmierifoods.com. Since 1920, the Palmieri family has been making pasta sauces, all natural, with no additives. At present there are twelve tomato-based sauces, along with horseradish and cocktail sauces, a salsa, a barbecue sauce, and a buffalo-chicken-wing dip, all distributed and sold around the state at Stop & Shop stores, Shaw's, and Geissler Markets and, in this area, at Robert's Food Center, Madison. The spaghetti sauce remains Palmieri's most popular item.

Stonington Red Shrimp Cocktail

Christopher Prosperi, chef-owner of Metro Bis in Simsbury (see the Hartford chapter), swears by the superfreshness of Stonington Seafood Harvesters and shared with us this recipe he makes using their famous red shrimp.

1 pound Stonington red shrimp
(or any small shrimp)

½ cup salt

Vinaigrette

2 cups tomato juice

1 cup horseradish

1 teaspoon black pepper

1 teaspoon sugar

2 tablespoons
Worchestershire sauce

3 dashes Tabasco sauce

2 tablespoons olive oil

Pickled Onions

½ cup thinly sliced onions

¼ cup white vinegar

Pinch of salt

Pinch of sugar

Garnish

¼ cup good-quality vodka

For shrimp:

1. Bring 1 gallon water to a boil with ½ cup salt.

Pasta Cosi, 3 Linden Avenue, Branford, CT 06405; (203) 483–9397. Pasta Cosi, a line of nine robust, flavorful Italian sauces, was developed in a cozy little Italian restaurant, Billy's Pasta Cosi, at this Branford location. The sauces—which include roasted garlic, white clam, vodka, arrabbiata, puttanesca, amatriciana, bolognese, marinara, and blue crab—are sold at Bud's Fish Market in Branford and Stop & Shop stores throughout the state. They are also available at the restaurant, as are seven types of fresh pasta (angel hair, penne, fusilli, lasagna, linguine,

2. Blanch peeled and deveined shrimp, then shock in ice water. Drain shrimp and reserve.

For vinaigrette:
Mix all the vinaigrette ingredients together (works well when mixed in a martini shaker).

For pickled onions:
Put thinly sliced onions in a shallow dish and cover with white vinegar, salt, and sugar. Let sit for ten minutes.

To assemble:
Divide the shrimp evenly into 6 martini glasses. Add the onion mixture evenly. Top each serving with vinaigrette and then with 2–3 tablespoons of vodka.

Serves 6.

Metro Bis

7B Simsburytown Shops
928 Hopmeadow Street
Simsbury, CT 06070
(860) 651–1908
$$

rigatoni, and fettuccine). At the restaurant alone are five fresh sauces, including fresh blue crab, which is available only when the crabs are—in summer.

Sankow's Beaver Brook Farm, 139 Beaverbrook Road, Lyme, CT 06371; (860) 434–2843; www.beaverbrookfarm.com. With 350 lambs gamboling over her 175 acres, Suzanne Sankow operates a double-pronged business. She uses the wool from her Romney sheep to make sweaters, caps, hats, scarves, and mittens, which she sells in the wool shop on the grounds. She milks her East Frisian sheep and four Jersey cows to make seven extraordinary farmstead cheeses (among them Camembert, Summer Savory, feta, Farmstead, and Pleasant Cow), ricotta, and thick, rich yogurt, all of which are for sale in her Farm Market shop, along with her USDA-inspected lamb roasts, chops, patties, and lamb sausages (salami, Land Jäger, pastrami, and garlic-fennel). Stuart London, former chef at the Old Lyme Inn, runs the farm's kitchen. His shepherd's pie, lamb-curry stew, lamb-and-feta cheese turnovers (with a wonderful flaky pastry), a variety of cheese spreads (try the horseradish ricotta and tzatziki), and delicious vanilla and Belgian chocolate ice cream (the Belgium chocolate is made with the premier Callibaut chocolate) are all terrific. Sankow's is one of the few dairies in the state licensed to sell raw milk. Pleasant Valley, a premier, aged sheep cheese, is the most popular, but Sankow's makes a fine white Stilton at Christmas and other special-occasion cheeses. The shops are open from 9:00 A.M. to 4:00 P.M. daily, and Sankow products are sold at farmers' markets in Stonington and Greenwich in summer. The last weekend in November/first in December Sankow's has an Annual Farm Day. Visitors come to watch sheep being shorn, try hand spinning, sample the meats and cheeses, and take a free horse-drawn hayride through the farm.

Stonington Seafood Harvesters, 83 Cutler Street, Stonington, CT 06378; (860) 535–8342; www.scallopstogo.com. This small, one-family company is famous among discerning Connecticut restaurateurs for its sea scallops, which Captain Billy Bomster Jr. and his brothers Joe and

Mike dredge from the Atlantic Ocean depths on their western-rigged scallop trawler, the *F/V Patty Jo*. What makes the Bomster scallops different is that they are shucked by the crew and flash frozen in heavy, one-pound plastic pouches within minutes of coming on board, instead of sitting on ice in the hold for two weeks before the boat lands. This quick process protects the flavor, color, and firmness. Family patriarch Bill Bomster is convinced they are the "world's finest all natural, unadulterated, scrumptious sea scallops." Judge for yourself. You can order from the Bomster Web site or via e-mail (ssh-inc@snet.net), with UPS next-day delivery to your door. The scallops come in five one-pound pouches shipped in a reusable foam box that keeps them in perfect condition. At the Bomster self-service freezer (address above), the scallops, along with fresh-frozen local seafood (cod, flounder, tuna steaks, handcut salmon fillets), are for sale on the honor system. You can also enjoy them at Boom restaurant in Stonington or buy them from McQuade's Marketplace in Mystic, among many other area outlets. Seasonally, from July to November, the Bomsters also sell the much-prized, deep-water red shrimp. Open year-round every day, twenty-four hours a day.

Specialty Stores & Markets

Atlantic Seafood, 1410 Boston Post Road, Old Saybrook, CT 06475; (860) 388–4527. What it lacks in space, this spic-and-span seafood store makes up in quality, with the freshest of fish and shellfish presented in immaculate trays in refrigerated display cases. Our local foodie friends swear by it. A case of frozen seafood dishes—stuffed clams, clam chowder, lobster bisque, marinated mussels, and others (all made in-house)—catches your attention as well. "Only the Freshest" is the shop motto, and you are urged to call ahead to find out what piscine wonders have just arrived from Port Judith, Rhode Island, the seagoing source of all these nautical gems.

Bon Appetit, 2979 Whitney Avenue, Hamden, CT 06518; (203) 248–0648; www.bonappetitct.com. In 1971 Roland and Andrea Blakeslee opened their gourmet food shop and have stayed ahead of the curve ever since. Today this attractive, well-organized shop is like a wish list of every delicacy you can imagine: condiments, dips and spreads, dessert sauces, deli meats and salads, jams, mustards, oils, olives, rices, teas, vinegars. A large international cheese assortment is flanked by glass-covered displays of fresh croissants, bagels, danish, pastries, cookies, and luscious cakes. Tables, cupboards, display cases, even wine barrel tops are covered with good things to eat from all over the world, including Connecticut.

The British Shoppe, 45 Wall Street, Madison, CT 06443; (203) 245–4521. A clapboard house that dates back to 1690 seems an appropriate backdrop for a British shop, er, shoppe. There are three small rooms chockablock with British imports. Many are food products: Stilton, cheddar, Sage Derby, Royal Windsor, Wensleydale, and other English cheeses; Fortnum & Mason, Jackson's of Piccadilly, and other English teas, as well as marmalades, jams, shortbreads, crackers, and even bangers (traditional English breakfast sausages). A fourth room, the Front Parlour, has a stone fireplace, weathered pine boards, overhead exposed wooden beams, and eight glass-topped tables, a cozy setting where light lunches (try the shepherd's pie, and the ploughman's or miner's lunch) and afternoon teas are served. An authentic "British Tea" consists of thinly sliced finger sandwiches, cakes, currant-studded scones with jam and Devonshire cream, and a choice among seven loose teas, served in Crown Victoria floral porcelain teapots and cups. The teas bear the shop's own Rather Jolly Tea Company label. This is as close to Britain as it gets, unless you hop a plane to London.

Chabaso, 360 James Street, New Haven, CT 06513; (203) 562–7205; www.chabaso.com. When Charles Negaro opened the cafe in his Atticus Bookstore in New Haven in 1981, he produced yummy pastries, bars, and cookies but tried in vain to find top-quality sandwich bread. So in 1995 he started his own bakery: Chabaso (named after his three children). Chabaso turns out a variety of breads—three kinds of ciabatta (plain, wheat, and with olive oil), pugliese, seven-grain, Normandy rye, country sourdough, three kinds of baguettes (wheat, seeded, and Parisian)—and scores of delicious rolls, sweet rolls, and desserts. More than just supplying Atticus, Chabaso now wholesales its breads to more than fifty stores in Connecticut, including Nica's in New Haven, Cilantro in Guilford, and Stony Creek Market in Branford. Julia Child once said, "How can a nation be great if its bread tastes like Kleenex?" With Chabaso around, Julia can stop worrying.

The Cooking Company, Swing Bridge Market Place, 1610 Saybrook Road, Haddam, CT 06438; (860) 345–8008. Subtitled "A Prepared Food Market," this is no small-potatoes operation. Three trained chefs, including owner Susan Bauer, prepare a vast panoply of delicious foods for customers to take away, reheat, and consume at home. (It is also possible to do your noshing at a table just outside the store.) Fresh salads (like grilled chicken Caesar pasta, Greek, or Cobb), soups, prepared entrees (Greek chicken, stuffed Portobello mushrooms, Florentine chicken, among others), frittatas, sandwiches (the likes of roast beef and Boursin cheese, Black Forest ham and Brie), and multilayered wraps are a few of the freshly made possibilities. There are deli items (Genoa salami, maple-smoked turkey, spicy capocollo ham and others) and a frozen-foods section, where soups and entrees have been made up in advance. For the sweet tooth, there are fruit pies, cookies, brownies, and cakes. A coffee bar with Daybreak coffees is just inside the entrance, and a rear room is stocked with fancy gourmet goodies: olive oils, vinegars, pickled vegetables, preserves, and other comestibles.

4 & Twenty Blackbirds, 610 Village Walk, Guilford, CT 06437; (203) 458–6900. At wicker chairs and tables outside, next to flower-filled window boxes, patrons sit and read the *New York Times* while sipping a cup of coffee and nibbling on a fresh-baked croissant. That is the modus operandi at this nifty bakeshop. If you sit inside, you will inhale all the delicious baking aromas and might even catch a batch of cookies, cakes, pastries, or pies (sorry, no blackbirds) emerging from the oven, which is visible behind the counter. Fruit tarts follow the local growing season. Saturday is specialty-bread day, but the scrumptious cakes and cheesecakes are daily delights. Principally known for its exquisite desserts, the shop also sells a small, select array of chocolates, olive oils, imported pastas, and other high-end comestibles.

Fromage Fine Foods and Coffees, 1400 Boston Post Road, Old Saybrook, CT 06475; (860) 388–5750. Into this minuscule, inviting shop, which has been at this location since 1992, Christine Chesanek has packed fifty to seventy different international cheeses, a truly awesome selection, along with a number of compelling cheese spreads. Also for sale are Hudson Valley coffees, Harney teas, eighteen different types of olives (in open containers to make selection easy), condiments, and many comestibles. A frozen-food case has scores of phyllo hors d'oeuvres by the tens or dozens. For a party, Fromage makes easy one-stop shopping. Christine's customized gourmet  gift baskets are wonderfully inventive and appealing.

Hallmark Drive-In, 113 Shore Road, Old Lyme, CT 06371; (860) 434–1998. What is better on a summer day than stopping at an old-fashioned ice-cream stand along the shore? That's what Hallmark is, an unpretentious drive-in on the way to the beach. WE MAKE OUR OWN, the sign proclaims, and they do, five gallons at a time, in twenty-five flavors, like strawberry and fresh peach in season, ginger (made with ginger from Hong Kong), grape nut, mint chip, banana nut, pistachio, raspberry, Hockey Fight, and peanut-butter-cup crunch. You can get

MYSTIC PIZZA . . . MAYBE
ONLY JULIA KNOWS FOR SURE

We don't intend to stoke fires of rivalry, but Mystic Pizza, a pizzeria in Mystic, claims it is the site and inspiration for the movie *Mystic Pizza*, which catapulted Julia Roberts to fame. But don't tell that to folks in Stonington, who claim the movie was filmed at a pizzeria, now defunct, on Water Street in their town, not Mystic.

tasty grinders and clam rolls, too. Inside are a few tables with breakfast service, a sheltered spot on windy shore days.

Hong Kong Grocery, 67 Whitney Avenue, New Haven, CT 06510; (203) 777–8886. Narrow, cluttered aisles and crammed-together cans, bags, and jars of all kinds of Chinese foods do not deter the crowds from this diminutive, if confusing, market. A prime source of fresh Chinese produce, steamed dim sum, twenty-five-pound sacks of rice, and scores of hard-to-find Chinese and other oriental items, it is no wonder the place is jammed most of the time. There is even a small restaurant—Great Wall—in the rear.

Judies European Bakery, 63 Grove Street, New Haven, CT 06511; (203) 777–6300; www.judies.net. For a big, wide, wonderful world of breads, look no farther. Daily Judies bakes peasant baguettes (asiago and shallot, red onion and garlic), sesame breads, Italian baguettes, and panini. Each day brings two or three special breads, like English oatmeal and Russian black (Mondays), mill hollow and Scottish raisin (Tuesdays), English cheddar and Portuguese corn (Wednesdays), challah and potato (Thursdays), orange ricotta, Moravian sugar, rosemary and kalamata-olive and brioches (Fridays) and rosemary and kalamata-olive (Saturdays). Judies also does pastries, cakes, and wedding cakes. Its plain but agreeable coffee/tea room serves breakfast, lunch (soup and a variety of sandwiches), and Sunday brunch (crepes, omelets, French toast, salads) and is a popular place for a cup of Lavazza coffee, espresso, or cappuccino. Judies breads are sold throughout the New Haven area, at Buds in Branford, Bishop's Orchards in Guilford, and Bon Appetit in Hamden, among other places.

Lee's Oriental Market, 432 Williams Street, New London, CT 06320; (860) 443–9665. What this small market lacks in size it makes up for in variety and orderliness. A fresh-food case has, among other veggies, napa cabbage, daikon, Korean radishes, bitter melons, lemongrass, and soy-bean sprouts. The freezer reveals frozen soybean kernels, egg-roll wrappers, gyoza skins, fish and fish cakes, grated cassava, and shumai dim sum. There are shelves full of teas of various kinds, a wide range of rice (including twenty-five-pound sacks of Thai jasmine rice and sticky rice), dried mushrooms, roasted sesame seeds in quantity, gallon tins of soy sauce, packaged soups, and assorted kinds of candies and sweets. Chinese foods dominate, but there are Japanese, Filipino, Korean, and Thai goods as well, all neatly presented in well-kept surroundings.

The Life of Riley Irish Imports, 880 Boston Post Road, Old Saybrook, CT 06475; (860) 388–6002 or (800) 404–7956; www.lorirish imports.com. Begorrah, all kinds of Irish goods, perfumes, Celtic jewelry, Galway Irish crystal, figurines, walking sticks, books, and cards are dis-

I Scream, You Scream, We All Scream for Ices, Italian Ices

In New Haven the name Libby's is synonymous with Italian ices. Liberato Dell Amura began making gelatos and granitas in 1922, and his family continues the tradition.

In this unassuming little Wooster Street shop (next to Frank Pepe's Pizzeria), you will find twenty-five flavors of intensely delicious Italian ices. Besides the usual flavors, there are piña colada, blue raspberry, sambuca, amaretto, mango, and cranberry. Libby's also sells delectable Italian pastries. Signatures are the twenty varieties of Sicilian cannoli and ten types of biscotti.

Libby's Italian Pastry Shop

139–141 Wooster Street
New Haven, CT 06511
(203) 772–0380

Inside the shop is the small **Caffè Villa Gina**, where patrons enjoy various coffees and desserts in the evening.

played in Tracey Riley's compact shop devoted solely to the Emerald Isle. Food products include Bewley's and other Irish teas, biscuits, cookies, scone mixes, McCann's Irish oatmeal, Irish Village brown bread, butter toffee, jams, mustards, cheeses, and frozen foods like Galtee bacon, bangers, and black pudding (blood sausage). The shop opened in 1986 and is still going strong.

Old Lyme Ice Cream Shoppe, 34 Lyme Street, Old Lyme, CT 06371; (860) 434–6942. Some locals call the ice cream here the best ice cream

in the area, and it is certainly high on the list.
There are twenty-four flavors. You will also find a
few tables and chairs inside and in front where
you may enjoy the ice cream, take-out soups, sandwiches—like a
Snoopy (toasted beagle, er, bagel with melted provolone cheese and
tomato slice) or a Dagwood (roast beef, bacon, and Swiss cheese with
tomato and lettuce on a Kaiser roll)—muffins, and danish pastries, all
sold here as well. A self-serve coffee bar is just inside the door.

ROE, ROE, ROE YOUR BOAT GENTLY DOWN THE RIVER

The shad season is so short (officially between April 1 and June
15, when the fish run from the ocean up the Connecticut River
to spawn) that it is here and gone before you can say "I'll take a
pair of roe" at the fish market. Many markets don't even carry
this fish, which in colonial times was so common and cheap
(about a penny a fish by present-day prices) that society people
ate it on the sly, pretending it was only for "poor folk." The pesky
bones (some 1,000 per fish) are forbidding, but there is nothing
inhibiting about the delicious roe, which we like to sauté with
bacon and eat with lemon juice sprinkled liberally over it. A good
place to buy fresh-from-the-river shad is at **Spencer's Haddam
Shad Shack**, Route 154, Haddam—"shack" is an apt description
for a small shed that is open only during the shad season.

TEA AND COMPANY

Tucked away on a back road in Higganum, Sundial Gardens, our favorite teatime treasure, is worth the hunt. Proprietor Ragna Tischler Goddard is both a tea and garden expert, and a visit is a chance to enjoy both. Her free tea tastings, which are held once a month or so, provide a sampling of some of the many teas she imports and sells under her own Sundial Gardens label. At each tea tasting, a few delicious nibblies, like fresh-made scones or tea cakes, are served, made by Ragna's husband, Tom Goddard, a master pastry chef. There are also several special-occasion and "theme" teas (Mother's Day, Autumn Festival, Valentine's Day), at a fixed price, with the works: tea, scones, lemon curd, tea cakes, and cucumber and other tea sandwiches. There are three formal architectural gardens to view: knot, eighteenth century, and topiary. In a small shop attached to the tearoom are all kinds of teas for sale, as well as herbal tisanes, unusual teapots from China, tea accessories, and Bavarian pewter Christmas ornaments. Check the Web site or phone for tea dates and to make a reservation.

Sundial Gardens

59 Hidden Lake Road
Higganum, CT 06441
(860) 345–4290
www.sundialgardens.com

Saeed's International Market, 461 Bank Street, New London, CT 06320; (860) 440–3822. This average-size storefront shop has shelves full of foods from around the Middle East and Mediterranean and a large deli case in the rear (with meats, spinach and cheese pies, cheeses from Albania, Bulgaria, Syria, Greece, Italy, and the Canary Islands, and rows of baklava and other honeyed Greek pastries). In the front by the window are five tables where you may enjoy a hot sandwich (try the Mediterranean Delight, with lamb gyros, hummus, and tomato on pita bread) or salad. Olive oils from all over the Mediterranean (including Israel) are a strong suit at Saeed's (some in five-gallon tins), as are other oils (walnut, almond, grape seed, basil, sesame, hazelnut, and pepper), various vinegars, twelve bins of different types of briny olives, couscous, mograbyeh (Israeli toasted couscous), lentils, and other grains, spices, dried nuts, seeds, and fruits, a variety of Turkish delights, Italian candies, panettone, and other sweets. Greek yogurt and tara-masalata can be found in the frozen-food case. We enjoy navigating around the shelves, listening to taped Greek background music as we do, making discoveries of new, exotic-looking products.

Simon's Marketplace, Main Street, Chester, CT 06412; (860) 526–8984. Tiny as Chester is, it has lately blossomed into a real "foodie" town. Credit this large, wonderfully inclusive market for some of the local excitement. The spacious store has tables in front for noshing and a wide range of groceries, many of them organic foods (including milk, yogurt, cream cheese, and butter), in the high-ceilinged rear. A delicatessen case with salads, meats, and sausages by the pound; an appealing cheese selection; bins of granola, nuts, and

Sundial Gardens
Ginger Brandy Tea Cake

At a Sundial Gardens tea, you might well be served this delicious tea cake, a specialty of chef Tom Goddard, who was willing to share his recipe with us.

½ cup unsalted butter

1 cup sugar

2 large eggs

½ teaspoon salt

¼ teaspoon vanilla extract

1 teaspoon ground ginger

½ to ¾ cup coarsely chopped crystallized ginger

1 cup coarsely chopped walnuts (optional)

2 cups unbleached white flour

2½ teaspoons baking powder

¼ cup brandy

½ cup milk

Glaze

2 –4 tablespoons unsalted butter

¼ cup brandy

¼ cup sugar

1. Butter a 9-inch molded cake pan or Bundt pan and dust lightly with flour. Invert pan and tap gently to remove excess flour. Set pan aside and preheat oven to 350°F.

2. Cream the butter and sugar with an electric mixer until light and fluffy, about 3–5 minutes. Add the eggs, one at a time, beating slowly after each egg is added. Add salt, vanilla, ground ginger powder, crystallized ginger, and nuts and mix slowly until all ingredients are well blended.

3. In a separate bowl, sift flour and baking powder together. Using a wooden spoon, alternately fold the brandy and milk into the flour mix-

ture until fully blended. Do not overmix. Fold this mixture into the egg/sugar/spices mixture until well mixed but not overbeaten.

4. Spoon the batter into the prepared cake pan. Tap pan several times on the countertop to remove air pockets. Bake in the center of the preheated oven for 45–50 minutes until firm. Check from time to time by inserting a thin straw or skewer into the cake; when the straw comes out clean and the cake is slightly firm, it is done.

5. When the cake is baked, place the pan (with the cake still in it) on a rack to cool for 15–20 minutes. While the cake is cooling, prepare the glaze. (*Note:* Instead of the glaze, the cake can be dusted all over with powdered sugar.)

6. In a small saucepan mix the brandy and sugar and bring to a boil. Let simmer for 2–3 minutes; then add the butter. Stir until completely melted and well blended.

7. Turn the cake upside down onto a large plate. Tap the sides of the pan gently to help ease the cake from the pan to the plate.

8. With a small skewer or toothpick, prick the cake all over and brush on the glaze with a pastry brush. Repeat until all the glaze has been used.

9. Serve, if desired, with lightly whipped cream, garnished with sprigs of mint. This cake keeps well and freezes well. It tastes better if served a day or two after it is baked, as the flavors have had time to meld together.

Makes 1 large molded Bundt-style cake.

Sundial Gardens

59 Hidden Lake Road
Higganum, CT 06441
(860) 345–4290
www.sundialgardens.com

seeds, and ten flavors of Salem Valley Farms ice cream; these are a few of the attractions here. All the take-out dishes are made on the premises by Simon's three professional chefs in residence. This is no rinky-dink operation; it's first rate all the way.

Star Fish Market, 650 Village Walk, Guilford, CT 06437; (203) 458–3474. We really are not out to sea when we state unequivocally that this sterling little store in an upscale shopping complex may be the prettiest seafood store we have ever seen, with displays so artistic you might think you are in an art studio. The types of fish available are displayed on plates in the refrigerated glass case, one fillet or fish per plate, sometimes with a single sprig of herb adorning it—sea-fresh, pristine, immaculate. The rest of the shop is just as beautiful, with shelves and tables full of deluxe products: olive oils, dried pastas, sauces, seafood accoutrements. A frozen and smoked fish, sausage, and chicken section is also inviting, as are the small but choice cheese selections and bread display. Star Fish is a work of art, a still life of pure perfection.

Farmers' Markets

For up-to-the-minute information about dates and hours, which can change from year to year, call Connecticut Department of Agriculture at (860) 713–2503, visit the Web site at www.state.ct.us/doag, or e-mail at ctdeptag@po.state.ct.us.

Branford Farmers' Market, parking lot behind Town Green, Branford. Sundays from 10:00 A.M. to 1:00 P.M., mid-June through October.

Deep River Farmers' Market, 184 Main Street (Route 154), Deep River. Saturdays from 8:30 A.M. to noon, end of May through mid-October.

Dudley Farmers' Market, 2351 Durham Road, North Guilford. Saturdays from 9:00 A.M. to 2:00 P.M., last week of June through October.

Essex Farmers' Market, Town Green, Main Street, Essex. Fridays from 3:00 to 6:00 P.M., first week in June through October.

Groton Farmers' Market, Groton Shopping Plaza, next to Post Office (Route 1), Groton. Wednesdays from 2:00 to 6:00 P.M., second week in June through October.

Mystic Farmers' Market, Quiambaug Fire House, Route 1, Mystic. Tuesdays from 3:00 to 6:00 P.M., early June through October.

New Haven Farmers' Market, Temple Street Plaza, across from Omni Hotel, New Haven. Wednesdays from 8:00 A.M. to 2:00 P.M., Saturdays 8:00 A.M. to 1:00 P.M., late June through October.

Lee White's Super Simple Salad Dressing

With all the diverse home-grown greens available at farm stands in this part of the state, here is a great and simple salad dressing to toss with them. Its creator, Lee White, is a cookbook author and food consultant and one of our most generous "foodie" friends.

1 cup rice vinegar
⅓ cup white vinegar
⅓ cup Dijon mustard
1 tablespoon minced garlic
¾ cup sugar
1 cup olive oil
1 cup vegetable oil

In a large blender, combine vinegars, mustard, garlic, and sugar and blend well. In a separate bowl combine the oils. With the blender running, pour oil mixture in a slow, steady stream into the blender until all ingredients are well integrated. Share this dressing and make friends or store in the refrigerator to use as needed; it keeps a month or two easily.

Makes about 4 cups.

New London Farmers' Market, Municipal Parking Lot, Corner of Eugene O'Neill Drive and Pearl Street, New London. Tuesdays and Fridays from 9:30 A.M. to 2:00 P.M., early July through October.

Old Saybrook Farmers' Market, Cinema Plaza, 210 Main Street, Old Saybrook. Wednesdays from 10:00 A.M. to 1:00 P.M., mid-June through October.

Pawcatuck/Westerly Farmers' Market, Pawcatuck Park on the river, West Broad and Mechanic Streets, Pawcatuck. Thursdays from 2:00 to 6:00 P.M., early July through October.

Stonington Farmers' Market, Town Fishing Fleet Pier, Stonington. Saturdays from 9:00 A.M. to noon, early June through October 12.

Wallingford Wal-Mart Farmers' Market, Wal-Mart parking lot, Wallingford. Sundays from 10:00 A.M. to 2:00 P.M., early July through October.

Wallingford II Farmers' Market, Railroad Station Green, intersection of Routes 5 and 150, Wallingford. Saturdays from 9:00 A.M. to noon, mid-July through mid-September.

West Haven Farmers' Market, West Haven Green, West Haven. Thursdays from noon to 6:00 P.M., July 11 through October.

Farm Stands

Bishop's Orchards, 1355 Boston Post Road, Guilford, CT 06437; (203) 453–2338; www.bishopsorchards.com. This is one BIG (320 acres) operation. Five generations of Bishops have farmed here since 1871. There are 140 acres of apples alone, twenty-two acres of peaches, twenty-seven of pears, plus strawberries, blueberries, raspberries and pumpkins. You may pick your own from June through October. Bishop's has a special 'round-the-clock phone number for the latest fruit ripening and pick-your-own information: (203) 458–PICK. Check their Web site and sign up for their *Pick-Your-Own Newsletter.* Seasonal fruits are offered as they ripen: strawberries first, in mid-June; blueberries next, July to September; raspberries and peaches, in mid-August; pears and apples the end of August; and apples and raspberries continuing into mid-October. Oh yes, pumpkins ripen in late September and are around for Halloween. Bishop's sizable year-round farm market—more like a mini-supermarket—sells their produce, along with pies and breads from their bakery, their own apple cider, apple butter and other preserves with their label, cut flowers, fruit baskets, and gift packs (which they will ship). The market also sells a range of grocery products made elsewhere. The farm market is open year-round, Sunday from 9:00 A.M. to 6:00 P.M., Monday through Saturday from 8:00 A.M. to 6:00 P.M.

Bishop's has a second, seasonal location at 1920 Middletown Avenue in Northford (203–458–PICK). It specializes in apples

Cranberry Conserve

Connecticut's cranberry bogs were never much competition for those in Massachusetts, but the last-known commercial cranberry bog in the state is on Pond Meadow Road in Killingworth. "We figure a package of Killingworth Cranberries costs us about $100 to produce," says Sandy Evarts, "but we continue to do so because it has been a family tradition since 1896, when my husband Ken's grandfather started the bog." The Evartses' five daughters, their husbands, and ten grandchildren love pitching in during the harvesting season—picking, putting the berries into the sorting machines, which blow the chaff away, then sorting by hand and packaging.

Whether you buy one of the Evartses' one-pound cranberry packages from Bishop's Orchards (the only outlet) or not, here is one of our favorite and simple recipes for this wonderfully tart seasonal crop.

1 large California navel orange (sweet, with no seeds)
1 pound fresh cranberries
¼ cup honey
½ cup sugar
1 cup sultanas (golden raisins)
2 teaspoons coarsely chopped sugared ginger
½ cup coarsely chopped walnuts

Cut orange into quarters and put through a food processor, along with the cranberries. Add the remaining ingredients and mix thoroughly by hand. Chill in the refrigerator until flavors blend, about 3 hours minimum. Serve as an accompaniment to poultry or game.

Makes 4 cups.

(which you can pick on weekends). Also on sale are the other fruits as they ripen, likewise seasonal vegetables, dairy products, and fresh-baked breads and pies from Bishop's Guilford location. Open August through October on weekends 9:00 A.M. to 5:00 P.M.

Drazen Orchards, 251 Wallingford Road, Guilford, CT 06437; (203) 272–7985; e-mail: gordraz@aol.com. The Drazens have been farming their thirty-acre spread for fifty years. Now son Gordon, with the weekend help of *his* son and local workers, grows eighteen varieties of apples (including McIntosh, Empire, Liberty, Janagold, Gingergold, Gala, Mutsu, and Cortland), eight types of peaches, both yellow and white, nectarines, and two types of pears, all of which are available for picking from mid-August until the end of October. Note that the apples are dwarf varieties for easy picking. The fruits, along with sweet corn, tomatoes, and cider, are also sold at the Drazen farm stand. Open from the second week in August until Thanksgiving from 10:00 A.M. to 5:30 P.M. daily.

Four Mile River Farm, 124 Four Mile River Road, Old Lyme, CT 06371; (860) 434–2378. Teaching history for years in Hamden wasn't enough for Nunzio Corsino II, so in 1991 he began to farm his eighteen acres, raising, without chemicals or growth hormones, Yorkshire pigs (twelve at a time), Angus cattle (a herd of thirty to thirty-five), and land hens (one hundred). The certified beef and pork is processed and vacuum-packed in Stafford Springs. He markets directly from his farm, at the Stonington Farmers' Market, and the new Lyme Farmers' Market on Bill Hill Road, Lyme, which he helped establish for local farmers. The Corsino farm stand (with a freezer inside one of the outbuildings) has fresh eggs, steaks in various sizes, beef patties, beef kielbasa, other

CHEWING ON HAMBURGER HISTORY

New Havenites insist that the hamburger was born in their city, the creation of Louis Lassen in 1900. According to Louis's grandson Ken, it was midday when a man dashed in to Louis' luncheonette and breathlessly asked for a quick meal he could eat on the run.

Louis' Lunch

261 Crown Street
New Haven, CT 06510
(203) 562–5507
www.louislunch.com

$

Louis rose to the challenge by slapping a freshly broiled beef patty between two slices of bread, and the customer rushed away, unaware of his role in this epochal event. Louis' Lunch (pronounced "Louie") today is a pocket-size landmark, now on the National Register

of Historic Places. Moved from its original spot in 1967, the wee redbrick building with its red-shuttered windows was reconstructed, with bricks contributed by hundreds of nostalgic devotees. Ken Lassen still uses Louis' original recipe, broiling each patty of fresh-ground beef on the antique vertical cast-iron grill, serving it between toasted bread slices. Cheese, fresh tomato, and onion are the garnishes of choice, the old-fashioned Louis way. Mustard and ketchup are no-nos to purists.

beef cuts, mulch hay for landscaping, and handcrafts made by Irene, Nunzio's wife—sold on the honor system. Pigs are special orders; customers may request in advance the desired division: chops, roast, ham steaks, bacon, and the like.

Hindinger Farm, 835 Dunbar Hill Road, Hamden, CT 06514; (203) 288-0700. From the hills, you can see across Long Island Sound. Bill and Ann Hindinger and their family have had this view for years, as did Bill's grandfather when he bought the farm in 1893. The Hindingers raise fruit and vegetables with modern techniques. Their farm stand sells freshly picked apples, peaches, pears, strawberries, and vegetables as they ripen, including asparagus, rhubarb, peas, cucumbers, beans, eggplant, and especially sweet corn and tomatoes. All these and fresh flowers are at the stand, as they ripen, beginning May 1 right up to Christmas, from 9:00 A.M. to 6:00 P.M. daily, except Mondays. Each year the family holds a Peach Festival the third week in August, with peach shortcake, ice cream, and pies, plus hayrides using the two tractors—and those wonderful views; call for date and time.

Holmberg Orchards, 1990 Route 12, Gales Ferry, CT 06335; (860) 464-7305; www.holmbergorchards.com. Here's another big farm and orchard beckoning you to pick your choice of fruit as it ripens. Yours to pick: fifteen varieties of apples, peaches, pears, nectarines, blueberries, raspberries, and pumpkins in season. You can finish up at the big Farm Market building for its freshly baked pies, turnovers, muffins, applesauce and apple crisp, newly harvested vegetables, and fresh-pressed apple cider. In the fall you may want their bales of hay, gourds, corn stalks, winter squash, and dried flowers. Open year-round, daily from 9:00 A.M. to 6:00 P.M., with pick-your-own available from July through October.

J. DeFrancesco & Sons, Forest Road, Northford, CT 06472; (203) 484-9708; e-mail: farmerjoed@aol.com. Joe DeFrancesco began truck farming here in the 1900s and expanded the farm and the family with his wife, Raffaela, over the years. At present, their son Joe Jr., his wife, Linda, and their four sons run the one hundred acres that now include four acres of greenhouses for flowers. Outdoor plantings of fruit and vegetables include peas, beans, strawberries, tomatoes, cantaloupes, watermelons, a dozen varieties of sweet corn, and pumpkins. These are sold to stores, restaurants, and at the farm stand, over which Raffaela still rules as queen. The stand is in a venerable old barn and is open daily from Palm Sunday through Halloween from 7:00 A.M. to 6:00 P.M.

Maple Lane Farm & Market, 57 Northwest Corner Road, Preston, CT 06365; (860) 887-8855; www.maplelane.com. This onetime pasture for dairy cows has evolved into a 120-acre farm where you can pick your own strawberries, raspberries, and blueberries all summer long, plus apples and peaches into fall. Alternately, if you phone or e-mail your order a day ahead (info@mapleline.com), your choices will be picked for you and kept at the Farm Market. There, tree-ripened peaches, apples, and pumpkins are for sale, along with a variety of vegetables, fresh home-baked breads and pies, maple sugar, honey, and dairy products. During the fall pumpkin season, there are weekend hay rides. Open April through December, daily, from 9:00 A.M. to 6:00 P.M.

Medlyn's Farm Market, 710 Leetes Island Road, Branford, CT 06405; (203) 488-3578. Here the vegetables include eggplant, beans, peas, sweet corn, tomatoes, squash, potatoes, peppers, and pumpkins.

Movable Feasts

The **Cedar Street Food Carts,** at the corner of Cedar and York Streets, New Haven, are a phenomenon. As many as twenty-two food carts with their shade umbrellas, arranged on both sides of Cedar in a minipark setting, sell a smorgasbord of ethnic foods between noon and 2:00 P.M. every weekday. Their location near Yale–New Haven Hospital is no accident. The reason so many of these vendors arrived here in the first place was to provide a quick, easy, and inexpensive lunch to hospital personnel and visitors. So take a stroll and take your pick: Japanese, Chinese, Malaysian, Thai, Mexican, Caribbean, Indian, Pakistan, soul food, Ethiopian, Middle Eastern, hot dogs, Italian ices. It is a short trip to some fun gastronomic adventures. Some carts are outposts of fine local restaurants—like Roomba, Bangkok Thai, Sandra's Soul Food, Lalibella—giving a sample of what you might find at the source and a chance to enjoy one of New Haven's best-kept secrets.

You won't go home disappointed. The market also has melons, rhubarb, and strawberries in their growing seasons. Open June to December, Monday through Friday from 10:00 A.M. to 6:00 P.M., Saturday and Sunday from 9:00 A.M. to 6:00 P.M.

Scott's Yankee Farmer, 436 Boston Post Road (Route 1), East Lyme, CT 06333; (860) 739–5209. For more than twenty-seven years, Karen and Tom Scott have been growing apples, strawberries, and blueberries for you to pick fresh during the growing season, June through October. For sale in their roadside store are all of the above, along with vegetables, cider, jams, honey, cheese, pies, and more (including weekend wagon rides in autumn). Open daily from 9:00 A.M. to 5:30 P.M. year-round.

Food Happenings

February: **Make Mine Wine,** Lyman Allyn Art Museum, 625 Williams Street, New London, CT 06320; (860) 443–2545 or (860) 447–5783. The year 2000 was the first annual *Make Mine Wine* event, which is now being held the last Friday in February at this site. Live jazz and a buffet dinner accompany the tasting of fifty different wines (available for sale at a discount) and a silent auction. Sponsored by the Waterford Rotary Foundation, proceeds go to New London charities and scholarships. Tickets to this one-night gala must be bought in advance. Hours: 7:00 P.M. to 10:00 P.M.

May: **Fine Wine & Food Festival,** Garde Arts Center, 325 State Street, New London, CT 06320; (860) 444–6766; www.development@gardearts.org. Leading restaurants, caterers, bakeries, and wine merchants provide their best offerings to be sampled and enjoyed by donors in this annual fund-raiser. The money goes to Garde's performing arts, film, and education programs; the fine wines and gourmet cuisine are consumed by the donors. Call for the full story or visit the Web site.

FOOD LOVERS' TIP

Our state is the biggest producer of clams on the East Coast. The state clam is officially a *Mercenaria mercenaria*, better known throughout New England as a quahog. A sign of summer and the fried clam season is when all the clam shacks along U.S. 1 from Branford to the Rhode Island line open their windows and begin their ritual deep-frying of bucketsful of ocean-fresh clams. Whose are the best? You decide.

May: **Taste of the Nation—New Haven,** New Haven Lawn Club, New Haven, CT 06512; (203) 469–5000; www.strength.org. Usually a mid-May event, this is New Haven's largest, most successful annual fund-raising event, going strong since 1987. Many of the area's finest restaurant chefs participate each year, with more than fifty different wines available for the sampling, as well as cooking demonstrations, a champagne seminar, and a chef auction.

June: **Shad Festival,** Connecticut River Museum, 67 Main Street, Essex, CT 06426; (860) 767–8269; www.ctrivershore.com. Essex salutes this Connecticut native with an annual two-day event, usually held the first weekend in June. Demonstrations of cooking shad, shad history, and hands-on activities are held at the museum (admission charge). A plank-baked shad dinner is served by the Essex Rotary Club at the Essex Elementary School.

June: **Branford Festival,** Town Green, South Main Street, Branford, CT 06405; (203) 488–5500 or (203) 488–8304. For more than twenty-three years, this has been a tasty (and tasting) perennial three-day event around Father's Day, the second weekend in June. It begins Friday evening with food, music, and entertainment. Saturday's highlight is a festival within a festival: A tent on the Green houses the Strawberry Festival, sponsored by the local Historical Society. From 10:30 A.M. to 1:30 P.M., homemade shortcakes are for sale, and the minifestival ends when the last berry is bought or consumed. Then the larger Branford Festival continues through Sunday. Call for schedule and details.

June: **Greater New Haven Pizza Fest,** New Haven Green, New Haven, CT 06519; (203) 776–9900. During the New Haven Arts & Ideas Festival the last two weeks in June, Also-Cornerstone, a nonprofit community-service organization, holds an annual fund-raiser on the Green, with some ninety pizzerias from the Greater New Haven area donating their specialties. Any weekday between noon and 1:30 P.M., you can wander around the Green, enjoy a free concert, and sample pizzas provided by ten or so different pizzerias each day. How's that for a twofer? You can become a pizza expert (everyone in New Haven is) and support a good cause at the same time.

July: **Lobster Festival & Arts & Crafts Show,** Pennsylvania Avenue, Niantic, CT 06357; (860) 739–2805 or (860) 739–6931. If it is the Fourth of July, it must be Niantic's annual Lobster Festival and the craft show that has accompanied it for more than twenty-five years.

The major event is lobster enjoyment (meaning consumption)—which is tackled with gusto, along with clam chowder and steamed clams, by young and old alike. Expect to find music, entertainment, and a juried arts-and-crafts competition also, but everyone knows the real headliner: lobsters, of course. Hours are noon to 6:00 P.M. both Saturday and Sunday, on or close to the fourth. Call for dates.

August: **Bluefish Festival,** Town Dock, Clinton, CT 06413; (860) 664–4229 (Chamber of Commerce). This town has gone all out for bluefish for more than twenty-five years and is proud of its sobriquet "Bluefish Capital of the World," bestowed by a Connecticut governor after a rousing bluefish tournament. The two-day festival each year (usually about August 15–16) begins on Friday, from 6:00 to 10:00 P.M., with a boat parade at dusk, and picks up again Saturday noon until midnight. There are booths with food from fifteen restaurants (including fried dough and fish chowder) and live music both days. And all the while, fishermen compete, trying to land the biggest bluefish ever. Call to verify dates and times.

August: **Adam's Garlic Fest,** Adam's Garden of Eden, 360 North Anguilla Road, Pawcatuck, CT 06379, (860) 599–4241; e-mail:adamsgarden1@aol.com. Everything you ever wanted to know about garlic you are likely to find out (or taste or inhale) at this popular two-day event, usually held the second weekend in August. Ed Adam started the fest modestly in 1994, and it has expanded into an exposition. Irresistible garlicky aromas dance through the air as a dozen local chefs demonstrate

ADVICE NO GARLIC LOVER PAYS ATTENTION TO ANYMORE

"And most dear actors, eat no onions nor garlic, for we are to utter sweet breath."

—William Shakespeare

their creations of thoroughly garlicked spring rolls, pierogies, and other delicacies. Farmers display their multitype garlic harvests while medical doctors, folklorists, and others report garlic's advantages, with either a jazz or string band playing in the background. There are even booths where craftspersons offer jewelry and pottery with garlic themes. All this because of the hardy, liliaceous plant that reigns supreme everywhere in this festival, from 10:00 A.M. to 6:00 P.M. each day. Admission fee; free parking.

August: **Market "En Plein Air,"** at Florence Griswold Museum, 96 Lyme Street, Old Lyme, CT 06371; (860) 434–5542; www.flogris.org or www.historiclymestreet.com. This is an event within an event. Historic Old Lyme celebrates an annual town-wide Midsummer Festival, usually the first Saturday/Sunday in August, when about 6,000 people attend. On Saturday, from 8:00 A.M. to 3:00 P.M., the locale is the beautiful grounds and gardens of the Florence Griswold Museum, when the attraction is "En Plein Air," a French-style, open-air market as its title indicates. It bursts with top-quality Connecticut products—fresh produce, flowers, breads, fine cheeses, meats, and specialty foods—as well as imaginative fun projects and activities and a chance to visit the museum at reduced admission. There is usually a Friday-evening concert, and festivities continue through Sunday. Call for dates and hours.

September: **Boats, Books, and Brushes . . . With Taste,** New London, CT 06320; (800) TO ENJOY; www.sailnewlondon.com. What began in 2000 as a boat show in Mystic has now cruised over to New London to become a food extravaganza as well. It is a three-day gala held the first weekend in September after Labor Day on the waterfront in New London, surrounded by tall ships. Some thirty restaurants offer samplings. There are cooking and boating demonstrations, cookbook authors on hand, live entertainment on two stages, a regatta, tall-ship tours and cruises, and more, much more. Check the Web site for details.

September: **Best of Connecticut Party,** Oakdale Theater, Wallingford, CT 06492. This annual event, usually attended by 1,500 to 2,000 people, is a combination cocktail party and vendor show, showcasing those chosen by a *Connecticut* magazine readers' poll as the "Best of Connecticut" in a variety of categories, including foods, restaurants, and specialty-food shops. The party is cosponsored by *Connecticut* magazine and the March of Dimes, with proceeds going to the latter. For tickets and details, call Suzanne Galotti, March of Dimes at (860) 290–5440, extension 306.

October: **Annual Apple Festival,** Town Green, Route 85, Salem, CT 06420; (860) 859–1211. Having held these celebrations since 1969, Salem's Congregational Church sure knows the drill. Traditionally held the last Saturday in October, this exuberant festival opens at 9:00 A.M.,

Best Dining with River Views

Chefs have come and gone at the Gelston House, but the view is forever. This magnificent Victorian wedding-cake–style restaurant-inn was built in 1853 on a hilltop high above the Connecticut River, adjacent to another Victorian "wedding cake," the Goodspeed Opera House. Both were built by William Gelston, an entrepreneur and opera buff, to lure music lovers from New York by steamboat. Nowadays, huge windows on three sides of the Gelston's River Grill, the main dining room, provide majestic views of all the boating action on the river below. Though the views trump the food, don't underestimate the new American menu, with its Italian undercurrents, now under the competent management of Hartford's Carbones Restaurant Group. Braised cod loin in a rosemary/garlic/plum-tomato reduction, salmon fillet in tomato aioli with risotto, and prime ribs au jus are three among the worthy dishes you might enjoy. If you are in a hurry to get to a Goodspeed musical production, the Tavern, with a pared-down menu (and prices to match), and the casual outdoor Beer Garden are both quick and handy alternatives.

Gelston House

8 Main Street
East Haddam, CT 06423
(860) 873–1411
e-mail: info@gelstonhouse.com
$$

though church volunteers have been busy for weeks making apple pies, turnovers, crisps, brownies, Bettys, crumbs, Swedish apple puddings, applesauce cakes, and other apple goodies for the big event. In the Grange building are booths selling various apple treats: the Apple

Olé for the State's Best Tapas

And then there were none. Not at first, not a single Spanish restaurant in Connecticut. But within the past fifteen years, there has been a mini-explosion of them. Ibiza began life as Pika Tapas, specializing in the delectable morsels that in Spain are served with drinks, to stave off hunger and endure the long wait that precedes lunch or dinner there. Pika Tapas has morphed into Ibiza and is now an elegant, full-fledged restaurant. Tapas are no longer on center stage, but a tapas menu features at least nine creative ones. Though the

Ibiza

39 High Street
New Haven, CT 06510
(203) 865–1933
$$

selection changes often, you will usually find wood-roasted piquillo peppers stuffed with codfish, garlic, and onions in a tomato sauce; grilled baby squid; and *boquerones* (marinated fresh anchovies on toasted bread with aioli and fresh fish roe). Whatever is available is almost guaranteed to be delicious.

Fritter booth, the Apple Sundae & Hot Dog booth (in which apple sauerkraut is served with the wieners), and the Piece of Pie booth (apple pie with or without cheddar cheese). At the crafts booths, stuffed teddy bear dolls wear an apple theme: an aged Granny Smith, a slick Jonathan, a Delicious femme fatale with feather boa. The Tea Room features hot apple pancakes, served with tea or coffee. There is continuous music in the Gazebo and games for the kids. The party's over when all the apple goodies have been sold, usually by around 1:00 P.M.

October: **Celebrate Wallingford,** Downtown Wallingford, c/o 261 Center Street, Wallingford, CT 06492; (203) 284–1807; e-mail: wallingford centerinc@msn.com. For more than sixteen years, "Celebrate Wallingford" has been a popular annual event, in which local restaurants offer their outstanding specialties. The celebration, held the first weekend of October, runs for two days, and each year it is in a different location, showing off a newly renovated area of town and featuring live entertainment, arts, crafts, cars, and activities for children and by civic groups. Hours are usually Saturday from 11:00 A.M. to 6:00 P.M. and Sunday from noon to 6:00 P.M. Locale changes; call or e-mail for this year's location.

October: **Annual Apple Festival & Country Fair,** Town Green, Main Street, Old Saybrook, CT 06475; (860) 388–1957. Usually held the first weekend in October, this is a joyful outdoor event held on Main Street. The entire town green is chockablock with food booths peddling apples in many delicious and enticing forms, plus all kinds of other tempting edibles. There is always a petting zoo, as well as pony rides and entertainment. Usually held from 10:00 A.M. to 4:00 P.M. Call to verify date and time.

November: **Star Chefs Auction of Greater New Haven,** Omni New Haven Hotel, 155 Temple Street, New Haven, CT 06510. Held late in October or early November, this fabulous food event is a major annual fund-raiser for the March of Dimes. Chefs from area restaurants and other vendors set up gourmet tastings and a silent auction. Later, a live auction with a celebrity master of ceremonies gavels off to the highest bidder packages donated by chefs and others, such as cooking lessons with a master chef, a cocktail party for thirty guests in a local restaurant, a wine dinner with two wine experts, lunch with a local television personality, a catered dinner for forty in your home. For tickets and specifics, call Suzanne Galotti at the March of Dimes, (860) 290–5440, extension 306; e-mail: sgalotti@marchofdimes.com.

Learn to Cook

Fourteen Lincoln Street, 14 Lincoln Street, Niantic, CT 06357; (860) 739–8180; www.14lincolnstreet.com. In a sparkling, fully commercial kitchen in the culinary studio of a nineteenth-century church, which she has converted into a four-bedroom, bed-and-breakfast inn, Cheryl M. Jean conducts themed cooking-class weekends (Mexican, Japanese, Burmese, for example) throughout the year. A Culinary Institute of America graduate, Cheryl emphasizes cooking fundamentals, new techniques, northern Italian, French, Japanese, Mexican, and regional New England in her courses, occasionally using guest chefs. The fee is for two nights, two four-course breakfasts, and a five-hour cooking class, followed by a sumptuous meal. Other individual classes can be scheduled for groups of six or more on request. For a schedule or details, phone or e-mail (fourteenlincoln@aol.com).

Institute of Gastronomy and Culinary Arts, University of New Haven, 300 Orange Street, West Haven, CT 06516; (203) 932–7362 or (800) 356–3803, extension 328. Patrick Boisjot, noted chef and restau-

Jacques Pépin's
Honeyed Sweet Potatoes

French chef and longtime Connecticut resident Jacques Pépin, a frequent guest chef at the Institute of Gastronomy and Culinary Arts, shares this recipe from Jacques Pépin's Simple and Healthy Cooking *cookbook (published by Rodale Books, 1994) and is reproduced with the permission of the publisher. It makes a great garnish for turkey, duck, or game, a natural at the holiday season. It can be prepared a day ahead and reheated just before serving. The potatoes can be peeled if you prefer.*

5 sweet potatoes (about 3 pounds)
2 tablespoons canola, corn, or safflower oil
¼ teaspoon freshly ground black pepper
3 tablespoons honey

1. Scrub sweet potatoes and remove eyes or damaged areas with a paring knife. Cut the potatoes on a crosswise slant into 1½-inch slices.
2. Place the potato slices in a large saucepan with enough water to cover them by ½ inch. Bring the water to a boil, reduce heat to medium or low, and boil potatoes gently for 5 minutes. Drain.
3. Heat the oil in a large skillet (or two smaller ones). When the oil is hot, add the potato slices in a single layer, sprinkle with pepper, and sauté them over medium to high heat for 2 minutes on each side.
4. Add the honey. Reduce heat to low and cook for 2½ minutes longer on each side. Remove from pan and serve.

Serves 6.

SEAFOOD BY THE RIVER

Situated at the edge of a boatyard, the Blue Oar doesn't look like much, but from its tiny kitchen come forth grilled seafood dinners (like Cajun catfish) that attract the likes of *60 Minutes* reporter Morley Safer and chef Jacques Pépin. What adds to the appeal is the halcyon setting, facing a quiet marina on the Connecticut River. You sit at pastel-painted picnic tables on an open-sided deck or under a shade tree on the patio—no frills, but at one with nature. If there is a better way to enjoy steamers and lobster rolls than al fresco, we can't think of it. *Caveat*: BYOB and no credit cards.

The Blue Oar

16 Snyder Road
(off Route 154)
Haddam, CT 06438
(860) 345–2994
$

rateur, founded the institute in 1997. Beginning in September 2003, full-time students may earn a B.S. degree in Gastronomy, Culinary Arts, or Kitchen Management. But even hobbyists may study here. There are weekly two-hour cooking demonstrations by well-known regional chefs throughout the school year, from September through December and from the end of January to May. Demonstrations and other classes are held in the first-rate Delia Inc. teaching/training center at 4 Laser Lane, Wallingford. Call for the registration form for specific classes.

Mystic Cooking School, 1305 Pequot Trail (Route 234), Stonington, CT 06378; (860) 536–6005; www.mysticcooking.com. Tucked into the Old Mystic section of Stonington, this cooking school offers a number of recreational cooking classes with guest instructors: regional and foreign chefs, caterers, cookbook authors, and other culinary experts. There are approximately sixty-five "stand-alone" classes a year, conducted in a modern facility with granite countertops, a European-style fireplace, and topnotch appliances and cabinetry. Started in 1993 by Annice Estes, the school has featured cuisines as diverse as Burmese, Korean, Brazilian, and Greek, as well as classes in pastry making, seafood specialties, cooking with wine, and easy entertaining. Classes are usually held Wednesday evenings from 6:00 to 9:00 P.M. and occasionally on weekends from 1:00 to 4:00 P.M. For a schedule and details, call or check the school Web site.

Mystic Seaport, 75 Greenmanville Avenue, P.O. Box 6000, Mystic, CT 06355; (860) 572–5322; www.visitmysticseaport.com. We can't think of a better place for learning "Open Hearth Cooking" than in the kitchen of the Buckingham-Hall House, an authentic 1830s farmhouse in Mystic Seaport. The basic course, usually offered in October and February, teaches cooking methods—baking, roasting, frying, boiling—and the specific utensils required for an open-hearth or beehive oven. An entire meal is prepared, and the class then sits down to enjoy it. An advanced three-day course is often taught as well. Call for details and dates.

Learn about Wine

Mt. Carmel Wine & Spirits Co., 2977 Whitney Avenue, Hamden, CT 06518; (203) 281–0800; www.mtcarmelwine.com. For five years in a row, this splendid shop has been voted "Connecticut's Best Retail Wine Shop" by *Connecticut* magazine, for the range of its selections from all over the world. Mt. Carmel has had plenty of time to get its act together.

When Prohibition ended in 1934, Sydney Levine turned a corner of his family's general store over to wine and spirits, which eventually took over the entire store. Descendants Ben and Bob Feinn now run the business. The store is a source for rare wines, specialty wines, and "value wines" (those representing the best value for their price), taste tested and often imported exclusively and directly from small wineries in France and elsewhere. Hard-to-find older vintages are a specialty—notably Bordeaux, red and white Burgundies, Rhones, and Ports. French wines are here in great depth, but the entire wine world is well represented. Mt. Carmel's Web site is a helpful source for upcoming wine events— tastings and dinners—in the area. It also lists the store's excellent weekly wine specials, with frank appraisals of specific wines.

Landmark Eateries

Atticus Bookstore Café, 1082 Chapel Street, New Haven, CT 06510; (203) 776–4040; $. What began in 1981 with a couple of tables, a counter, and display cases at the edge of the bookstore has insinuated its way into one third of the store. Now there are eighteen tables-for-two and two large tables for groups, proof that readers and shoppers like a handy place for a wholesome sandwich or quick pick-me-up. Fresh-tasting, nutritious soups and sandwiches and delicious muffins, cookies, and tarts are the modus operandi here. A good deal is the combo of a cup of soup and a huge half-sandwich. The breads and baked goods come directly from Chabaso Bakery, a felicitous spin-off owned by Atticus.

Abbott's Lobster in the Rough is low on the radar screen, but for more than thirty years multitudes have braved the hairpin-twisting, convoluted shore route to find this little tucked-away gem that faces a picture-pretty marina at Noank, facing Fishers Island Sound. Fortunately, the road is well signposted. Once you have arrived at this modest place, the drill is simple: You order at the counter, wait briefly, then take your goodies to a picnic table inside the "shack" or outside on the deck or grassy lawn. Accoutrements are basic plastic and paper, but a heads-on view of the boats and water is so sublimely peaceful you might feel you are at the upper reaches of Maine. Though Abbott's has other choices, including a respectable clam chowder, Bay of Fundy steamers, or oysters on the half shell, the magnet is lobster. Our preference is the lobster roll, a toasted, buttery bun piled high with luscious, tender, pure lobster meat, but lobster mavens with bigger appetites crave the whole lobster—from one-and-a-quarter-pounders up to ten-pounders—steamed and served with drawn butter, cole slaw, and potato chips. Abbott's claims a "more humane" approach to cooking its lobsters: in a cooker in which the lobster is steamed above the boiling water, not in it. Tell that to the lobster. You can also order take-out lobster bakes in a canister

**Abbott's Lobster
in the Rough**

117 Pearl Street
Noank, CT 06340
(860) 536-7719
www.abbotts-lobster.com
$

(with live lobsters, steamers, mussels, corn on the cob, white and sweet potatoes, all nestled in damp seaweed), which is all ready to pop on the stove, outdoor grill, or campfire. Open daily from June 1 through Labor Day, thereafter on three-day weekends through Columbus Day.

Bentara, 76 Orange Street, New Haven, CT 06510; (203) 562–2511; www.bentara.com; $$. We warmed to this Malaysian restaurant immediately. With its baskets, shadow puppets, bamboo screen, and beautiful ceramic pots, it reminded us of our many happy years spent in the Far East. Aside from its artistic arrangements in a spacious restored building, Bentara's menu is a delight as well. Helpfully, each dish is carefully described on the menu. As befits a Malaysian restaurant, the menu is as polyglot as the country, with Chinese, Indonesian, Indian, and Thai influences. We recommend especially the curry mussels, *rendang* (chicken with tofu, Chinese eggplant, and green beans in a lemongrass-spiked coconut curry), and *udang goreng pedas* (hot and spicy shrimp with slivered onions and green beans).

Caffé Adulis, 228 College Street, New Haven, CT 06511; (203) 777–5081; $. In this college town with all its diversity, it may not surprise you to find an Ethiopian restaurant, a rarity in Connecticut. Caffé Adulis is even more specific; its food is Eritrean, from a region of Ethiopia, and Adulis is the name of an Eritrean port. The well-seasoned, peppery dishes are served on *injera,* which are large pieces of a spongy, crepe-thin bread, spread out to cover a large tray. The drill is to scoop everything up with pieces of the *injera,* using it instead of utensils. This can be a lot of fun, even jollier as a communal experience for groups of four or more. If you don't know how to order (few of us do), rely on the gracious, helpful staff. The setting is simple and attractive, making this an unusual and pleasing culinary adventure.

A Trio of "Inn" Experiences

The days of "quaint"—relish trays and cottage cheese—at Connecticut country inns are long past. Now some of the loveliest modern food is served at inns whose decor is at least two centuries older. The following threesome, clustered together near the Connecticut River, are known even more for their food than their period surroundings.

The Bee & Thistle Inn, 100 Lyme Street, Old Lyme, CT 06371; (860) 434–1667; www.beeandthistleinn.com; $$$. A favorite romantic getaway, this vintage inn has food as appealing as the Americana decor is charming. The cuisine is modern American, with a few oriental touches (Thai curry seafood stew and sesame-roasted salmon, for instance), and each of the four dining rooms has its own quiet character.

Copper Beech Inn, 46 Main Street, Ivoryton, CT 06442; (860) 767–0330; www.copperbeechinn.com; $$$. Easily spotted by the giant copper beech tree in its front yard, this impeccably maintained inn has been on a gustatory roller-coaster ride in the recent past but has finally found firm ground again with notable French food (like *cassoulet, carré d'agneau,* and *ris de veau*) and a remarkable wine list. Dining here is both elegant and romantic.

Old Lyme Inn, 85 Lyme Street, Old Lyme, CT 06371; (860) 434–2600 or (800) 434–5352; www.oldlymeinn.com; $$$. Inside the handsome, nine-teenth-century house are two dining rooms; both have the same modern American/continental menu, with many New England seafood dishes, like Stonington sea scallops, grilled Atlantic salmon, and Maine lobster tail. The casual Tap Room is open for lunch and dinner; the long, more formal Winslow Room is open only on weekends for dinner.

Flanders Fish Market & Restaurant, 22 Chesterfield Road, East Lyme, CT 06333; (860) 739-8866 or (800) 242-6055 (Connecticut) or (800) 638-8189 (nationwide); www.flandersfish.com; $$. What started as a modest fish market in 1983, when Paul and Donna Formica began selling her clear clam chowder at the fish counter, little by little expanded to a restaurant with 150 seats in a modern building with wraparound dining areas and a wooden deck with tables and sun umbrellas. At the restaurant entrance are the market's refrigerated display cases, filled with sparkling fresh shad and shad roe in season, cod, catfish, salmon, sea bass, and dozens of other denizens of the deep. Both market and restaurant bustle all day long. The restaurant is cheerful and simple, with lots of windows and nautical prints on the walls. We especially enjoy the clam roll with whole clam bellies on a toasted square roll (served with Flanders-made tartar sauce), fried calamari and oyster platters, and the velvety lobster bisque, a signature dish. As if they weren't busy enough, Flanders also caters old-fashioned New England clambakes and ships any size lobster anywhere in the country by next-day air.

Randall's Ordinary, Route 2, North Stonington, CT 06359; (860) 599-4540; $$. There is something about open-hearth cooking that has near-universal appeal. Kids are fascinated by its evocation of "olden times," and even jaded adults feel a twinge of nostalgia for simpler days. This eighteenth-century farmhouse (with parts dating back to 1685) was converted in 1987 into a country inn (or "ordinary," as it would have been called in its time) and named after the house's original owner, John Randall. The wide hearths in the three low-ceilinged, exposed-beam dining rooms are perfect for hearth cooking, which is done at all

Hunt Breakfast at "The Gris"— A Connecticut Tradition

Probably the best-known, and most reasonable, Sunday brunch in the state is the Hunt Breakfast at the historic eighteenth-century Griswold Inn in Essex. The Hunt was started when the British commandeered the inn during the War of 1812. The prix-fixe Hunt breakfast consists of approximately eighteen dishes. You can be sure there will be scrambled eggs, bacon, sausages, grits, several salads, fresh fruits, and an array of fresh-baked breads, coffee cakes, and desserts. In addition, there might be pan-fried chicken, a pasta dish, hunter's stew, a fish special of the day, pecan French toast, cheddar hash browns, corned-beef hash, creamed chipped beef, English muffins, and corn bread. You must reserve ahead, as the inn is a mob scene every Sunday. You are seated in one of three charming dining rooms; the wood-paneled Library with fireplace, the musket-laden Gun Room, or the Steamboat Room, which resembles the dining salon of an old steamboat. A staffer takes your drinks order, and you are free to meander to the buffet line, returning for seconds if you like (most people do). There is no charge for children under six years. Consider this brunch Sunday dinner. You won't be hungry again all day.

Griswold Inn

Main Street

Essex, CT 06426

(860) 767–1776

www.griswoldinn.com

$

Every time we visit Branford's well-named Le Petit Café, which seats a mere fifty, we wonder how chef-owner Roy Ip manages to serve a first-rate, five-course prix-fixe dinner for such a modest price.

Another surprise: how quickly and smoothly the staff moves around in a closetlike space without losing their smiles and their cool. We also like the clever way huge mirrors are used to give the illusion of a larger room. There is nothing illusory, however, about the appealing French food served.

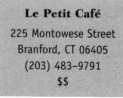

Le Petit Café

225 Montowese Street
Branford, CT 06405
(203) 483–9791
$$

Though the salad and appetizers are pre-set, guests have a choice among six diverse entrees and six dessert choices. The menu changes twice a month, so you may not encounter the zesty soft-shell crab *grenobloise,* sautéed in brown butter with lemon and capers, that we enjoyed, nor the Angus steak *au poivre* in a luscious brandy-peppercorn sauce. Nor a dessert gem like the rum-flavored bread pudding baked with Burgundy-poached pears, prunes, raisins, and almonds, served with a scoop of crème Chantilly. Never mind; there will be choices equally delicious on your visit. You can count on it.

three meals—breakfast, lunch, and dinner. You might watch the corn bread cooking in a black iron "spider" pan right over the open fire. At dinner a three-course prix-fixe menu usually includes at least one vintage dish, like our favorite, Thomas Jefferson's authentic bread pudding, laced with Bourbon and served warm with fresh-whipped cream, made from his family "receipt." If it is on the frequently changing menu, try the roast capon with wild-rice stuffing. An a la carte dinner menu is also available. Waitresses in long skirts, rooms lighted by mirrored wall sconces, candles, and the hearth embers add to a rare dining experience for the entire family. Home sweet hearth indeed.

Restaurant Bravo Bravo, 20 East Main Street, Mystic, CT 06355; (860) 536–3228; $$. Small, smart, and stylish, Bravo Bravo is a surprise to find in a much-visited tourist town like Mystic, where faster food is the norm. Chef-owner Bob Sader's Italian-accented menu more than lives up to the urbane interior of white walls, mirrors, oak floors, and tables. We think the pasta dishes are the most inspired, especially the chicken and walnut ravioli Marsala, if it is on the menu when you visit. Black-pepper fettuccine tossed with grilled scallops and sun-dried tomatoes in a Gorgonzola Alfredo is another knockout, and we are partial as well to the osso buco and veal medallion stuffed with garlic, spinach, and cheese.

Restaurant du Village, 59 Main Street, Chester, CT 06412; (860) 526–5301; $$$. Discreet, with its lace cafe curtains shielding the windows, and elegant, with fresh flowers, fine napery, cushioned chairs, and expertly trained staff, this restaurant in the small and charming town of Chester deserves high praise for its superior French fare, the creation of Alsatian chef-owner Michel Keller and his wife Cynthia. In what might be an outpost of France, you may dine on roast leg of lamb, quail with green grapes, or pan-seared tuna with a tapenade. The menu changes often, but virtually everything is top-notch. Desserts, like the breads and nearly all else, are made on the premises.

Roomba, 1044 Chapel Street, New Haven, CT 06510; (203) 562–7666; $$. When Roomba (yes, *Room*-bah) opened in 2000, it introduced to Connecticut Caribbean cooking with a hip modern beat, melding tropical ingredients with European cooking techniques: in short, Caribbean fusion cooking that is smart, fun, and sometimes fantastic. A basement locale has been converted into several stylish, soft-lit dining areas with banquettes, from which you can watch the action in the open kitchen. Part of the fun at Roomba is the plate presentations—citrus-marinated ceviche served in a coconut shell boat with plantain and yucca chip "sails" and smoky, slow-roasted pork loin stacked in a "pyramid," come to mind. Desserts, too, have a Latin beat, especially the *tres leches* and *churros*. All right, everybody, one-two-three, let's Roomba!

Union League Café, 1032 Chapel Street, New Haven, CT 06510; (203) 562–4299; www.unionleaguecafe.com; $$$. This isn't just the handsomest dining room in New Haven (in our view), it is also in one of the city's historic structures, the Sherman Building, erected in 1860 on the site of the house of Roger Sherman. He was New Haven's first mayor and the only man to sign all three founding documents of the fledgling United States. Stately, neoclassic, with pink-granite columns, a welcoming fireplace, and wide windows overlooking Chapel Street, the room makes a worthy stage for the polished French-brasserie cooking of chef-owner Jean-Pierre Vuillermet. His moules marinières

Best Bookstore-Cafe

Bookstore cafes are often utilitarian places for a quick bite while shopping. That isn't the case at R.J. Café, whose delicious quiches, soups, and sandwiches make it a favorite lunch destination for locals. A creative menu, with daily soups and quiches, makes R.J.'s special, as dothe friendly staff and helpful manager, Mike Quinn. The cafe snuggles in the rear of R.J. Julia Booksellers on Madison's main street, but it has its own patio and parking lot. The well-known bookshop stages many events with celebrity authors like Garrison Keillor and Anne

R.J. Café
768 Boston Post Road
Madison, CT 06443
(203) 318–0706
$.

Rice, many of whom pop into the cafe for a snack or coffee after their book signings, a bonus that cafe patrons seem to enjoy. With only seven tables inside and nine on the patio, you will feel lucky if you manage to snare a table with a window seat, covered with cushions, in front of a bow window. The big bowl of soup and half-sandwich combination is good value. We are partial to the chicken sandwiches, namely the herb-roasted chicken breast and lemon-basil chicken salad. There are sandwiches for the kids, too. The cafe is open all day until 9:00 or 10:00 P.M. most nights, making a light supper possible. Call ahead just to be sure.

and coquilles St. Jacques are mouthwatering ways to begin a meal, followed by seared wild king salmon, roasted duck breast with figs, or roasted monkfish. Crepes aux marrons, bittersweet chocolate mousse, and house-made ice creams complete a meal that you will probably long remember (we certainly did). *Note:* There is a succulent raw bar and also a less elaborate, less pricey bistro menu available in the bar on weeknights.

Brewpubs & Microbreweries

BAR (or BruRm@BAR), 254 Crown Street, New Haven, CT 06510; (203) 495–8924; www.niteimage.com/clubs/BAR. You don't have to be an Eli to enjoy the funky atmosphere of this multiplex a couple of blocks from Yale University. Nor is a degree in Beer Appreciation 101 required. This is a favorite watering hole for Yalies (and other thirsties) because of such attractions as Toasted Blonde, Damn Good Stout, a pleasingly bitter Pale Ale, plus an Amber Ale that has overtones of caramel malts (which goes down well with the top-notch house pizza). The building began life in 1915 as an upscale auto showroom, later had many other tenants, and then was empty for years. Randal Hoder and Stuart Press decided to brighten up the city's nightlife in 1991 by opening BAR here, a handsome discotheque for dancing where the fancy autos once reigned. Later, BruRm ("brew room") was added, as the city's first—and

only—brewpub. Lunches are served Wednesdays through Fridays and dinners Saturdays through Thursdays. The Front Room has a DJ for '60s-to-'90s–style dancing and an acoustic band on Sunday. The Back Room, flooded with music and lights, is dedicated to dancing, dancing, dancing, with a DJ. Call for schedule of hours.

Our Favorite Onion Rings

People can argue from here to eternity about the quality of onion rings, so let's be up front about our preferences. Not for us are those thick-cut onion rings in a batter so heavy they resemble Michelin tires. We like our onion rings cut razor-thin and lightly fried to golden, gossamer crispness. This is why the red-onion rings at Boom in Westbrook give us such pleasure. Skinny as shoestrings, Boom's rings are crispy and wonderful. Using red onions provides such flavor that the rings don't even need the horseradish-honey-mustard remoulade dip that is served with them. And delicious as other dishes are at Boom, we can happily make a meal of what are listed on the menu as "very thin red onion rings." What an understatement for such heavenly little circles.

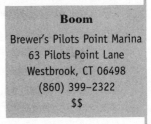

Boom

Brewer's Pilots Point Marina
63 Pilots Point Lane
Westbrook, CT 06498
(860) 399–2322
$$

Race Book Bar at Mohegan Sun, 1 Mohegan Sun Boulevard, Uncasville, CT 06382; (860) 233–4545. After navigating your way through the thicket of slots, tables, aisles, falling water, and "Indian theme" decor, you may locate the Race Book Bar, a brewpub in a casino. There you can watch races on the video screen and order your brew (featuring "extract brewery" ingredients—malt-syrup extracts that shortcut the process of finishing it on-site): namely, slightly dry Sachem Ale (malty with a touch of hops), Matagha Lager (plain and simple), or Cold Moon Ale (really cold, but light). Or hedge your bets and order a Bud or Sam Adams. The Bar has light food, but for serious eating you can dine on the casino premises at one of more than eleven restaurants, buffets, and food courts offering gourmet, casual, or serve-yourself fare. Race Book Bar hours: daily, 11:00 A.M. to race finales at 1:00 A.M.

Wine Trail

Connecticut Wine Trail, www.ctwine.com, offers three trail plans that show where ten of the state's wineries are located, how to reach them, and important information about each one (hours for tastings, tours, picnicking, nearby points of interest). In this area, Chamard, Jonathan Edwards, and Stonington are the wineries included in Connecticut Wine Trail, Trip 2, which can be printed from the Web site listed above. At this writing, Haight's Mystic "Vineyard" was not yet listed for printout.

Chamard Vineyards, 115 Cow Hill Road, Clinton, CT 06413; (860) 664–0299; www.chamard.com. William Chaney (CEO and chairman of Tiffany & Co., New York) and his family planted their first five acres of vines in 1984 at their Chamard property just 2 miles inland from Long Island Sound. Clinton was an old seaport town in colonial days, and its location has a maritime microclimate that is mild in winter with a lengthy growing season. These factors, plus rich, stony soil, favor European grapes such as the Chardonnay, Cabernet Sauvignon, Pinot Noir, Merlot, and Cabernet Franc that Chamard grows. Their first wine for the market was a

1998 Chardonnay, released for sale the next year. Now expanded to twenty acres, Chamard has devoted much of its land to Chardonnay, which has won kudos and gold medals in competitions. The impressive chateau-style main building gives a panoramic overview of the vineyards. Don't miss the airy tasting room with its impressive stone fireplace and soaring cathedral ceiling, built with wooden beams from ancient trees that were cut on the property. Tours and tastings are offered year-round, Wednesday through Saturday, from 11:00 A.M. to 4:00 P.M.

Haight Vineyard—Mystic, Coogan Boulevard, Mystic, CT 06355; (860) 535–1222; www.haightvineyards.com. This Haight "Vineyard" is located just off I–95, exit 9, across the Olde Mistick Village parking area from the Mystic Acquarium. Its "winery" is more of a sales point and tasting room for the main Haight vineyard's output in Northwest Connecticut. Displays of winemaking history cover the walls, Haight wines are sold, and visits to the "mini-apple winery," Tank Room Wine Bar, and gift shop are invited. Free tastings and self-guided tours are available Mondays through Saturdays from 10:00 A.M. to 6:00 P.M. and Sundays from noon to 5:00 P.M. in summer.

Jonathan Edwards Winery, 74 Chester Maine Road, North Stonington, CT 06359; (860) 535–0202; www.jedwardswinery.com. One of Connecticut's newest wineries was established in one of its old whaling villages (Stonington) in 2001 by the Edwards family. The panoramic view of Long Island Sound is possible from the winery's hilltop complex. Part of the complex is an 1880 vintage dairy barn that Jonathan Edwards converted into a unique winery. While living in Napa Valley, California, he selected specific vineyards and grapes he wanted in his

Finding Stonecroft is not easy, tucked into the wooded countryside as it is, a short, convoluted, off-the-track ride from Foxwoods Casino, but light years away in spirit. Even when you have found the country-inn complex, the dining room itself seems devilishly elusive, until you learn the trick of walking around the building and entering through the terrace on the far side (otherwise you are going up and down stairs needlessly). Once inside the dining room, the pleasure unfolds seamlessly. With its fieldstone walls, pine floors, gas fireplace, and lounge chairs for waiting, the room has a manorial aspect. The American food, though, is decidedly

Stonecroft

515 Pumpkin Hill Road
Ledyard, CT 06339
(860) 572-0771
$$$

modern, with such dishes as pan-roasted duck breast with duck confit, braised pork shoulder on Gorgonzola ravioli, and grilled filet mignon over a truffled-oyster-mushroom ragout. Chef Drew Egy, son of the owners, knows what he is doing and does it with flair. If you want to spend the night—and considering the difficulty of finding your way in, it is not a bad idea—there are ten attractive guest rooms.

own wines. He then contracted with vintners for hand picking and processing of these grapes into "young wine." This is transported in refrigerated trucks to his Connecticut winery for barrel aging and bottling. The result is "Napa Valley/Connecticut" wines of Chardonnay, Merlot, Cabernet Sauvignon, Syrah, and Zinfandel grapes. Meanwhile, as the Edwardses' vines here mature, their grapes will be used in locally produced Chardonnay, Riesling, Gewürztraminer, and Cabernet Franc wines. Visitors may sample Napa-bred wines in the tasting room Wednesdays through Sundays year-round, from 11:00 A.M. to 5:00 P.M. Tours are at 2:00, 3:00 and 4:00 P.M. on those days, and picnicking is encouraged. Mrs. Edwards invites visitors to their Spring Fest in early June and their Harvest Fest in mid-October, when fresh food and music augment the enjoyment of the wines.

Stonington Vineyards, 523 Taugwonk Road, Stonington, CT 06378; (800) 421–WINE or (860) 535–1222; www.stoningtonvineyards.com. In 1987 Nick and Happy Smith, impressed by the maritime microclimate and long, cool growing season of the area, bought south-sloping Stonington uplands for their vineyard. Conditions were comparable to those in Bordeaux, and the Smiths have focused their twelve acres on European-style wines and have won awards for their barrel-fermented Chardonnay, as well as their Pinot Noirs and Rieslings. They also grow Gewürztraminer, Cabernet Franc, and Fumé Vidal Blanc grapes. Their sprawling assembly of buildings includes modern processing machinery and tanks. There is a free, forty-five-minute conducted tour of the winemaking process at 2:00 P.M. The Smiths host several winery events during the year: Spring Cellar-bration and Barrel Tasting is held in May (they originally called it the Bud-Break Celebration but a herd of thirsty "bikers" descended, looking for "the beer blast"). There is a Summer Cellar-Bration Clambake in late July and an October Harbor Festival, which includes picking grapes and watching the crush. With each event, expect live bands, food from participating restaurants—and plenty of wine. A tasting room is open year-round, from 11:00 A.M. to 5:00 P.M. daily (at a small charge); also for sale are New England food products, jellies, jams, crackers, honey, and maple syrup.

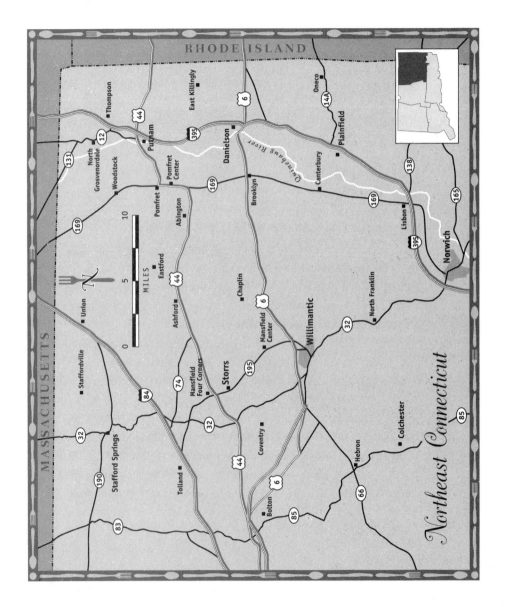

RHODE ISLAND

Thompson

44

12

North
Grosvenordale

131

Woodstock

169

Union

Staffordville

32

Stafford Springs

190

Tolland

83

84

74

32

44

6

Bolton

85

East Killingly

6

Putnam

395

Danielson

Pomfret
Center

Pomfret

Abington

Eastford

Ashford

44

169

Chaplin

Mansfield
Four Corners

Storrs

195

Mansfield
Center

6

Brooklyn

Quinebaug River

Willimantic

Coventry

Oneco

14A

Plainfield

138

Canterbury

169

169

Lisbon

395

165

Norwich

North Franklin

32

Colchester

85

Hebron

66

MASSACHUSETTS

MILES

N

10

5

0

Northeast Connecticut

Northeast Connecticut

Connecticut is a state composed of scores of small towns, most with a single zip code. This is quickly apparent in the northeast area, sometimes called "the quiet corner." "Peaceful" or "tranquil" would be just as appropriate a sobriquet, for this is a land of rolling hills, woodlands, marshes, ponds, brooks, small streams, and clusters of state forests and state parks like Mashamoquet Brook near Pomfret. It is also a land of dairy farms, pasturelands, an abundance of apple, peach, and pear orchards, and fields and fields of strawberries and blueberries. The largest grower of organic mushrooms in the United States is here.

Such expansive farmland is punctuated with hamlets and villages whose historic original names can be found on a map of the world: Lebanon, Hebron, Lisbon, Coventry, Canterbury. Yet each of these towns is quintessentially New England. Many have deep roots in American history, like Coventry, where hero Nathan Hale was born and his family farmhouse can be visited. Also in Coventry is a large herb farm, famous for its herb lunches and lectures. In Norwich, on the Thames River, traitor Benedict Arnold was born. Norwich was also home to Col. Christopher Leffingwell, a supplier for Washington's Continental Army; his historic home is open to view. The town's current claim to fame is a spa-and-inn complex, considered the most elegant spa in the state.

In Lebanon, with its town-long green, George Washington stabled his horse during the American Revolution. The Wadsworth stable is still there, still viewable. The state's only colonial governor, Jonathan Trumbull, lived in this town; his house, too, is open to visitors. Peaceful Canterbury has the restored home of Prudence Crandall, an intrepid Quaker who established the first school for African-American girls in pre–Civil War America.

Quiet does not mean somnolent, as the presence here of so many farmers, dairymen, and food entrepreneurs attests. There is even a new distillery in the area, dedicated to making eau-de-vie. The University of Connecticut in the bucolic hills around Storrs began life as an agricultural land-grant college and is now a prestigious university with two famous basketball teams (male and female), but the rich homemade ice cream sold at the university's dairy bar is almost as popular in the region as the Huskies mascot.

Brooklyn and Pomfret are pastoral New England villages, whose environs now encompass vineyards, a bison farm where American buffalo roam free, maple sugarhouses, scores of orchards, and a unique restaurant in the middle of a working farm. On the green in Woodstock is one of the most unusual historic houses in the state—the vibrant-pink Roseland Cottage, a rare example of Gothic Revival outside and in. Its many celebrated nineteenth-century visitors included four U.S. presidents. Food lovers in Woodstock may be almost as delighted by one of the area's largest apple orchards and farm store across the green.

Nearby Putnam, named for American Revolutionary War hero Israel Putnam, is a classic example of the Connecticut enterprising spirit. When its large textile-manufacturing companies moved out of state, Putnam didn't just sit passively and expire. Over the past ten years, it has reinvented itself and become the major antiques center of southern New England. With all the antiques buffs descending on the town, new restaurants and food suppliers soon followed. Presently, Putnam fairly bustles with renewed Yankee spunk. In Willimantic, what was once the largest thread mill in the United States has been converted into a museum of the textile industry, but of even greater interest to beer drinkers is the way the town's old post office has been recycled into a lively brewery, brewpub, and cafe.

As we were saying, *quiet* in this area is no synonym for *boring*, as the following pages will reveal.

Made or Grown Here

Bibelicious Sauces, Inc., 26 Hawks Landing, Hebron, CT 06248; (860) 228–0745. Frank Parseliti has a track record in the marinara-sauce business, having developed his first commercial sauce in 1993 from recipes used over the years in his family's restaurant, Frank's, in Hartford. In 1995 the restaurant closed, and Frank, son of the original Frank's, began expanding his line. Now there are four sauces: Marinara,

Basil & Roasted Garlic, Spicy Fra Diavolo, and Vodka. Several factors make his chunky, textured sauces so fresh tasting: all natural ingredients, no added sugars, and the use of whole peeled tomatoes and extra-virgin olive oil. The sauces and Frank's new garlic bread are distributed to 600 stores throughout Connecticut. In this area, you will find them at Stop & Shop and Highland Park Market in Coventry.

Cato Corner Farm, 178 Cato Corner Road, Colchester, CT 06415; (860) 537-3884; e-mail: catocornerfarm@mindspring.com. Elizabeth MacAlister and her son Mark Gillman produce some remarkable artisan farmstead cheeses from the raw milk of a small herd of seventeen-to-twenty-five Jersey cows, pasture fed and raised without hormones or chemical fertilizers. Half of the seventy-five-acre farm is pastureland, so these Jerseys have a carefree, free-ranging life, which is probably why their cheese is so delicious and distinctive. Raw-milk cheese must be aged at least sixty days, so Elizabeth, who began making cheeses in 1997 (joined by Mark two years later), built an underground cave for the eleven different types of cheese to age properly at a temperature of 50 to 55 degrees. Their most popular cheese is the creamy Bridgid's Abbey, made from a traditional Belgian recipe. Newest is the earthy Petite Vâche, which is well paired with wine. Various cheeses are sold at Priam Vineyards in Colchester and at Lyman Orchards, Middlefield. You might taste them also at the Golden Lamb Buttery in Brooklyn and at the Restaurant du Village in Chester. Elizabeth and Mark sell their cheeses at farmers' markets in the area and in New York City and directly by e-mail or phone, with one- or two-day delivery via UPS. On Saturday mornings from Thanksgiving to Christmas, you may buy right at the farm.

Creamery Brook Bison, 19 Purvis Road, Brooklyn, CT 06234; (860) 779–0837; e-mail: dtanner@neca.com. You may not think of Connecticut as the home where the buffalo roam, but Deborah and Austin Tanner are raising bison (American buffalo) on their one-hundred-acre farm, so if you happen to be driving by and see 110 bison grazing in a meadow, you are not hallucinating. Deborah praises buffalo as "the original health food" because the red meat is all-natural, low-fat, with fewer calories and less cholesterol than the usual beef, chicken, and turkey. The animals are fed only corn, grain, and grass, absolutely no growth hormones or antibiotics. The Tanners sell their meat (processed for them in Stafford Springs) at Rain Desert in Danielson and Nature's Way in Lebanon, but mostly they sell directly from the shop on their farm. Frozen steaks, ground meat and patties, short ribs, Texas ribs, and shanks and boneless ribs and steaks are all available. Tours of the fields to see the free-roaming bison by wagon are conducted Saturdays at 1:30 P.M. from July to October. Shop hours are April through October, Monday through Friday from 2:00 to 6:00 P.M. and Saturday from 10:00 A.M. to 2:00 P.M. Off-season, November through March, the hours are the same, but the shop is closed on Mondays and Tuesdays.

Fish Family Farm, 20 Dimock Lane, Bolton, CT 06043; (860) 646–9745. Driving up to the dairy store at this beautiful 211-acre farm, you will see Jersey cows grazing in the meadows. In 1981 Don and Sharon Fish bought what was then a "gentleman's farm" and turned it into a real working farm with a forty-five-cow herd of registered Jerseys. They built a bottling plant, and they now process, pasteurize, homogenize, and bottle their own milk, which they sell to Highland Park Market in Manchester and to Munson's Chocolates in Bolton, which uses the milk and cream in chocolate making. Don Fish jokes that "our milk has been in outer space, because our astronauts made a gift of Munson's Chocolates to the Russian astronauts on the space station." Inside the spotless little store is a freezer, where the premium-quality Fish Family Farm Creamery Ice Cream is sold by the quart. There are eight rich flavors: vanilla, maple walnut, coffee, peanut butter chip, cherry vanilla, chocolate chip, Heath bar, and chocolate. There are also a few jams and jellies for sale. Sales are on the honor system most of the year, but in summer, high-school students are hired to scoop and serve the ice cream. Hours are from 8:00 A.M. to 6:00 P.M. daily, except Sunday; summer hours are from 8:00 A.M. to 8:00 P.M., also except Sunday. There are no organized tours of the farm, but visitors are invited to wander around on their own and may watch the 4:30 P.M. milking if they wish.

Foxfire Farm, 85 South Bedlam Road, Mansfield Center, CT 06250; (860) 455-0739. Elisa Santee and her family run a 140-acre dairy farm, with a herd of twenty-five Jersey cows, bottling and selling their licensed raw milk and farmhouse cheese to health-food stores and to the Willimantic Food Cooperative in Willimantic. The Santees' aged farmhouse cheese (made from raw milk) is an old Polish recipe from Elisa's family. It has a high butterfat content and melts nicely for cooking. The farm's ten pasture-raised Dorset sheep provide lamb products that are also sold to many Connecticut health-food stores. Though

Foxfire has no sales facility at the farm, if you call Elisa, she will tell you where the public can buy their products.

Westford Hill Distillers, 196 Chatey Road, Ashford, CT 06278; (860) 429–0464; www.westfordhill.com. Margaret Chatey and husband, Louis, have gone in for "artisan distilling" on the 200-acre hilltop farm that the family has worked since 1919. In a huge New England barn, they have installed a state-of-the-art distillery that produces eau-de-vie—the clear, fruit-flavored liqueur that is a popular tradition in Europe. "We were licensed in 1998," says Margaret, who runs the project from mashing to marketing, "and sold our first fruit spirits in 1999." The line of eaux-de-vies includes cherry (kirsch), raspberry (framboise), strawberry (fraise), plum, apple, and pear (Pear William), which won a gold medal in one competition. Their liqueurs, in beautiful elongated bottles with the appropriate fruit charmingly depicted on the label, are now in liquor stores and restaurants throughout the state. Distillery visits can be arranged if you call ahead.

Specialty Stores & Markets

Caprilands Herb Farm, 534 Silver Street, Coventry, CT 06238; (860) 742–7244; www.caprilands.com. This fifty-acre herb farm, with shop, gardens, greenhouse, and tearoom, was developed by the late Adelma Grenier Simmons and is still being maintained by her husband, Edward Cook. At the Gift Barn, you can buy packets of the herbs grown

MARY POPPINS
IN AN HERB GARDEN

We were fortunate to meet Adelma Grenier Simmons back in the 1970s, when we visited Caprilands for several of her herb lectures and herbal lunches and subsequently wrote magazine articles about her. A short, stocky lady whose dress usually had a cape, she had the fey charm of a pixie and the "take charge" character of a reliable governess. We half-expected her to unfurl a Mary Poppins umbrella and fly away. She was a respected herbalist, horticulturist, lecturer, and author of many books on herbs. Her lectures about the herbs in her various gardens—Silver Gardens, Shakespeare, Victorian, Curious Knotted Garden, among others—were marked by spicy comments, a mischievous twinkle, and reams of folk wisdom. "Caraway seed," she said, "was once fed to straying husbands to get them to return home. If you don't want him back, hide the caraway." In showing silver rosemary, she observed, "It is tasty in tea, but if you don't drink tea, you can wash your hair in it." Pointing to nasturtiums in a vegetable garden, she said, "We decorate salads with them, but the *real* reason they're with the vegetables is to keep aphids away." "Why the name Caprilands?" we asked her. The name stemmed from the fact that goats were raised on the farm when her family bought it in 1929 ("capri" is the Latin root for "goat"). Her interest in herbs began as a hobby, grew into a passion and finally into a business, which still exists, pretty much as she left it.

on the grounds, Adelma's paperback cookbooks with her herb recipes, other books, and many herb-related gifts. At the Greenhouse are plants and a complete line of herbs for sale. And if you have made advance reservations, you might enjoy a Caprilands afternoon tea (Sundays at 2:00 P.M.) or herb lunch with lecture (Saturdays), from early May to Christmas. At lunch every dish contains an herb or two grown on the grounds. Both tea and lunch in the eighteenth-century farmhouse are served in three rooms, which are decorated with potpourris, herb bouquets, wreaths, and big wooden bowls filled with rose petals, lavender, lemon verbena, and other herbs.

Colchester Bakery, 96 Lebanon Avenue, Colchester, CT 06415; (860) 537–2415. In a large building on a side street, some of the area's best Jewish rye bread, Russian pumpernickel, challah, Vienna bread, rye, and babka are turned out daily. In the showroom in front, on any given day the display cases are full of fresh fruit pies, coffee cakes, brick-oven-baked bagels (garlic,  sesame, onion, among them), turnovers, biscotti, crispy elephant ears, assorted Danish pastries, black and whites, éclairs, and other pastries. There is a self-serve coffee bar along one side, convenient for a drink along with a Danish.

Martha's Herbary, 589 Pomfret Street (junction of Routes 44, 97, 169), Pomfret, CT 06258; (860) 928–0009; www.marthasherbary.com. Just across the road from the Vanilla Bean Café, this unusual shop, located behind the old house where shop owners Richard and Martha Paul live, sells herbs and herb books, along with rare teas and various nonedibles. The parking lot is behind the house on Route 169 and leads into the shop. There you will find eighteen types of fresh basil, tarragon, sorrel, and other herbs, as well as clothes, scarves, jewelry, hats, potpourris, and other gift items. Visitors are free to wander through the herb gardens and admire the sunken garden, the pond with a waterfall, and the birdhouse fence.

Mrs. Bridge's Pantry, 136 Main Street, Putnam, CT 06260; (860) 963-7040 or (888) 591-5253; www.mrsbridgespantry.com. In relatively cramped space, Diana Jackson and Veronica Harris have packed an entire world of imported British goodies. There are teas like Fortnum & Mason, Jackson's of Piccadilly, Yorkshire, London Herb & Spice, and Metropolitan. Other offerings include McVities and other biscuits, Cadbury chocolate bars (imported), Fry's chocolate, Uncle Joe's mint balls, and preserves and jams. A freezer contains English bangers, (made by an English butcher in California), sausage rolls, meat pies, Cornish pasties, steak and kidney pies, and blood sausages. There are English teapots, accessories, and gift items for sale as well. Connected to the shop is a tearoom that seats twelve at four tables (with outdoor tables in warm weather) and serves lunch (Cornish pasties, ploughman's lunch, vegetable curry, shepherd's pie,

Tipsy Pudding

Diana Jackson, co-owner of Mrs. Bridge's Pantry in Putnam, recommends this recipe for Tipsy Pudding, which comes from a vintage (1936) English cookbook. Such pudding, similar to trifle, has a long pedigree in England. Depending on how liberally you sprinkle it with wine, rum, or brandy, it could make you tipsy. No problem with that in this recipe, which we have modified.

3 ounces plus 1 teaspoon sugar

3 ounces butter

3 ounces flour

3 lightly beaten eggs

2 tablespoons rum or brandy

1. Cream 3 ounces of sugar with the butter and work in the flour. Mix lightly. Add eggs and mix thoroughly.
2. Pour mixture in a well-buttered cake tin, sprinkled lightly with sugar. Place in a preheated 350°F oven. Bake 40 minutes, or until cake has risen and is golden brown. Remove to a rack and let it cool briefly (10 minutes at most).
3. Sprinkle all over the top with rum or brandy and remaining spoonful of sugar. If you want more of a kick, add an additional tablespoonful of liquor. Serve warm with a dollop of whipped cream on top.

Serves 4.

Mrs. Bridge's Pantry

136 Main Street
Putnam, CT 06260
(860) 963-7040
www.mrsbridgepantry.com

among other dishes) and afternoon tea (with crumpets, scones, clotted cream, pastries made locally, Eccles cake, tea sandwiches, and house-made strawberry jam from the owner's own berry patch). Diana and Veronica have moved their shop five times since they opened in 1991 with five shelves in a corner of the town's first antiques shop. Having been seven years in their present location, they consider it permanent.

Munson's Chocolates, Route 6, P.O. Box 9217, Bolton, CT 06043; (860) 649–4332 or (888) 686–7667; www.munsonschocolates.com. When Ben and Josephine opened their first candy store in 1946 in Manchester, they called it the Dandy Candy Company. Ben mixed up batches of creams and caramels and hand dipped them in chocolate; then Josephine would package assortments for sale. Their young business caught on and is now the largest retail chocolate manufacturer in Connecticut, run by the third generation of Munsons. The myriad assortments are sold via mail order, on-line, and in the twelve Munson shops. Among the boxed assortments are gourmet truffles, chocolate-layered truffles, pecan-caramel patties, butter crunch, and chocolate cordial cherries. There are also candy bars, fudge in four flavors, peanut brittle, boxed fruit slices, and chocolate-covered pretzel rods. In the spanking-clean main shop at the Bolton factory, factory seconds of chocolate indulgence are sold. There is even a sugar-free chocolate line. If it can be made in chocolate, Munson's probably makes it.

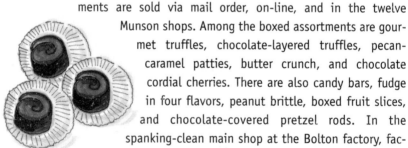

Maple Shortbread

While we usually make this shortbread at Christmas, it satisfies a sweet tooth any time of the year.

Bottom Layer
  ½ cup sugar
  2 cups flour
  ½ teaspoon salt
  1 cup (½ pound) chilled butter

Top Layer
  1¼ cups tightly packed brown
    sugar

⅔ cup pure maple syrup
2 eggs
4 tablespoons melted butter
1 teaspoon vanilla extract
1 teaspoon maple extract
½ teaspoon salt
2 cups chopped pecans

1. Heat oven to 350°F.
2. In a mixing bowl combine sugar, flour, and salt for the bottom layer. Cut in the chilled butter with a knife until the mixture is crumbly. It should not be smooth. Press as evenly as possible into a 9-by-13-inch baking pan. Bake until the surface is lightly browned but not thoroughly cooked, approximately 10 minutes. Remove from the oven and cool slightly, about 5 minutes.
3. While the bottom layer is in the oven, mix together all the ingredients (except the pecans) for the top layer: brown sugar, maple syrup, eggs, melted butter, vanilla, and maple extracts, and salt. Mix well until smooth. Spread the top layer over the cooled bottom layer. Sprinkle the pecans evenly over the entire top. Bake until the top layer is firm, 20 to 30 minutes. Cool on a rack about 10 minutes before cutting into squares or oblongs.

Makes approximately 36 bars.

Roy Apiary, 280C Killingly Road, Pomfret, CT 06259; (860) 928–6618. Mary and Joseph Roy's interest in honey began about twenty years ago, when a neighbor asked them to clean a swarm of bees out of an attic. Intrigued, Mary bought a hive and began cultivating the bees for honey. Now the Roys have thirty hives, with between 60,000 and 80,000 honeybees per hive, and sell their natural wildflower honey and three blends Mary has created: garlic, hot pepper, and mint honey. Mary's mint honey is her best-seller and has won awards two years in a row at the Connecticut Food Association. She sells the honey from home and at the Roy Family Pools & Billiards store, 570 Putnam Road, Plainfield (860–774–7702). Hours at both locales are from 9:00 A.M. to 6:00 P.M. daily. You may buy the honey by the half pound or up to a sixty-pound pail. Who buys such a large quantity of honey? Colchester Bakery for one, to use in their baking.

University of Connecticut Dairy Bar, 3636 Horsebarn Road Extension (off Route 195, Storrs), Storrs/Mansfield, CT 06268; (860) 486–2634; www.canr.uconn.edu/ansci/dairybar/dbar.htm. Fans consider this the best ice cream in this part of Connecticut, which may be why the simple store draws more than 100,000 visitors a year and has been a UConn icon for generations. Devotees love the ice cream for its creaminess and 14-percent butterfat content (with no additives). Since 2003 the trip to the Dairy Bar isn't necessary; the ice cream is now made by Royal Ice Cream, a small family-owned Manchester factory, and is at Stop & Shops and other supermarkets throughout the state. Twenty of the twenty-four flavors are still being made at UConn as well. The most famous flavor is

Jonathan the Husky Dog (vanilla swirled with peanut butter and choco-late-covered peanuts), named for UConn's mascot. Also popular are Scholar Chip, Midnight Madness, chocolate cappuccino, coffee espresso crunch, peanut butter cup, and peppermint stick.

Farmers' Markets

For up-to-the-minute information about dates and times, call Con-necticut Department of Agriculture at (860) 713–2503, visit the Web site at www.state.ct.us/doag/, or e-mail at ctdeptag@po.state.ct.us.

Danielson Farmers' Market, Killingly Memorial Library, 25 Wescott Road and Route 12, Danielson. Wednesdays from 4:00 to 6:00 P.M. and Saturdays from 9:00 A.M. to noon, mid-June through October.

Norwich Farmers' Market, Uncas on Thames (Route 32), Norwich. Wednesdays from 10:00 A.M. to 1:00 P.M., mid-July through October.

Plainfield Farmers' Market, Recreations Office, Senior Center, 482 Norwich Road (Route 2), Plainfield. Tuesdays from 4:00 to 6:00 P.M., mid-June through October.

Putnam Farmers' Market, Kennedy Drive and Bridge Street, Putnam. Mondays and Thursdays from 4:00 to 6:00 P.M., mid-June through October.

A CAUTIONARY TALE

Back in the late eighteenth century, Connecticut's Mohegan Indians asked the state assembly for relief, as their once-plentiful food supplies had been ruined by the European immigrants. The Mohegans explained that their forefathers could run into the woods and kill deer, raccoon, fowl, and bear, and in the rivers and along the seashores could fill their canoes with fish and shellfish. Wild fruits, nuts, and beans were available for the taking. But with the arrival of the white man, all this had changed.

Stafford Springs Farmers' Market, Mocko's Lot (junction of Routes 32 and 190), Stafford Springs. Thursdays from 1:00 to 4:00 P.M., early July through October.

Storrs Farmers' Market, St. Mark's Episcopal Church, 42 North Eagleville Road, Storrs. Saturdays from 3:00 to 6:00 P.M., first week in May through mid-November.

Tolland Farmers' Market, Tolland Green, Tolland. Saturdays from 9:00 A.M. to 1:00 P.M., first week in June through October.

Willimantic Farmers' Market, corner of Main and Jackson Streets, Willimantic. Tuesdays from 1:30 to 5:00 P.M. and Saturdays from 7:30 A.M. to noon, mid-June through October.

Bats of Bedlam Maple Syrup, 101 Bedlam Road (on Route 198), Chaplin, CT 06235; (860) 455–9200; e-mail: dubos@neca.com. It's not bats but maple syrup that Pat and Bob Dubos have focused on for thirty years on their Bedlam farm, turning buckets of top-quality maple sap from acres of "sugar bush" dedicated maple trees into syrup and sugar for waffles, pancakes, and other tasties. Their first-of-the-year run of syrup and sugar begins in March and continues into April. You will find the maple sweets by the posted sign at their address, but call ahead. And don't worry . . . no bats. That name refers to the years that Bob Dubos was a vertebrate zoologist and curator of the research collection, which included bats, at the University of Connecticut.

Blackmer Farm, 438 Quinebaug Road, North Grosvenordale, CT 06255; (860) 923–2710; e-mail: rblackmer@poweruser.com. With ten greenhouses, forty cows, forty acres of sweet corn, a roster of fresh vegetables, and a farm stand on their family farm, Myrtie and Randy Blackmer really need the help of sons Tod and Mark and nieces, too. It is not a pick-your-own place, but you will find these vegetables are harvested fresh daily when in season: cauliflower, eggplant, broccoli, peppers, summer squash, wax beans, melons, pumpkins, loads of sweet corn and tomatoes, as well as plants and flowers. Their farm stand is open from mid-July to frost, daily from 10:00 A.M. to 6:00 P.M. Take Route 12 north, then left on Route 131 north.

Buells Orchard's
Apple Walnut Cake

Patty Sandress, wife of Jeffrey of Buells Orchard, has a favorite recipe, using the apples for which Buells is famous.

3 eggs	½ teaspoon baking powder
1 cup cooking oil	1 teaspoon baking soda
2 cups sugar	¾ teaspoon nutmeg
3 teaspoons vanilla	3 teaspoons cinnamon
3 cups flour	2 cups chopped apples
1 teaspoon salt	1 cup chopped walnuts

1. Preheat oven to 300°F and grease and flour a bundt pan.
2. Beat eggs and add oil, sugar, and vanilla. Cream until fluffy. Add dry ingredients and mix thoroughly. Stir in chopped apples and nuts.
3. Put batter into the bundt pan and bake for 45 minutes at 300°F. Increase heat to 325°F and bake 20 minutes longer. Cool for 15 minutes and remove from pan.

Serves 6.

Buells Orchard

108 Crystal Pond Road
Eastford, CT 06242
(860) 974-1150

Buells Orchard, 108 Crystal Pond Road, Eastford, CT 06242; (860) 974–1150. Henry Buell bought 120 acres here in 1889 and planted Rhode Island Greening apples. Even today his great-grandchildren, Jonathan and Jeffrey Sandness, have followed his lead. They now raise twenty types of apples (Macouns are their best seller; Ginger Gold and Honey Crisp are their newest). They also have two acres of blueberries and grow peaches, pears, strawberries, cantaloupe, tomatoes, peppers, yellow and green squash, eggplant, and pumpkins, all available for picking, except the pears, which are sold (with the other produce) at the store inside one of the farm buildings. Also for sale there are jams, jellies, local honey, and, in fall, fresh-cut chrysanthemums. A big treat for visitors is watching the candied-apple-processing machine. Buells is New England's only seasonal processor and from late August to Halloween three quarters of a million apples go through the machine—forty-five to fifty apples per minute—entering as naked, unadorned apples and emerging rolled in cinnamon-flavored caramel with coconut topping, taffy-covered with Heath bar chunks, Jazzy (with fall sprinkles embedded all over), or covered in peanuts or sprinkles. It is a fascinating process to watch. The store (off Route 198 via Westford Road) is open mid-June into May the following year. Check for days and hours, which change each season.

Chase Road Growers, 174 Chase Road, Thompson, CT 06277; (860) 923–9926; e-mail: chaserdgrowers.@aol.com. Jayne and Warren Reynolds have a nursery that specializes in flowers until fall, but their big red barn is where they sell fresh vegetables in season. Expect sweet corn, tomatoes, peppers, cucumbers, and other vegetables as they ripen, with pumpkins and gourds available later on. Open mid-July to October from 10:00 A.M. to 5:00 or 6:00 P.M.

Fort Hill Farms, 260 Quaddick Road, Thompson, CT 06277; (860) 923–3439. What was once an Indian fortress has been a busy farm for the past century. Kristen and Peter Orr have put scientific research on disease-resistant, sweet strawberries to maximum use on their eight acres, producing seventeen varieties of berries whose antecedents hail from France, England, and Chile. The Orr berries ripen at various times and make their season, which begins in May, unusually long. It is wise to call to find out when the berries are ripe for your picking. Two acres of blueberries are pickable from July into September. In addition, on their 410 acres, Kristin and Peter have 400 cows, sixty-two gardens bursting with flowers in summer, and an unusually large nursery for perennials. The flowers are for sale from May through November.

Franklin Mushroom Farms, 931 Route 32, North Franklin, CT 06254; (860) 642–3000; www.franklinfarms.com. In the rolling hillsides around Franklin, it is hard to miss the sprawling white building occupying eight acres where a variety of organic mushrooms are grown year-round in a controlled environment, without pesticides. Because of the need for such a regulated environment, it is not possible to tour the

facility, but you may buy the various mushrooms in two-pound bags at the farm store near the road. Portobellos, "pleurotes" (oyster mushrooms), maitakes, shiitakes, enokis, beech, criminis, and white buttons (also known by their Latin name *Agaricus bisporus*) are all available, as well as veggie burgers, veggie and soy meatballs, and jars of marinated, spicy garlic and baby portobello mushrooms. Even if you miss a farm visit, you are probably buying Franklin Farm mushrooms when you shop at Shaw's, Stop & Shop, and other markets. The mushrooms are distributed throughout New England, one of Connecticut's few agricultural crops exported to other states. In fact, Franklin Farms is the largest grower and harvester of certified organic mushrooms in the United States. Open year-round, 8:00 A.M. to 5:00 P.M. daily.

Lapsley Orchard, 403 Orchard Hill Road (Route 169), Pomfret Center, CT 06259; (860) 928–9186. John Wolchesky has been farming this 200-acre farm for the past twenty years and can provide you with a wide variety of fruit and vegetables. There are twenty-eight types of apples, for instance, ranging from the popular McIntosh and Macouns to the new Honeycrest and Braeburns. The prize is the century-old apple tree that still produces Gravensteins. Pick-your-own-ers are welcome to tackle the apples as soon as the earliest ones ripen—the Jerseymacs usually are first in early August—continuing into October. John has sixteen varieties of peaches, twelve of pears, and also nectarines. His twenty acres of vegetables include sweet corn, tomatoes, and pumpkins and fresh flowers for cutting from mid-July onward. His farm stand sells jams, jellies, and sweet cider, as well as all the produce. In addition, there are free horse-drawn hayrides on Sundays in September and October. Open daily, July–December, 10:00 A.M. to 6:00 P.M.

Adelma Simmons's
Spicy Pumpkin Bread

The late Adelma Grenier Simmons called this "a quick baking powder bread." We have adapted it from A Witch's Brew, *one of her many recipe books published by Caprilands Press and still in print.*

3½ cups flour	¼ cup shortening or butter
3 teaspoons baking powder	1¼ cups brown sugar
1 teaspoon baking soda	2 eggs
1 teaspoon ground ginger	1 cup canned pumpkin
1 teaspoon salt	1 cup raisins
½ teaspoon cinnamon	½ cup nuts
½ teaspoon grated whole nutmeg	1 cup milk

1. Sift all the dry ingredients together. Mix well.
2. Cream the shortening or butter with the brown sugar, whip in the eggs, and add the pumpkin, raisins, and nuts. Add the dry ingredients and mix well. Add milk; mix well and beat for 1 minute.
3. Spoon mixture into two 9-by-5-inch loaf pans and bake in a preheated 350°F oven until lightly browned on top and firm, about 30 minutes. Serve warm with butter.

Makes 2 small loaves.

Mik-Ran's Sugarhouse, 86 Stetson Road, Brooklyn, CT 06234; (860) 774–7926; e-mail: king@cyberzone.net. Open year-round by appointment, this large, low-slung, knotty-pine shop off Route 6 sells all kinds of maple products made on the grounds: maple syrup, maple cream, maple candy, maple granulated sugar, maple butter, and maple popcorn, as well as a few foods, like mustards and barbecue sauces made elsewhere in New England. Stenciled wooden gift boxes and baskets filled with maple food products are also for sale, along with a few handcrafts, including mushrooms carved out of wood. There are free demonstrations of maple-syrup production in the nearby sugarhouse on weekends in February and March. Call for times.

Norman's Sugarhouse, 387 County Road, Woodstock, CT 06281; (860) 974–1235; e-mail: r.norman@snet.net. Richard and Avis Norman have been putting 1,200 taps into the sugar maples on their fifty acres during each of more than thirty years (and processing the results into delectable edibles). Their most recent results can be seen, sampled, and carried home from their sugarhouse, where you will find maple syrup, granulated maple sugar, maple cream, maple jelly, and candies. Call ahead if you want to witness "the boil," which transforms maple sap into syrup; it goes on from Presidents' Day in February for six or eight weeks. After that, you are welcome to visit Saturday or Sunday from 1:00 to 5:00 P.M. or Monday through Friday from 3:00 to 6:00 P.M.

Palazzi Orchard, 1393 North Road, East Killingly, CT 06243; (860) 774–4363. Not only are there twenty varieties of pick-your-own apples here, but Mark and Jean Palazzi give hayride tours on weekends at harvesttime. You'll savor the four-state views from the hill, and nearby is a Revolutionary War cemetery with the old Charter Oak tree. Open daily, September to October, 9:00 A.M. to 5:30 P.M.

River's Edge Sugar House, 326 Mansfield Road (Route 89), Ashford, CT 06278; (860) 429–1510; www.riversedgesugarhouse.com. Driving up a long dirt road (1.5 miles south of Route 44), you will know you have arrived at River's Edge when you see the horses in the field next to a log house and, in the parking area, a neat wooden building that is both shop and processing plant. In February and March you may watch the syrup being made. The rest of the year, stop by for Bill and Amy Proulx's maple products: syrup, candy, and cream. It is best to call ahead.

Wayne's Organic Garden, 1080 Plainfield Park (Route 14A), Box 154, Oneco, CT 06373; (860) 564–7987. Wayne's is best known for certified organic vegetables that are truly exotic and expensive. The fingerling-size purple Peruvian potatoes (try saying it fast), pink-outside/yellow-inside Laratte potatoes, Walla Walla onions (similar to Vidalias), and

 Italian Cipollini, and Borretana onions are among the specialties Wayne's grows and sells at Putnam and Danielson farmers' markets. From the end of May through mid-July, Wayne's heirloom tomatoes, garlic, and green-

house vegetable plants are for sale at this Plainfield location. Call for days and times.

We-Li-Kit Farm Ice Cream Stand, 728 Hampton Road (Route 97), Abington, CT 06230; (860) 974-1095. Just opposite the milking center is the We-Li-Kit farm stand, with remarkably rich ice cream. Whimsical names like Ape's Delight (banana with chocolate chips and walnuts), Guernsey Cookie (coffee with Oreos), Holstein (chocolate studded with white chocolate chips and almonds), and, most popular of all, Road Kill (vanilla with cherry swirl, white chocolate chips, and walnuts) don't detract from the creamy ice cream's popularity. There are twenty-five flavors, about seventeen available on any given day. Farm-fresh eggs are the stand's other attraction, but it is the ice cream that is the magnet for miles around. The stand is open from early April to the end of October.

Windy Hill Farm, 164 Hillhouse Road, Goshen, CT 06756; (860) 491-3021. The Allens have been providing freshly harvested vegetables on their farm for the past twenty years. Throughout the growing season Marianne and Doug supply sweet corn, tomatoes, potatoes, cucumbers, pumpkins, and other veggies, as well as their own maple syrup and fresh eggs. These are available at various times of the season (call ahead for specific times) from mid-July to mid-October, daily from 9:00 A.M. to dusk.

Winterbrook Farm, 116 Beffa Road, Staffordville, CT 06076; (860) 684-2124; e-mail: juddfarm@juno.com. Here on Beffa Road you will find a big red barn and farmhouse that have been on this spot since the 1700s. This is where Kirby and Laura Judd have been raising Dorset sheep for years to supply Easter lambs to churches in the

Green Corn Pudding

This corn pudding is easy to make and can brighten up a Sunday breakfast or brunch.

1 quart milk
½ teaspoon sugar
5 eggs, beaten until foamy
12 ears of fresh corn, cut off the cob (or 2 10-ounce boxes of fresh-frozen corn kernels)

1. Preheat oven to 300°F. Butter the bottom and sides of an 8-by-12-inch glass baking dish.
2. Add the milk and sugar to the beaten eggs in a large mixing bowl. Add the corn kernels and mix well.
3. Pour the corn-milk mixture into the buttered baking dish and bake for approximately 2 hours or until firm. Serve hot with dabs of butter over the dish along with bacon or ham.

Serves 8.

area and to others who savor lamb meat. You can order your own in January and have it cut to your specifications for delivery the week before Easter. The Judds also have homemade maple syrup (after March) and hay (in June), and you can call ahead for the days and times to pick your own blueberries from their fields (July through September). Open mid-July through September, dawn to dusk daily.

Woodstock Orchards, 494 Route 169, Woodstock, CT 06281; (860) 928-2225. On a road that shoots off from the Green in the center of Woodstock is the Apple Barn, Woodstock Orchards' neat roadside shop where Harold and Doug Bishop sell the fresh vegetables, blueberries, peaches, pears, and twenty-five types of apples (Ida Red, Red Delicious, Russet, Empire, McIntosh, and Cortland among them) that they grow on a sixty-five-acre spread. Harold seems especially proud of his Crisp-Aire apples, which are kept in a controlled atmosphere in a Crisp Aire "vault" at a lowered atmosphere with less than 5 percent oxygen, which "puts them to sleep" for several months. When they "awaken," they are crispy-fresh. Also available at the store are glass jars of preserves, corn relish, pickled mushrooms, pickled garlic buds, and other foods with the Woodstock Orchards label, as well as the farm's own sweet cider (a huge seller) and locally made honey and maple syrup. You may also pick your own apples and blueberries.

Wright's Orchards & Dried Flower Farm, 271 South River Road, Tolland, CT 06084; (860) 872–1665. If you like to pick your own, you will find blueberries, raspberries, apples, peaches and (later) pumpkins that Todd and Joyclyn Wright grow here. Their dwarf and semidwarf apple trees make picking easier. The Wrights have been farming along the Willimantic River for more than twenty years, growing tomatoes, cucumbers, squash, and other vegetables, as well as pick-your-own fruits. Flower lovers will appreciate how unusual and beautiful the Wrights' dried flowers look as they dry in the barn. The Wright farm stand, with its wide array of fruits, vegetables, flowers, fresh cider, preserves, and pies, is open for business from the first of August until Christmas, 12:30 to 5:30 P.M. every day but Wednesday and is open on Sunday 1:00 to 5:30 P.M.

 Food Happenings

March: **Annual Hebron Maple Festival,** held at six Hebron sugarhouses, Hebron, CT 06248; (860) 228–9503; e-mail: wellse1@mind spring. On the second weekend in March, there are self-guided tours to six sugarhouses: Dad's, Hope Valley, Pierces, Wells, Wenzel, and Woody Acres. Other family-oriented activities include a pancake breakfast, maple baked goods, and the sugar-making process. Call for details.

October: **Buells Orchard Annual Fall Festival,** 108 Crystal Pond Road, Eastford, CT 06242; (860) 974–1150. Ever since 1978 this annual harvest event has been held Columbus Day weekend. At the festival Patty Sandress, Jeffrey's wife, dispenses free cider and doughnuts. There are seven hayrides through the orchards to the pumpkin patch, which is open for pick-your-own. Hot dogs, chicken barbecue, desserts, and other foods are available, adding to a very rewarding day-at-the-farm experience for one and all. Check for day and hours.

October: **Annual Oktoberfest,** Wright's Mill Farm, 63 Creasey Road, Canterbury, CT 06331; (860) 744–1455; www.wrightsmillfarm.com. The oompahs and tootling you will hear at this *gemütlich* celebration are from the Jolly Kopperschmidts, a genuine German band, which keeps the music pumping as visitors enjoy the German traditional buffet banquet and German beer. So lift tankards in typical Oktoberfest fashion, which should put you in the mood for the yodeling contest. Prost! The festivities are held the last Sunday in October from noon to 4:00 P.M. at the Lodge on the 250-acre farm property, now used for special events.

Landmark Eateries

Altnaveigh Inn & Restaurant, 957 Storrs Road (Route 195), Storrs, CT 06268; (860) 429–4490; $$. Dating back more than 200 years, this old-fashioned inn, with its three dining rooms (two of them warmed in winter by fireplaces), has been a treat for generations of UConn students and their parents. The cooking is continental, and there are classics on the menu that we have neither seen nor heard of in aeons: beef Wellington, tournedos chasseur, lobster Newburg, veal Oscar. It is fun to become reacquainted with them and other dishes. Prices are extremely modest, considering that each entree comes with salad, baked potato or rice, and a vegetable. In warm weather, you can even dine outside on a pleasant patio. There are five guest rooms, too, so staying overnight can be a happy prospect.

Fireside Tavern at Sharpe Hill Vineyards, 108 Wade Road, Pomfret, CT 06258; (860) 974–3549; www.sharpehill.com; $$. Lunch or dinner in the eighteenth-century-style Fireside Tavern here evokes the past in looks and spirit, though the food—prepared on a wood-burning

stove by Catherine Vollweiler, the vineyard's co-owner—is deliciously modern. The ancient-looking barn-red building dates back only to 1998, but it illustrates Catherine's eye for American antiques and details. The cozy tavern, up a winding, marbleized wooden stairway, has a double fireplace in the center of the room, ladder-back chairs, and charming murals and seats a mere forty. There is a single large dining table on the ground floor near the bar for those who can't handle the stairs. There is also a spacious outdoor terrace, with four weeping cherry trees in the center, where meals are served in warm weather, a mere rabbit hop from the vineyards. Though the menu changes often, you may find such dishes as wood-grilled lamb chops with rosemary potatoes, sea-bass fillet grilled with rosemary and vidalia onions, or even spicy Jamaican chicken marinated in a fiery jerk sauce and wood-grilled. Look for an exceptionally attractive cheese platter, which includes English, French, and northeast Connecticut's Cato Corner Farm cheeses. Served at their full ripeness, the cheeses make a fine accompaniment to the vineyard wines. Lunch and dinner are served only on specific days, which change with the season. It is *essential* to call ahead to check dates and make reservations.

The Golden Lamb Buttery, 299 Wolf Den Road (Route 169), Brooklyn, CT 06234; (860) 774–4423; $$. This one-of-a-kind restaurant, ensconced in a big, rambling barn on a working farm of 1,000 acres, is unique in several ways. For one thing, it has been functioning as a restaurant since 1963 with the same owners (Jimmie and Bob

Booth), same chef (Jimmie), same host (Bob), at the same locale. In all these years the Booths, now into their eightieth decade, have never lost their enthusiasm for what they do. And it shows. Aside from pleasant lunches served on the deck, the prix-fixe dinner is indeed unique. The evening begins with drinks and a hayride (to live guitar accompaniment) through freshly mown fields, past the sheep, cows, horses, and donkeys grazing on the hillsides. Then guests drift into the converted barn, with its high ceilings, barn-siding walls, fireplace, and hayloft. Festooned with garden flowers, the dining room decor is best described as "sophisticated country casual." There is usually a choice of four entrees, accompanied by six or seven fresh garden vegetables, always prepared in interesting ways (for example, fresh peas tossed with mint, carrots in a white-grape sauce, celery braised with fennel). During dinner a guitarist strolls through the rooms, singing folk songs. This may sound corny, but the excellence of the food, the genuine friendliness of the staff, and the appealing country surroundings make an evening here a rare and memorable experience. The Golden Lamb is a destination in itself, an excursion that we never tire of repeating over and over again. Reservations are essential.

The Harvest, 37 Putnam Road (Route 44), Pomfret, CT 06260; (860) 928–0008; www.harvestrestaurant.com; $$. Slightly more formal than most places in this area, with dark floral wallpaper and soft-lighted wall sconces, the Harvest's biggest claim to local fame is as a steakhouse, with five superb choices, plus grilled pork tenderloin and lamb. You may have your steak cut to order, any size you would like, with a choice

Jimmie Booth's Broccoli Salad

Jimmie Booth, the eternally youthful chef of the Golden Lamb Buttery, is famous for the big wooden bowls of farm-fresh vegetables she serves with every dinner. These abundant veggie dishes are part of the mystique of the Buttery.

3–4 large, fresh broccoli spears
1 medium-size red pepper
10-ounce package frozen peas
½ cup butter
2–3 cloves garlic, mashed in garlic press
Salt and pepper to taste (optional)

1. Wash the broccoli, drain, and wipe dry.
2. Dice the red pepper in small pieces and place them in a bowl with the broccoli. Add the peas and set aside.
3. When ready to serve, heat butter and garlic in a skillet, and add the vegetables. Sauté, stirring frequently, just long enough to cook but not overcook the vegetables. Season as desired. Place in a serving bowl and serve immediately.

Serves 4.

The Golden Lamb Buttery
Route 169
Brooklyn, CT 06234
(860) 774-4423

of six sauces. An added feature is a Japanese chef, who plies his handy chopping knife at a sushi bar in the bar area, where there are several dining tables. Diners may choose a Japanese menu with a variety of sushi and tempura or the regular continental menu. We often mix and match, beginning with gyoza (Japanese dumplings), continuing with duckling in raspberry sauce, cedar-plank roast salmon with lemon-ginger butter, or one of the Harvest's tender, juicy sirloins. The Harvest has an admirable wine list, diverse, wide ranging, and surprisingly well priced. A relaxed Sunday brunch is a treat here, too, featuring a prix-fixe menu with ten entree choices.

The Inn at Woodstock Hill, 94 Plaine Hill Road, Woodstock, CT 06281; (860) 928–0528; www.woodstockhill.com; $$. There aren't many Connecticut inns as entwined with the town history as this one. It was built in 1816 by William Bowen, a descendant of one of the thirteen "Goers," those who founded the town in 1686. William was the grand-father of Henry Bowen, whose pink Victorian Gothic house, Roseland Cottage, is Woodstock's leading landmark. The inn, with twenty-two guest rooms, also serves meals in several bright and pleasant dining rooms. As you feast upon grilled duck breasts roosting atop wild-mushroom cous-cous or grilled pork tenderloin with cinnamon-spiced apples and onions, you might contemplate the fact that much of the surrounding hills and meadows still belongs to the Bowen family. The inn itself was in the same family until 1981. That's continuity for you!

Kathy-John's Ice Cream and Sandwich Shoppe, 643 Middle Turnpike (corner of Routes 44 and 195), Storrs, CT 06268; (860) 429–0362; $. Don't let the wall-to-wall gift shop, which leads off from the entrance to the right, deter you. Kathy-John's is a reliable place for sandwiches that taste homemade (we love the homey BLT, hot corned beef, and roast beef special) and a sinfully rich, old-fashioned ice-cream sundae or Banana Split Supreme (with five scoops of ice cream). There are fifteen ice-cream flavors to choose among. For a big helping of nostalgia, you might tackle a root-beer float, an extra-thick shake, or a brownie a la mode. The brownies are truly decadent. There are kiddie portions on the menu as well, with prices to match. A cheerful, upbeat staff enhances a lunch visit.

Main Street Café, 967 Main Street, Willimantic, CT 06226; (860) 423–6777; www.willibrew.com; $. Partnered with the Willimantic Brewing Company, this pleasant cafe occupies the former workroom of the majestic, old 1909 U.S. Post Office building. The building had been vacant for almost thirty years when Cindy and David Wollner took it over, expanding their cafe and brewery to larger, more comfortable quarters. As you enjoy a casual flat-bread pizza, a sandwich, or even a full-fledged dinner (try the Gurleyville garlic-walnut chicken in a roasted garlic-cream sauce), you will observe post-office memorabilia as part of the decor, along with a monumental 12-by-17-foot mural.

Appropriately, the mural depicts Main Street as it was in the 1920s and was the work of Gordan MacDonald. Note also that most dishes on the eclectic American menu are named after northeastern Connecticut towns, so it is possible to order by zip code, as in "I'll have 06075" (Stafford sautéed sirloin tips) or "give me an 06334" (Bozrah Best BLT).

The Spa at Norwich Inn, Route 32, Norwich, CT 06360; (860) 886–2401; www.norwichinnandspa.com; $$$. In 1983 Edward J. Safdie, owner of the Sonoma Mission Inn & Spa in Sonoma, California, converted a rustic old inn in Norwich into an upscale spa and inn, with handsome public areas, rooms, villas, and grounds. The Mashantucket Pequot Indians now own the property, but little has changed. Kensington's is the major dining room, with graceful chandeliers, carpeting, and well-spaced tables. The food is modern American, peppered by the Far East, with attention paid to healthful eating. They aren't kidding about the spa: The amount of calories, fat, protein, and carbohydrates are listed under each dish on the menu so that you can choose accordingly (or not). We find it difficult to avoid the temptation of bourbon-sautéed scallops, oven-seared veal with grilled lobster tail, and hot, molten chocolate cake. Diet be darned! If you are there for lunch in temperate weather, the deck, shaded by huge trees, is a wonderfully relaxed place to eat. For a quicker, lighter meal, try Ascot's, a knotty-pine-paneled pub with fireplace, whose tasty items include five-onion bisque, Maryland lump crabcake, and burgers ($).

Traveler Restaurant: The Food & Book People, off Route 84 (exit 74), Union, CT 06076; (860) 684–4920; $. Situated right at the Connecticut-Massachusetts line, this is one of the most unusual restaurants in the state. Traveler is a restaurant and bookstore combined, entwined one might say. The plain, knotty-pine-walled dining room and glassed-in porch are awash in books—in bookcases, on ledges and counters, in fact, everywhere you turn. The books are secondhand, but the food is fresh at breakfast, lunch, and dinner. The gimmick, if you want to call it that, is that with every order of food, customers can help themselves to a free book. On Wednesdays, you may take three books; on Saturday, two. Art Murdock, the owner, told us he gives away 100,000 books a year, many of which he acquires through library sales. The food is hearty, generous, moderately priced, and appetizing, though in no way fancy. The mainstays we particularly like are the cheddar hot bites with explosive jalapeños, fried clam strips, and packed lobster roll at lunch. If you sit on the glassed-in porch, you can view an enormous wooden moose "grazing" on a grassy knoll, with a small pond and Massachusetts visible just beyond. After choosing your free books, wander down a short flight of stairs to browse in Traveler's bona fide secondhand bookstore (interesting tomes, but no freebies there!).

The Vine Bistro, 85 Main Street, Putnam, CT 06260; (860) 928–1660 or (860) 928–9958; $$. In a relatively short time, this modish cafe has made itself "the" scene in Putnam, especially for antiquers. Comfortable banquettes, soft lighting, wood floors, and colorful art on the walls all add to the relaxed mood of the Vine Bistro. The Italian food, served in

HAVE YOU BEEN TO THE BEAN?

At a rural crossroads (of Route 44, 97, 169), seemingly in the middle of nowhere, is the Vanilla Bean Cafe, inside a restored nineteenth-century barn. Looks are deceiving. "The Bean" is anyplace but "nowhere," but rather the most popular gathering spot for miles around. Faculty and students from nearby Pomfret School drop by in the morning for fresh-made warm muffins, bagels, and serve-yourself coffee or tea. At lunchtime it is burgers (which include garden burgers, black-bean burgers, and buffalo burgers, in addition to the usual types) or other house-made comfort foods, as well as extensive beer and wine lists. Our favorite room is the main one, with its old-fashioned, giant-wheeled bicycle mounted on an overhead beam; the huge blackboard listings of the daily salads, grilled sandwiches, homemade soups, and seductive pies and cakes; and the bentwood chairs and cozy window seat. If the weather is warm, we like to carry our salads and sandwiches to a picnic table on the brick-lined outdoor patio under sheltering pine trees, taking our "To Bean or Not to Bean . . . Is It Really a Question?" coffee mugs back inside for refills. On Friday and Saturday evenings, live entertainment is a "given," often folk-music concerts but sometimes poetry readings, jam sessions, and open-mike nights. Barry and Maria Jessurun opened the Bean in 1989 with sixteen seats. Now it is a northeastern Connecticut institution.

The Vanilla Bean Cafe

450 Deerfield Road
Pomfret, CT 06258
(860) 928-1562
www.TheVanillaBeanCafe.com
$

HE COULDN'T SAY THIS TODAY

James Fenimore Cooper, the nineteenth-century American author, once wrote: "The Americans are the grossest feeders of any civilized nation known. As a nation, their food is heavy, coarse and indigestible, while it is taken in the least artificial forms that cookery will allow. The predominance of grease in the American kitchen, coupled with the habits of hearty eating . . . are the causes of the diseases of the stomach which are so common in America." That was then.

gargantuan portions, helps, too; there is something about pasta, eggplant, mozzarella, and other Italian favorites that provide a high comfort level. This is a comfortable, laid-back place. Though the Vine's wine list is small, it has a few wines from Sharpe Hill Vineyards in nearby Pomfret that you might enjoy sampling.

Brewpubs & Microbreweries

Willimantic Brewing Co. & Main Street Café, 967 Main Street, Willimantic, CT 06226; (860) 423–6777; www.willibrew.com; $$. No matter how you "stamp" them, the beers at this brewery-cafe, ensconced in the town's old post office (a handsome limestone building, vintage 1909), arrive in "First Class" condition. From the light palate of Certified Gold and the smooth, dark Postage Porter to the fruity Most Wanted India Pale Ale and a rich, mochalike stout, the suds seem freshly set before you by "Special Delivery." In a sense they were, since the creative brewer and co-owner David Wollner crafts them on the premises and "express mails" them directly to the taps of the 60-foot mahogany bar that dominates the former customer lobby. David's seasonal suds include Rail Mail Rye, an unfiltered rye pale ale; an "aggressively" hopped, six-malt First Class Festive Ale; and Willi Whammer Barleywine, whose 10.4 percent strength is called "infamously powerful" locally. It is fun to explore all the postal memorabilia while sipping one of the house brews. The old post office's sorting room is now tastefully separated by a glass partition from the dining room, over which David's wife, Cindy, has presided since the Main Street Café opened in 1991. Not incidentally, the cafe offers dining-plus-beer events each month. Hours: Sunday and Monday, 4:00 P.M. to midnight; Tuesday through Saturday, 11:30 A.M. to 1:00 A.M.

Wine Trail

Connecticut Wine Trail, www.ctwine.com, offers one of three trail plans that show where the state's ten wineries are located, the best roads to reach them, and important information about each of them (their hours for tastings, tours, picnicking, nearby points of interest). In this area, Sharpe Hill is the only winery included in Connecticut Wine Trail, Trip 3, which can be printed out from the Web site (listed above). As you follow the trail, remember the old saying that "life is too short to drink inferior wine."

A Country Inn, Once Almost Lawless, Now Idyllically Sedate

Thompson, Connecticut, is so peaceful nowadays that it is difficult to imagine what it was like in the nineteenth-century, when the town was at the intersection of two turnpikes running into Massachusetts and Rhode Island. Thompson's main tavern was manned by Captain Vernon Stiles, who boasted that "more stage passengers dined there every day than at any other house in New England."

White Horse Inn at Vernon Stiles

Junctions 193 and 200
Thompson, CT 06277
(860) 923-9571
www.whitehorseinn.com

Stiles was a genial host, an adroit politician, and a justice of the peace. His barroom was the informal headquarters of the local Democratic Party, and, in addition to raucous politicians, it also attracted liquor salesmen, fugitives, and runaway lovers who crossed state lines to be married under Connecticut's more lax laws. The inn's long history even includes the Marquis de Lafayette and Rochambeau as earlier guests, but since Stiles's day it has had frequent changes in ownership.

Now called the White Horse Inn at Vernon Stiles, this charming old house, with its wide floorboards, post-and-beam construction, and antique-filled rooms, is open for banquets, weddings, and other special catered events, but it no longer serves meals to the public. Nor are its guest rooms open to politicians or overnighters (unless they happen to be brides having their big event in the inn).

Heritage Trail Vineyards, 291 North Burnham Highway, Lisbon, CT 06351; (860) 376–0659; www.heritagetrail.com. This "boutique-size" winery might have scandalized the original eighteenth-century owner of the land, the Reverend John Palmer. Such men of the cloth did not encourage anything so scandalous as wine or winemaking. In 1996 Diane M. Powell bought the property, which is on a National Heritage Corridor known for postcard-pretty New England villages. The main building is an eighteenth-century Cape Cod dwelling, and its wine-tasting room has antique beams, board floors, a stone fireplace, and views of the farm grounds. The vineyard plantings include Chardonnay, Cabernet Franc, Merlot, and hybrids Cayuga White and Vignoles grapes. Quinebaug White and Shetucket Red, named after local rivers, are just two of Heritage Trail's five current wines. All can be sampled in front of the fireplace in winter or on the sundeck in summer, while you enjoy garden views. Tours and tastings from January to April are by appointment; May to December from 11:00 A.M. to 5:00 P.M. Friday through Sunday.

Priam Vineyard, 11 Shailor Road, Colchester, CT 06415; (860) 267–8520; e-mail: priamvineyards@earthlink.net. This winery was started from scratch in 1998, when Gloria Priam and Gary Crump bought twenty-seven acres of hillside, near Colchester, that has a 35-mile view. Gloria's grandfather was in the wine trade in his native Budapest, Hungary, in the 1800s, so she was simply following family tradition when she and Gary decided to turn their property into a vineyard, first planting Seyval, Chardonnay, and Cayuga grapes. Their production is small but growing, and in 2001 their Salmon River White, a handcrafted blend, won a

Easy Lemon Squares

In the Connecticut climate, teatime in any season is a welcome way to enjoy the late afternoon. There are a number of tea shops throughout the state, but tea at home is just as delightful a way of relaxing for an hour or so with friends at the end of a day. These lemon squares are easy to make and are among our old faithfuls for serving with afternoon tea (or almost any other time we crave something sweet, but not too sweet).

Dough
- 1 cup all-purpose flour
- ¼ cup powdered sugar
- ¼ pound chilled butter, cut into cubes

Filling
- ⅓ cup fresh lemon juice
- 2 large, lightly beaten eggs
- 1 cup granulated sugar
- 2 tablespoons all-purpose flour
- ½ teaspoon baking powder
- 1 tablespoon lemon zest (or more for a really tart, lemony flavor)

1. Preheat oven to 325°F. Lightly grease a 9-inch-square cake pan.
2. Combine the flour, powdered sugar, and butter and blend well in a food processor. Pour or scrape mixture into the pan and pat it so that it is distributed evenly in the pan. Dough should be slightly firm, not runny. Bake 10–15 minutes, or until the dough is lightly baked and lightly golden on top. Remove it from the oven.
3. While the dough is baking, combine the filling ingredients in a food processor and blend well. The mixture should be slightly runny. When you remove the pan from the oven, completely cover the dough with the filling, spreading it evenly all over the top.
4. Bake 20 to 25 minutes or until the dough and topping are firm. Remove the pan from the oven and cool slightly. Cut into squares and serve at room temperature.

Makes 16 squares.

gold medal in an international competition. They also captured a bronze in 2002 for their Essence of St. Croix, a smoky Vineyard Reserve port-style wine. Their vineyard plantings now include Cabernet Franc, Gewrütztraminer, and Riesling grapes, and their current wines include a crisp Cayuga, a Bordeaux-style Salmon River Red, and a Late Harvest Riesling dessert wine. They opened the winery to the public in 2003 for visiting and tastings from March through December, Friday to Sunday and holidays, from 11:00 A.M. to 5:00 P.M. Call for summer hours.

Sharpe Hill Vineyards, 108 Wade Road, Pomfret, CT 06258; (860) 974–3549; www.sharpehill.com. It seems almost miraculous that Sharpe Hill Vineyards has been an active winery only since 1992. Not only have its poetically named "Ballet of Angeles" white wine, late-harvest Vignoles, and Chardonnays earned gold medals in international competitions, but the vineyards and barn-red buildings look as old as the one hundred acres of rolling hills surrounding them. The property rises more than 700 feet above the countryside, and on a clear day you can see forever, well, at least into Massachusetts and Rhode Island. Owners Steven and Catherine Vollweiler's Chardonnay and late-harvest Vignoles have drawn high praise from *The Wine Spectator* magazine, which also included their winery on one cover. Sharpe Hill's vines produce Chardonnay, Melon de Bourgogne, Vignoles, Cabernet Franc, St. Croix, and Carmine grapes. To sample, the Tasting Room—handsomely furnished in eighteenth-century style—is open from 11:00 A.M. to 5:00 P.M., Friday through Sunday, year-round. The curving drive from Route 97 to Sharpe Hill is 1.5 miles under a canopy of trees. The vineyard delivers to 400 package stores and restaurants in New England.

Appendix A: Food Happenings

February

Annual Taste of Stamford (Stamford), 29

Make Mine Wine (New London), 197

Taste of the Nation (New Haven), 198

Taste of Ridgefield (Ridgefield), 29

March

Annual Hebron Maple Festival (Hebron), 254

Maple-Syrup Making Demonstrations (Woodbury), 84

April

Hotter Than Heck Festival (Waterbury area), 85

Taste of the Nation (Stamford), 30

Wine on Ice (Hartford), 139

May

Dionysos Greek Festival (New Britain), 139

Fine Wine & Food Festival (New London), 197

Taste of the Nation (New Haven), 198

June

Branford Festival (Branford), 199

Greater New Haven Pizza Fest (New Haven), 199

North Canton Strawberry Festival (North Canton), 140

Old-Fashioned Strawberry Festival (Plantsville), 140

Shad Festival (Essex), 198

Secrets of Great PBS Chefs (Norwalk), 31

Appendix B: Wine Happenings

If you want to observe or even be part of the winemaking process, some wineries invite you to help them. Others stage special events, such as early-wine evaluating, grape stomping, and tastings, which might also include live music, hayrides, food, and exhibits of crafts and art. Here is a calendar of some of the offerings you may enjoy. Call ahead to verify dates and times. Information about each winery can be found in its respective chapter.

February

Olde Fashioned Winter Celebration, Haight Vineyard, Litchfield; (800) 577–9463. Sample prerelease wines; reservations essential.

March

Barrel Tasting, Haight Vineyard, Litchfield; (800) 577–9463. Early sampling of prerelease wines; reservations essential.

April

Barrel Tasting, Haight Vineyard, Litchfield; (800) 577–9463. Early sampling, continued; reservations essential.

May

Spring Cellar-Bration & Barrel Tasting, Stonington Vineyards, Stonington; (860) 421–WINE. Savor last year's harvest, with live music and food from local restaurants.

June

Spring Fest, Jonathan Edwards Winery, North Stonington; (860) 535–0202. Wine, food, and music.

Taste of Litchfield Hills, Haight Vineyard, Litchfield; (800) 577–9463. Cooling off with wine.

July

Summer Jazz series, McLaughlin Vineyards, Sandy Hook; (203) 270–8349. Live music, plus wine, of course.

August

Summer Jazz series, McLaughlin Vineyards, Sandy Hook; (203) 270–8349. The music continues (the wine too).

Summer "Cellar-Bration Clam-bake" in late July, Stonington Vineyards, Stonington; (800) 421–WINE. Live bands, food from nearby restaurants.

September

"Grape Stomp," DiGrazia Vineyards, Brookfield; (203) 775–1616. Third week in September. You, too, can get blue feet.

Harvest Celebration, Hopkins Vineyard, New Preston; (860) 868–7954. Mid-month event: wine tastings, meet the winemaker, live music, buffet; admission charge.

Harvest Festival, Haight Vineyard, Litchfield; (800) 577–9463. Saturday–Sunday at end of the month. Live music, artisan crafts, outdoor cafe, pony rides, hayrides, grape-stomping contests; admission charge.

October

Harvest Fest, Jonathan Edwards Winery, North Stonington; (860) 535–0202. Wine, food, and music.

Harbor Festival, Stonington Vineyards, Stonington; (800) 421–WINE. Day includes picking grapes and seeing them go through the crush; live bands; food from nearby restaurants.

Appendix C: Specialty Foods and Produce

The following businesses, farms, and shops are especially known for these items that they produce or grow.

Almonds

Dr. Lankin's Specialty Foods (Groton), 167

Apple Cider

Bishop's Orchards (Guilford), 190

Blue Jay Orchards (Bethel), 25

Bushy Hill Orchard & Cider Mill (Granby), 128

Holmberg Orchard (Gales Ferry), 194

Lyman Orchards (Middlefield), 131

Roberts Orchard (Bristol), 82

Woodland Farm (South Glastonbury), 138

Woodstock Orchards (Woodstock), 253

Wright's Orchards (Tolland), 253

Baking Mixes

Arugula (West Hartford), 109

Gluten Free Pantry, Inc. (Glastonbury), 111

Barbecue Sauce

Rick Trading Company (Ridgefield), 10

Sally's Specialty Products (Hartford), 113

Sassy Sauces (Avon), 114

Beef and Pork Products

DiBacco's Food Imports (Hartford), 117

Drotos Brothers Market (Fairfield), 14

The Egg & I Pork Farm (New Milford), 62

Four Mile River Farm (Old Lyme), 192

Breads and Bakery Goods

Bantam Bread Company (Bantam), 66

Chabaso (New Haven), 175

Colchester Bakery (Colchester), 235

Lamb Products

Foxfire Farm (Mansfield Center), 232

Sankow's Beaver Brook Farm (Lyme), 171

Winterbrook Farm (Staffordville), 251

Maple Syrup and Other Maple Products

Bats of Bedlam Maple Syrup (Chaplin), 243

Lamothe's Sugar House (Burlington), 80

Mik-Ran's Sugarhouse (Brooklyn), 249

Norman's Sugarhouse (Woodstock), 249

River's Edge Sugar House (Ashford), 250

Warrup's Farm (West Redding), 28

Milk

Cato Corner Farm (Colchester), 230

Fish Family Farm (Bolton), 231

Foxfire Farm (Mansfield Center), 232

Town Farm Dairy (Simsbury), 115

Mushrooms

Franklin Mushroom Farms (North Franklin), 246

Pestos

Bear Pond Farm (Washington Depot), 61

Pierogies

Krystyna's Specialties Inc. (East Berlin), 112

Salad Dressings

Newman's Own (Westport), 7

Pearl's Salad Dressing (Westport), 10

Salsas

Giff's Original (Cheshire), 110

Sauces

Bibelicious Sauces (Hebron), 229

Newman's Own (Westport), 7

Palmieri Food Products (New Haven), 169

Pasta Cosi (Branford), 170

Shellfish

Briar Patch Enterprises (Milford), 3

Mohegan Aqua Culture (Stonington), 168

Stonington Seafood Harvesters (Stonington), 172

Smoked Meats/Game/Fish

Nodine's Smokehouse (Goshen), 64

Sally's Specialty Products (Hartford), 113

Teas

Chaiwalla (Salisbury), 91

Caprilands (Coventry), 233

Harney & Sons, Fine Teas (Salisbury), 70

Simpson & Vail (Brookfield), 20

Sundial Gardens (Higganum), 182

Appendix D: Unusual Chain Stores

We have nothing against chain-food stores. We rely on many for our standard staples and supplies, but you do not need our guidance in finding them. Though we have concentrated mostly on one-of-a-kind food sources in this book, there are a few unusual stores with multiple outlets that we have not included in our text (Trader Joe's is a unique exception) but that are worth calling to your attention here with their Connecticut locations, as follows:

Ashley's, famous in the New Haven and shore areas for ice cream in twenty-three flavors and a wide selection of toppings. Four stores in Connecticut:
1016–18 Main Street, Branford;
(203) 481–5558
942 Boston Post Road, Guilford;
(203) 458–3040
2100 Dixwell Avenue, Hamden;
(203) 288–7497
280 York Street, New Haven;
(203) 776–7744

Food for Thought, natural-foods supermarkets, which started in Albuquerque, New Mexico. Three stores to date, one in Connecticut:
596 Westport Avenue, Norwalk; (203) 847–5233

Garelick & Herbs, gourmet food stores with delicatessen and frozen-food sections, sizable baked-goods and take-out-foods sections. Three stores in Connecticut:
44–48 West Putnam Avenue, Greenwich;
(203) 661–7373
97 Main Street, New Canaan;
(203) 972–8200
1799 Post Road East, Westport,
(203) 254–3727

Hay Day Markets, gourmet food stores, known for their fine fresh produce, excellent baked goods, fresh ready-made dishes, and take-out meals. Eleven stores on the East Coast, three in Connecticut:
1050 East Putnam Avenue, Greenwich; (203) 637-7600
21 Governor Street, Ridgefield; (203) 431-4400
1385 Post Road East, Westport; (203) 254-5200 or (203) 319-3925

Mrs. Green's Natural Market, New York–New England chain of ten natural food stores, two in Connecticut:
1916 Post Road, Fairfield; (203) 255-4333
960 High Ridge Road, Stamford; (203) 329-1313

Pralines, seven popular Connecticut-based ice-cream parlors, with some thirty-five flavors, including unusual ones like Lemon Pie, Reese's Nightmare, Cotton Candy, in these locations:
Pralines of Berlin, 1179 Farmington Avenue, Berlin; (860) 828-3626
Pralines Ice Cream, West Farms Mall, Farmington; (860) 521-9333
Pralines of Meriden, 1245 East Main Street, Meriden; (203) 237-4303
Pralines Ice Cream of Westfield Shopping Town, 470 Lewis Avenue, Meriden; (203) 235-7454

Pralines of Southington, 1143 Meriden-Waterbury Road, Plantsville; (860) 621-4823
Pralines Café, 50 Center Street, Southington; (860) 620-9226
Pralines of Wallingford, 1122 West Colony Road (Route 5), Wallingford; (203) 269-1860

Wild Oats Natural Marketplace, supermarkets of natural foods, with enormous variety and 102 stores nationwide, these two in Connecticut:
340 North Main Street, West Hartford; (860) 523-7174
399 Post Road West, Westport; (203) 227-6858

Willoughby's, first specialty coffee roaster in Connecticut, now with four shops:
550 East Main Street, Branford; (203) 481-1700
752 Boston Post Road, Madison; (203) 245-1600
258 Church Street, New Haven; (203) 777-7400
1006 Chapel Street, New Haven; (203) 789-8400

Connecticut Eateries Index

Recipe Index

General Index

About the Authors

Perhaps it was the food rationing in Britain during their studies at the University of London that first fired the interest of Patricia and Lester Brooks in good food. "There's only so much you can do with cabbage," they found, and they have purposely sought and eaten more interesting, unusual fare ever since in their travels and writing. As newlyweds, they lived in Asia, where Pat studied Chinese cooking, and both reveled in what, at the time, seemed exotic foods and beverages. Once back in New York and then living in Connecticut (since 1956), they continued their shared interest in food and in travels throughout the United States and abroad.

Pat and Les have reported on cuisines, wines, and dining customs from Mandalay to Madrid, Bangkok to Bridgehampton, and St. Moritz to Santa Fe for *Bon Appetit, Food & Wine, Travel & Leisure,* and other national publications. Pat has written three cookbooks. Since 1977 she has been the *New York Times* Connecticut restaurant reviewer, reporting over time on more than 1,400 restaurants around the state. Among her twenty-three books are *Best Restaurants of New England* and *Connecticut's Best Dining and Wining.* Meanwhile, Les studied wine and beverages with the Sommelier Society of America and has written about wines and wineries for the *New York Times* and other publications. Together, the Brookses have written guidebooks about Spain, Portugal, Britain, New York City and State, and New England—all of them featuring valuable information about food, dining, and restaurants.